The Globalization of TERROR

The Globalization of TERROR

The Challenges of Al-Qaida and the Response of the International Community

Yoram Schweitzer
Shaul Shay

Viva Books

New Delhi | Mumbai | Chennai | Kolkata | Bangalore | Hyderabad | Kochi | Guwahati

This Paperback edition published in 2010 by

VIVA BOOKS PRIVATE LIMITED

- ï 4737/23 Ansari Road, Daryaganj, New Delhi 110 002
  E-mail: vivadelhi@vivagroupindia.net, Tel. 42242200
- ï 76, Service Industries, Shirvane, Sector 1, Nerul, Navi Mumbai 400 706
  E-mail: vivamumbai@vivagroupindia.net, Tel. 27721273, 27721274
- ï Jamals Fazal Chambers, 26 Greams Road, Chennai 600 006
  E-mail: vivachennai@vivagroupindia.net, Tel. 28290304, 28294241
- ï B-103, Jindal Towers, 21/1A/3 Darga Road, Kolkata 700 017
  E-mail: vivakolkata@vivagroupindia.net, Tel. 22836381, 22816713
- ï 7, Sovereign Park Apartments, 56-58, K. R. Road, Basavanagudi, Bangalore 560 004
  E-mail: vivabangalore@vivagroupindia.net, Tel. 26607409, 26607410
- ï 101-102 Mughal Marc Apartments, 3-4-637 to 641, Narayanguda, Hyderabad 500 029
  E-mail: vivahyderabad@vivagroupindia.net, Tel. 27564481, 27564482
- ï First Floor, Beevi Towers, SRM Road, Kaloor, Kochi 682 018, Kerala
  E-mail: vivakochi@vivagroupindia.net, Tel: 0484-2403055, 2403056
- ï 232, GNB Road, Beside UCO Bank, Silpukhuri, Guwahati 781 003
  E-mail: vivaguwahati@vivagroupindia.net, Tel: 0361-2666386

www.vivagroupindia.com

Published by arrangement with

Transaction Publishers
RutgersóThe State University
35 Berrue Circle
Piscataway, New Jersey 08854-8042

ISBN 978-81-309-1380-3

Published by Vinod Vasishtha for Viva Books Private Limited, 4737/23, Ansari Road, Daryaganj, New Delhi-110 002. Printed and bound by Swan Press, New Delhi.

Contents

Foreword

This volume by Yoram Schweitzer and Shaul Shay constitutes an important contribution to academic research dealing with the phenomenon of international terror. It uniquely describes the phenomenon of "Afghan alumni" in the overall texture of the development of modern international terror, against the background of radical Islam's militant worldview. The book presents the unique worldview of Bin-Laden and his ultimate goal, and exposes the organizational structure that Bin-Laden aspired to build in order to realize the vision of establishing a world Islamic Caliphate in practical terms. The book examines the background and causes that led to the attacks of September 11 and the objectives that they were intended to achieve. The terror assault in the United States integrates smoothly within the route navigated by Bin-Laden in order to realize his apocalyptic prophecy. Schweitzer and Shay expose Bin-Laden's intention to evoke "a great provocation" designated at causing a frontal confrontation between the Western world and the Moslem world as part of his revelation of the clashing of civilizations.

The circle of countries that support terror is analyzed extensively in this volume, but particularly noteworthy is the part of Shiite Iran, which has played a central role in the dissemination of radical Islam and made use of terror as a central tool for its promotion. Iran has not only contributed heavily to the spreading of terror in the world since the beginning of the eighties to date, but at the present time also serves as an important factor in the fostering of terror groups from various ideological streams.

Dogmatic Iran has demonstrated a remarkably pragmatic policy in all matters relating to terror organizations, even when they are affiliated with a rival school of thought. Thus, despite the hostility between Shiite Iran and the Sunni Taliban regime associated with Bin-Laden, Iran aids the Al-Qaida organization and many Sunni terror organizations mentioned in the book that are affiliated with the World Jihad such as the Jama'a al-Islamiya, The Egyptian Jihad, the Algerian GIA, the Tunisian al-Nahada and others. Within its boundaries, Iran hosts members of Al-Qaida, and in the past year several terrorists affiliated with the Global Jihad were apprehended en route to perpetrating an attack, and their point of departure was Iran. After the apprehension of Abu-Zubeida, one of Bin-Laden's prominent associates (the end of March 2000), his interrogation revealed that he had also found refuge in Iran after the terror attack in the United States. The Lebanese Hizballah organization, which under Iran sponsorship spearheads its terror policy, maintains links with terror elements affiliated with Al-Qaida such as the Lebanese "al-Antsar Regiment."

Nonetheless, Iran is not the only country that encourages and makes use of these organizations. The circle of countries that support terror includes Syria, Lebanon, Iraq, and Libya, and to a lesser degree Sudan and Pakistan, which, according to past reports, supported the Taliban and Al-Qaida.

In general, it is important to note the dualism with which Moslem countries address the issue of terror. On the one hand, these states aspire to find pragmatic ways to diminish this phenomenon, sometimes while supplying financing and support, as well as aspiring to make use of the organization for internal purposes. On the other hand, Egypt, and to a certain extent Jordan, too, are waging a relentless war against these elements within their boundaries, but demonstrate "flexibility" towards them when they are located outside of their terrain.

An additional significant aspect vis-à-vis the fostering of terror is expressed in the granting of the religious stamp of approval by the Islamic clergy. Most religious authorities act freely and with little disruption in the Moslem countries and in the Western countries, and serve as a vital tool for the dissemination of ideas and the imbuing of radical concepts within Islam.

A crucial point influencing the successful handling of the phenomenon of international terror in general, and Islamic terror in particular, is the approach to the funding of terror. There exists a network of funds based on the various "zakat" organizations, which actually function without disruption both in the Moslem world and in the West. The countries of the free world have not yet succeeded in building effective tools to contend with this phenomenon.

Technological developments and the availability of non-conventional substances with the capability to cause unlimited destruction, in addition to the willingness of terror elements and their patrons to cause massacres in order to promote their political interests, must now be considered immediate challenges demanding an adequate response by world leaders. It is their duty to provide a strategic response to the systematic threat posed by terror against every citizen on the globe. There is a suitable response to the threat of terror, and it is dependent upon the decision and action of world leaders. The solution lies in the formulation of an effective and coordinated action strategy, which will significantly diminish the presence of terror on the international agenda and prevent it from growing into the monstrous dimensions that it approaches with such confidence.

The current struggle against the terror of both Shiite and Sunni Fundamentalist Islam, whose radical expressions are indiscriminate mass terror, is a struggle on behalf of values, lifestyles, and the quality of life, and not only a struggle for justice, as the terrorists attempt to portray it. There is no justice or justification for the cold-blooded murder of unarmed infants, children, women, and men. The threat posed by terror today is against human liberty, security, and dignity, and it is very real and pressing; therefore, it must be dealt with resolutely and inflexibly, the sooner the better.

Meir Dagan, Brigadier-General (res.)
Director of the Counter-terror Commission
of the Israeli Government, 1996-2000
Head of the Israeli "Mosad," 2002
August 2002

Acknowledgements

The authors would like to acknowledge: Good friends and colleagues who assisted with excellent advice, support, and encouragement in the publication of our book. Many thanks.

To Dr. Nancy Kobrin of Minneapolis, Beatriz Boza of Peru, and Ofer Lefler of Israel—our appreciation.

Our heartfelt gratitude to Haviva Ashkenazi whose meticulous professionalism, determination, and perseverance made it possible to publish this book in Israel around the first anniversary of the terror attack on the United States, an event that effectively changed the map of international terror.

And above all, we thank *our families* for their tireless support during the writing of this book.

Authors' Note

Today, a year and a half after the terror attack perpetrated in the United States on September 11, 2001, and following the international war against terror declared by President Bush in response to the attack, it would be accurate to state that the struggle to mitigate the poisonous sting of terror and diminish it to marginal proportions is at one of its peak. The main difficulty in regard to the battle against terror in the arena of international relations stems from the political considerations of countries that refrain from cooperating in and committing themselves to this war. Conflict of interests between various blocks, based upon different political and economic goals, constitute these main considerations.

This state of affairs is clearly reflected in the conflict between some of the NATO countries and the United States regarding the immediate ultimatum to disarm Iraq of its nonconventional weaponry and comply with the UN resolutions. At this particular point in time, it is possible to identify central incidents that have taken place since September 11 that reflect both the achievements and the complexity of the battle against international terror.

In the beginning of March 2003, Khaled Sheikh Muhammad, Al-Qaida's most prominent operational commander who supervised the planning of the terror assault on the United States, and Mustafa Ahmad al-Hazawi, the financer of this campaign, were apprehended in Pakistan and extradited to the United States. The apprehension of these two key figures is likely to provide the final pieces of the puzzle that are missing in the overall picture portraying the planning and implementation of the September 11 campaign.

This dramatic development came in the wake of a series of arrests of other senior Al-Qaida members, including Abu-Zubeida, the most senior liaison officer to coordinate contact between Al-Qaida and its terror networks and cells (March 2002), and the apprehension in the United Arab Emirates (November 2002) of Abdallah al-Nashiri, another leading operational leader who supervised the attack against the *USS Cole*. In addition, Al-Qaida terror cells and affiliates in Asia, Europe, and Africa were neutralized. All of these accomplishments may ultimately lead to the apprehension or termination of Al-Qaida's most senior commanders, led by Osama Bin-Laden and Ayman al-Thawahiri.

The apprehension in early 2003 of several European Al-Qaida-affiliated terror cells possessing nonconventional combat materials (including the ultra-toxic ricin) underscores the fact that for Al-Qaida and its affiliates the era of nonconventional warfare has already begun and that they intend to use these materials in order to attack their adversaries all over the world.

The pending war in Iraq may constitute a grave test for the United States in its fight against what President Bush calls "the Axis of Evil." Its results will undoubtedly have a direct impact on the continuation of the campaign against international terror, particularly in the area of combat against countries that support terror and the distribution of nonconventional weaponry into the hands of terror organizations.

It is abundantly clear that the global crisis triggered by the September 11 attacks and the ability to contend with the new characteristics of terror are still far from over and they will continue to hound us, at least in the first decade of the third millennium. The chosen method of contending with terror will affect the lives of all the inhabitants of this earth and will mold international relations throughout the twenty-first century.

March 2003

Introduction

The terror attack perpetrated in the United States on September 11, 2001, was a defining event in the history of international terror. A "defining event" is an occurrence that affects the characteristics of terror activity in the international arena in particular, and international relations in general, in an extraordinary and fundamental manner. This event has direct impact on the organization that sent its emissaries, on the country that supports the terror organization, and certainly on the country in which the attack took place. Moreover, it affects the counter-terror strategy of countries combating it.

In the history of modern terror several events are recognized as "formative events," for example, the killing of the Israeli athletes at the Munich Olympics in September 1972. This event left its mark on the way that Western countries and world opinion approach Palestinian terror, led to the establishment of specialized counter-terror units, to the handling of bargaining attacks with hostages, and also facilitated the crystallization of defense patterns regarding Israeli facilities abroad. Since the incident in Munich, all sports events with a large number of participants ("mega events") have become highly secured occurrences.

Another such incident was the explosion of the Pan-American aircraft, flight 103, over the skies of a town called Lockerbie in Scotland, which claimed the lives of 270 passengers and crewmembers (December 21, 1988). This event also served as a central milestone in the international struggle against terror, and upon the discovery of Libya's part in the attack, international sanctions were imposed upon that country. Unrelenting international pressure resulted in a halt of Libya's active support for international terror and in reduced activities of many terror organizations, which until then had enjoyed massive Libyan aid, such as the Abu-Nidal Organization ("Fatah the Revolutionary Council"), the Japanese Red Army, and others.

As a rule, the definition of a defining event necessitates a perspective of several years, so that its full significance can be completely understood. When it comes to the terror attack in New York and Washington on September 11, it is safe to state even now, only one and a half years after the event, that this attack constitutes a formative event and a central milestone in the war against terror.

The heavy toll in human life, over 3,000 casualties, the tremendous financial loss as a direct and indirect result of the attacks, and the media and psychological impact on public opinion throughout the world brought about a historical turning point in coping with terror. The United States, the only superpower, declared a war to the death against terror and placed this at the head of its international priorities.

The terror attack on the United States, which was based on a combination of the kidnapping of aircraft and their use as a platform to perpetrate suicide attacks and multiple deaths, must be studied as part of the development of "modern" international terror, which became a regular and influential "player" in the international arena at the end of the 1960s.

The hijacking of aircraft in order to achieve political goals became part of the repertoire of international terror immediately upon the introduction of the use of terror as an instrument to gain political achievements in the international arena. The "secular" Palestinian terror organizations, which were the pioneers of international terror and the dominant activating factor for about a decade and a half (between the years 1968 and 1982), were also the first to employ aircraft hijackings as a central and effective weapon aimed at positioning the Palestinian problem as a focal point on the global agenda. They perpetrated large-scale attacks and killings against civil aviation targets in order to shake up world opinion. This activity was conducted under the sponsorship of several Arab states that provided them with various means of support, such as training camps, diplomatic aids and papers. They even allowed the hijacked planes to land in their territory and offered the hijackers asylum after the completion of their mission.

From the beginning of the eighties, terror circles were joined by the Shiite terror organizations, led by the Lebanese Hizballah, which, while operating under Iran's backing, plucked the leadership away from the Palestinians (although the Palestinian terror organizations continued to perpetrate attacks in the international arena until the end of the eighties).

The Shiite terrorist organizations also hijacked airplanes, but their main contribution to the repertoire of international terror was in presenting a new and unique method of action—suicide attacks. From 1983 onwards, terror organizations in Lebanon carried out some fifty suicide attacks, half of which were perpetrated by the Shiite, Hizballah and "Amal" activists. This method of operation, in which the suicide terrorist detonates himself through the use of explosives that he carries on his body or in some kind of vehicle, has since become a widespread phenomenon, one that has been perfected by various organizations throughout the world. The enlistment of Fundamentalist terror cells and organizations of the Sunni stream, led by the Afghan "alumni,"[1] in terror activity within the international arena, turned them into the dominant component in the international field, starting from the early 1990s to the present. The Afghan alumni, mainly from within the Egyptian and Al-Qaida organizations, adopted the suicide pattern within their terror repertoire. The attacks in the United States, however, represented the combination of an airplane hijacking and a suicide attack, the first of its kind. The hijacked aircraft served as a platform for perpetrating a suicide attack, while taking advantage of the fact that its full gas tanks would effectively turn it into a cruising missile on wings, as it were. When it hit its target, the resulting huge explosion was far greater than any caused by explosives used in suicide attacks prior to September 2001. The combination of these two methods of operation and their horrific consequences raised the terror level to new and unprecedented dimensions.

Terror attacks perpetrated over the years by Palestinian, nationalist, ideological left and Shiite organizations were both murderous and deadly, but the intensity and level of activity were generally controlled by their supportive patron states, as determined by cost-benefit considerations of the countries that supported terror.

Countries were only partially able to control the terror of the Afghan alumni, thus allowing its perpetrators greater freedom than their predecessors. The targets of the Afghan alumni, as conceived by Osama Bin-Laden and his fellow leaders in the "The International Islamic Front for Jihad," dictated a worldwide, violent and relentless struggle between Islam and its foes, and the battlefront was defined as the entire globe. Although it was worded in terms of defending Islamic sanctity, the goal of the Afghan alumni is to turn the Western world into part of the Islamic nation, which will govern according to the Sunni Islamic religious laws—the Sharia. This concept maintains that the world is divided into two parts: Dar al-Islam

(The House of Islam)—the lands where Islamic rule prevails, and Dar al-Harb—all of the remaining lands ruled by infidels, who must be liberated in a holy war (jihad) through the use of "the force of the sword" and be converted to Islam. The struggle to capture them is "to the death" and upon its completion the Islamic caliphs will be reinstated according to the ways of Allah and his prophet Muhammad.

Terror is the tool with which Bin-Laden and his people aspire to make their vision a reality. Since the nineties, Afghan alumni have been involved in the majority of large-scale terror attacks all over the world. This terror system included the perpetration of terror attacks and mass killings. However, Bin-Laden's main contribution was the training of cadres whom he sent throughout the world after undergoing training in terror and guerrilla warfare at his camps in Afghanistan.

These terrorists were to serve as forerunners in the great, anticipated confrontation between the Islamic civilization and the Western civilization.[2] The organization chosen to lead the camp of Afghan alumni as the vanguard of the entire Islamic world was Bin-Laden's organization, "Al-Qaida." This organization served simultaneously as a terror group in every sense of the word, and also as a roof-organization for terror networks trained in Afghanistan, whose leaders were in charge of the training of military/terrorist forces of the Islamic Front and planners of a global terror system. The few, but qualitative terror attacks perpetrated by Al-Qaida in Africa and the Middle East were meant to demonstrate the power and damaging capabilities at the disposal of Islamic fighters in the United States to the "Islamic Front" branches spread worldwide. The United States was presented as the power symbolizing the West, and the terror activated against it was intended to expose the vulnerability of the leader of Western, secular culture and its helplessness in a confrontation with the fighting Islam so ready for sacrifice. The terror attacks perpetrated by Al Qaida were directed against American symbols of power; the embassies in Africa and the U.S. navy destroyer in Yemen, and constituted a prelude to the main attacks of September 2001 on United States territory. This great provocation was geared to escalate the inevitable confrontation with the West (headed by the United States) and draw all of Islam into it. The activities conducted since Bin-Laden announced the establishment of the "International Islamic Front for Jihad against the Jews and the Crusaders" in February 1998 all led to the crescendo of September 2001.

In Bin-Laden's apocalyptic scenario, the United States and her Western allies were designated a predetermined role, which, if followed closely, would help him to produce the manifestation that he sought to create between two extreme camps and two civilizations engaged in a struggle, which would culminate in a dichotomic confrontation over religious and cultural hegemony. His contained and temporary success in attacking the United States triggered a military confrontation between a U.S.-led international coalition and the Taliban regime in Afghanistan, and generated the launching of a global war against terror, a battle that threatens the very existence of Al-Qaida and Bin-Laden. The immediate results of this campaign have led to the removal of the Taliban regime, which served as Al-Qaida's patron for a period of five years, and resulted in a severe blow to the Al-Qaida infrastructure in this country.

It is reasonable to say that due to his actions, Bin-Laden brought tribulation upon himself, which will ultimately lead to his own destruction, and that with his own hands he caused the establishment of an international coalition determined to rip up the foul roots of the terror industry, which he had so carefully nurtured during the previous decade. The achievement of the goals of the campaign against Al-Qaida and its allies will take a long time, mainly because the malignant cells of the "Afghan" terror were left to multiply for such a prolonged period, and its offshoots have spread to many parts of the world. Only the proper management of this campaign can bring about its ultimate eradication, or at least significantly lessen its abilities to strike out.

Therefore, it is important to continue the momentum and contend with the overall components of the phenomena of world terror; this is the true challenge faced by the global war against terror. In order to "lure the terror genie back into its bottle" it is essential to assess correctly the problem's focal points and direct confrontation with them through effective international cooperation. This challenge lies at the doorstep of President Bush, who has undertaken in the name of the United States government, to lead the battle against one of the most vicious diseases to inflict human society in the twenty-first century.

It is noteworthy that on the operational level, the particularly violent terror attack ("mega terror") of September 11 was a "natural" outcome of the development of modern international terror in general, and of Afghan alumni led by Bin-Laden, in particular. The increasing potential violence, which is expressed in the use of more powerful and larger amounts of explosives, the sophistication of the terrorists' methods based on technological development, their efforts— which are already supported by Armageddon nihilistic ideologies—to attain non-conventional weapons clearly underscore this trend. Terror entities such as Bin-Laden and his cohorts never concealed their intention to carry out "mega" terror, and actually announced this fact in public.

In the current controversy within the United States regarding the performance of the American intelligence agencies vis-à-vis information that had accumulated during the period preceding the attack, American security entities, including the director of the FBI,[3] admitted that if handled properly, indications of a "warning nature," which were in the possession of American intelligence, might have pointed to a possible Al-Qaida attack using American aircraft. Information in the hands of various entities within the American intelligence operations—which was not presented to any single, central authority—included the entry of wanted terrorists into the United States; a disproportionate presence of "people from the Middle East" in flight schools in the United States, combined with a suspicion that this phenomenon was connected to Bin-Laden; and the arrest of a foreign citizen suspiciously linked with radical Islamic circles in Europe as well as Al-Qaida, who sought to learn how to fly a civil aircraft just three weeks prior to September 11.[4]

It is therefore reasonable to presume that the terror attack on the United States was an "expected surprise" on the strategic level. It was surprising in its timing, its sophisticated simplicity, and the ease with which it was achieved, while exploiting security breaches in the United States and the open, liberal lifestyle of American society in order to cause it harm.

The willingness of several terrorist factions currently active in the international arena to escalate their activities and cause mass carnage, without any restraints as to the applied means and operation methods, is an existing reality. This will affect the terror level of established terror organizations that are under the controlling "rein" of countries that support terror. In general, the direction in which terror is heading is a clear escalation that dictates the need to confront its threats directly and accurately. The war against terror must grapple with its operational threats as well as its conscious implications on the general public and on decision-makers in countries targeted by terror. At the same time, there is a need to provide a response to the basic problems that constitute a hotbed for the burgeoning of terror and a conservatory for recruiting new members of terror organizations, which include poverty, ignorance and socio-economic gaps.

The Globalization of Terror describes the preparations and performance of the terror attack in the United States and examines the attack against the background of the worldview of the Afghan alumni and the unique structure of the terror organizations and their cells, which acted in the name of the Global Jihad concept as perceived by Bin-Laden and his men. It describes the combat strategy against global terror, the anticipated stages of the struggle, and the problems presented by international terror and the countries that support terror; these will have to be faced by the international coalition, which aspires to contend with the threats of future terror that endanger all those who hold human rights and liberty dear while moving into the new era of the third millennium.

Notes

1. The term Afghan "alumni" relates to two categories: (1) volunteers from all over the Muslim world who participated in the Afghan Jihad against the Communist regime in Kabul and the USSR forces; (2) volunteers and recruits from all over the Muslim world who came to Afghanistan after the war and underwent training in terror and guerrilla warfare.
2. Shaul Shay and Yoram Schweitzer, *The Terror of Afghan "Alumni"—The Islam Against the Rest of the World*, The International Policy Institute for Counter-Terror, The Interdisciplinary Center, Herzliya, Issue 6, September 2000.
3. Dan Eggen and Susan Schnidt Mueller, *Clues That Might Have Led to the September 11 Plot*, *Washington Post* Internet edition, May 30, 2002.
4. Michael Isikoff and Daniel Klaidman, The Hijackers We Let Escape, *Newsweek* Internet edition, June 3, 2002, and Ronen Ratnesar and Michael Weusskopf, How the FBI Blew the Case—The Whistleblower, *Time*, June 3, 2002, pp. 26-32.

1

Islamic Fundamentalism and Bin-Laden

Islamic Fundamentalism—The Background

The origins of the expression "fundamentalism" are Christian Protestant. The word has been adopted by Western researchers, politicians, and the press as a term of reference for religious/ideological fanaticism; the term is also applied to the phenomenon of Islamic zealots.

Islamic fanatics regard the use of this term in reference to Islam as an expression of Western intellectual imperialism. The term that they use to refer to themselves is *Islamayun*—Islams or the faithful of Islam (in contrast to *Muslimun,* which means one whose religion is Islam, but whose lifestyle may be secular).[1]

The semantic meaning of "fundamentalism" refers to a fervor for the principles of religious beliefs, a way of life that stems from the latter and includes adherence to all of its manifestations; adopting religious symbols in daily life; behaving according to the normative codes of Islam, or organization and activity to preserve all of these principles and their dissemination in society.[2]

By their very existence, Fundamentalist organizations, associations and movements embody the full scope of this phenomenon's manifestations, signifying an ideology that facilitates its goals through the use of political means. The Fundamentalist movements are essentially ideological, and their worldview is based on the holy writings of the Islam.[3] This type of ideology, which is rooted in "divine revelation," is driven by a rejection of any other ideology, as the latter is the creation of human conception, which is inherently perceived as imperfect.

An expression of this type of rejection can be observed in various slogans such as "Islam is the solution" or "not east, not west," which are widespread in the Fundamentalist propaganda. Those faithful to Islam believe that "the realization of Allah's will on this earth," meaning the establishment of an Islamic society and state, is the only solution to the maladies plaguing human society.[4]

Islamic Fundamentalism is not made up of one single approach. It contains major differences in the interpretation of Islamic history (Sunni, Shiite), as well as in the interpretation of commandments deriving from the principles of belief and the operative approach that best serves the ideology.[5] The Fundamentalist movement may embody different characteristics, from violent activity patterns (jihad), severance of any connection with the infidels (hijra), or service in the form of an organization that regards an investment in education and indoctrination (Dawa) as its ultimate goal—each group adheres to its own approach.

The basic common denominator, shared by all of the movements, is the perception of Islam in its current state as a culture that is becoming extinct. This assessment feeds the sensation of emergency and pessimism, and constitutes one of the basic cultural-psychological motivations vis-à-vis their actions.

In the history of the development of Islamic Fundamentalism, several events and processes can be identified that have contributed to the crystallization of its approach and conceptions:

Encounter with the West. The expansion of Fundamentalism is thought to be rooted in this encounter, which also serves as momentum for its present escalated strength. The encounter with the West involves many facets: The military, technological, scientific and economic superiority of the West, cultural estrangement, the Imperialist "scheming," a modernism which alongside its blessings instigates major changes in traditional lifestyles. The problematic issues triggered by this encounter, which rapidly evolve into confrontation, make it possible to define Fundamentalism as one of the forms of addressing this issue, or as the Islamic response to Western culture.[6]

Physical confrontation with the infidels. This stems from the overall experience of the encounter with the West, but it contains significant inherent influences both because of the emotionally charged aspect of these confrontations, and because of the pointed emphasis placed on the inferiority of the Islamic East vis-à-vis the West.[7]

Confrontation with the government. This includes experiences that sometimes have major impact on the direction taken by the Fundamentalist movements. Persecution and oppression against the Islamic faithful by various governments, particularly hardship and torture during incarceration, have generally led to "a temporary lowering of profile" but have instigated renewed activism and radicalism in the long term.[8] The experiences during imprisonment have taught the Islamic faithful that their primary enemies are not the West, Imperialism and Zionism, but rather their own rulers. This conclusion clarified the need for activism and confrontation with the ruling government through political or forceful means in order to cause its downfall.

Thus, Fundamentalism represents a radical ideology, which negates the existing order and expresses an aspiration for a more just society. This constitutes a struggle for social and economic change as part of an overall battle to bring Islamic peoples back to their authentic roots. Fundamentalism combats a failing socioeconomic reality as well as modernism, which cannot meet the materialistic and social expectations that it arouses, and seeks a cure for the social maladies at the root of Islamic societies, according to traditional, authentic standards rather than foreign, Western and modern standards.

The basic foundations of the Fundamentalist worldview were already laid in the writings of Ibn Timia (1263-1328), which served as a source of inspiration for the Wahabian movement for renewal in the eighteenth century. Ibn Timia developed a theory that justified the de-legitimization of and rebellion against rulers who fail to adhere to the Sharia (like the Muslim-Mongolian rulers of his time).[9]

As noted above, Islamic Fundamentalism is not a new phenomenon, but it is customary to view the beginnings of the new Islamic era in the renewed encounter with Western culture, which apparently began at the time of Napoleon's invasion of Europe at the end of the eighteenth century. Regardless of the above-mentioned theory, there are those who argue that the reawakening of Islam began even earlier with the rebellion of the Wahabis in the Arabian Peninsula, without any direct connection to Western influence.[10]

Muhammad Ibn-Wahib launched his activities in Mecca, preaching against the Ottoman rule and its supporters in the Arabian Peninsula. He argued that the Ottomans had neglected the sites sacred to Islam, violated the commandments of the Koran, and in his eyes had become idol worshippers. Ibn-Wahib called for the purification of religion and a return to untainted Islam, and declared a jihad against the Ottoman rulers at the head of a small group of supporters. He made an alliance with Muhammad Ibn-Saud, and after the former's demise in 1787, Ibn-Saud continued the struggle against the Ottomans. He even succeeded in temporarily capturing Mecca,

Medina and Karbala (a sacred city to the Shiites). In 1813, Ibn-Saud was defeated by the Ottomans, but the revolt was not completely suppressed, and the Saudi monarchy was finally founded in 1932.

The Wahabian revolt shook the foundations of the Muslim world, and inspired the establishment of small groups throughout the Muslim world that preached the adoption of Wahabian religious principles.

In any event, from the nineteenth century onward we witness a reawakening of the Muslim community in various parts of the world as a result of its encounter with Western culture. The above-mentioned religious principles were partially adopted by Fundamentalist philosophers in the twentieth century, such as Hassan Al-Wahabi—founder of the Muslim Brotherhood, Al-Mawdudi—one of the leading Islamic philosophers in India, Sayyid Qutb—one of the followers of Al-Bana in Egypt, and others.

Among the prominent reactions to the encounter with the West, one must take note of the Modernist movement, which aspired to adapt the values of Muslim heritage to the modern worldview, in its European mode. This movement is generally associated with the philosophy and activities of individuals such as Jamal A-Din Al-Afghani (who died in 1897) and Muhammad Abdu, the Chief Mufti of Egypt.[11]

Muhammad Abdu preached absolute devotion to Islam and strict adherence to its commandments, but simultaneously permitted innovative interpretations of the Sharia, called for full equality for women, and demanded the abolishment of polygamy. Abdu was accused of heresy by religious zealots in Egypt and was forced into exile in France. From his place of exile, he founded a nationalist political movement that called for a renewed examination of the various aspects of Islam in order to turn the religion into a faith in the spirit of the modern era.

The Modernists tried in various ways to lead Islam into the adoption of Western lifestyles without deserting Islamic values. They experienced only partial and external success, as the adoption of Western lifestyle and technology did not serve as a satisfactory replacement for faith and the original values. As the direction taken by the Modernists did not provide an adequate solution for the challenges presented by the encounter with the West,[12] Sunni Islamic Fundamentalism started to grow simultaneously at several focal points in the Middle East (mainly Egypt) and in the Indian subcontinent. Despite the geographical distance, it is possible to find marked similarities in worldviews, when diagnosing the maladies of Muslim societies and the ways to correct them.

The main stepping-stone in the development of radical Islam was laid with the establishment of the Muslim Brotherhood (Al-ahwan al-muslimun) in 1929 by Hassan Al-Bana. Al-Bana sought to oust British control from Egypt, revise the secular constitution enacted in Egypt in 1923 under British influence, and to establish an Islamic state according to the spirit of the Sharia. He called for a return to Islamic orthodoxy while demanding that the government address social problems in the areas of education, economics and personal welfare, all in the name of Islam.[13]

A clear and candid definition of the worldview of the Muslim Brotherhood movement is found in a speech delivered by Hassan Al-Bana at the fifth conference of the Muslim Brotherhood held in Cairo in 1938:[14]

> We believe that the laws and regulations of Islam are universal, and that they regulate human matters in this world and the next. Those who believe that these regulations apply only to the spiritual aspect of worshipping God are mistaken. Islam is both an ideology and the worship of God, the homeland and civics, religion and state, spiritualism and practice...Islam is the entire, all-encompassing meaning and it must be given hegemony over all matters of life which will be of Islamic character.... All its rules and regulations must be observed if the nation aspires to be truly Muslim.[15]

Regarding the approach of the "Brothers" to the government, Al-Bana declared:

> The Islam in which the 'Brothers' believe regards government as one of its pillars. In our books of religious law, government is viewed as an ideological and fundamental element, and not a marginal or secondary religious edict. Islam is the governing authority and performance just as it is legislation and study, law and justice. The "Brothers" do not demand that they themselves govern, so that if anyone willing to undertake the responsibility of this duty can be found in the nation, and he will govern according to the Islamic way of the Koran, then the "Brothers" will serve as his dutiful and loyal soldiers; but if no one can be found, then government is part of the "Brothers" system and they will strive to extricate control from any government that does not observe God's commands.[16]

Al-Bana also defined the goal:

> Firstly, liberation of the Islamic homeland from any foreign government. Secondly, a free Muslim state will be founded in the liberated homeland, which will act according to Islamic law and implement its social system...

The jihad is one of the three central principles in the perception of the Muslim Brotherhood's movement; the other two are knowledge and education.

In an "Epistle about the Jihad," Al-Bana made his message clear:

> Oh, my Muslim brothers, this religion was founded through the jihad of your predecessors, who fortified themselves through the belief in Allah; for modesty when facing life's temporary temptations, for the preference of eternal life and the sacrifice of blood, the soul and money in order to support the truth, and for the love of death in the name of God.
>
> My Brothers!! The nation which is so intimate with the art of death, that knows how to die a pure death; this is the nation to which Allah will give the dearest life in this world and the eternal life of delight in the next world. Prepare yourselves for a great deed so that you shall have life. Know that there is no escape from death, which will not happen more than once. Thus, if you sanctify it in the name of Allah, you will gain life and will receive your reward in the world to come.... Act in favor of the honored death and you will be rewarded with the complete joy.... May we be blessed to receive the honor of the shuhada dead.[17]

Al-Bana succeeded in convincing his followers that death for Allah is desirable, and that he who sacrifices his life as a messenger of Islam will be blessed with eternal life in the Garden of Eden. The movement's members came from every stratum of Egyptian society, and it rapidly established itself in Egypt and spread throughout the Arab world. Organization members were careful to clothe themselves according to the spirit of Islam and strictly observed the religion's commandments and instructions.

In the thirties and forties, the Muslim Brotherhood initiated underground activity and terror targeted at the Egyptian government and the British presence in Egypt, as well as cultural and entertainment spots that were identified with Western life (bars, casinos, movie theaters).

In 1948, members of the Muslim Brotherhood enlisted to fight the war against Israel, and its members fought in the area of Ramat Rachel. Following the Arab defeat in the war against Israel, the Muslim Brotherhood initiated an open rebellion against the monarchy of King Farouk in Egypt, entered an alliance with Gamal Abd al-Nasser and played a central role in the success of the 1952 revolt, which put an end to monarchy in Egypt. After the death of Hassan Al-Bana in 1949 a crisis and resultant split took place in the organization's leadership; his followers were in full agreement regarding the goal and vision of the religious Islamic state, but they disagreed about the ways to achieve them.

Al-Bana's official heir, Hassan Al-Hadibi (who was appointed "chief mentor" of the Muslim Brotherhood in 1951), formulated a "moderate" theory during his years of incarceration in a Nasserite prison and recorded it in his book, *Preach But Do Not Judge*. The book signified a response to his adversary Sayyid Qutb, who formulated an opposing radical theory, which will be discussed below. The school of thought established on the basis of Hadibi's theory is referred to as "traditional Fundamentalism" by researcher Fuad Ajami.

This approach believes in a compromise with the political reality, whether it is democratic or dictatorial. The believer's realization of Islam is his own business, and only limited areas are under the control of the Islamic government. Hadibi maintained that the concept of jihad should only be adopted in its spiritual, moral and non-violent sense. The Muslim masses must be recruited in peaceful ways and not through violent or forceful means. Therefore, information and education are the central tools to reform society.[18]

Sayyid Qutb, the radical ideologist of the Muslim Brotherhood movement, was influenced by the worldview of Abu Ala-Al-Mawdudi (an Islamic religious law authority of Indian-Afghan descent) and his student Abu Al-Hassan A-Nadawi. Mawdudi's theory developed during the years of national struggle for India's independence. Mawdudi regarded nationalism and national states as a threat to the interests and identity of the Muslim faithful believers. In an article published in 1930, he argued that nationalism was not a new phenomenon, and that its roots were in the ancient world (Babylon, Egypt, Persia).

Nationalism has a permanent character and historical continuity, and its manifestations are expressed in the twentieth century in the form of the national state. According to Mawdudi, as nationalism is based upon joint race, language or interest, it leads to conflict and results in a reversion to the pre-Islamic absence of solidarity—the period of the social upheaval of the Jahilliya. Therefore, the nationalist state is a destructive and negative phenomenon that splits society into ethnic groups and thrusts barriers between them. On the other hand, Islam regards the world as a single social system to be shared by all of human culture as the representative of divine revelation on this earth.

To prove his point, Mawdudi raised the success of the prophet Muhammad, who was able to bridge tribal, family and economic rifts, which were characteristic of the Arabian Peninsula prior to the spreading of Islam. Therefore, Mawdudi translated the "Jahilliyan" reality typical of the period prior to Islam into the concepts and reality of modern nationalism in the twentieth century.[19]

Hassan A-Nadawi developed Mawdudi's theory into elitist patterns. In his opinion, the Muslims were appointed God's messengers to lead the world and humanity. Islam is the loftiest religion, so the Muslims cannot be subjugated or led by members of other religions. Therefore, A-Nadawi rejected cooperation with the members of other religions in order to reform society, as well as non-Islamic perceptions, and he believed that the return of Islam to dominance in human culture was a preordained, inevitable process.[20]

Sayyid Qutb's philosophy was influenced by the failure of the Muslim Brotherhood to contend with Nasser's regime in Egypt. This failure inspired Qutb's theories regarding Takpir, Hijra, Taliaa and the modern Abu Ala-Al-Mawdudi, all of which combined to lead the Islamic Fundamentalist into a relentless battle against the governing regime.

The origins of some of these concepts appear in Ibn-Timia's writings, while other components are based on the philosophy of Abu Ala-Al-Mawdudi. Sayyid Qutb describes reality in terms of *neo-Jahilliya*. According to classic Islamic conception, the Jahilliya (the period of ignorance) was limited to fixed and defined time dimensions—the period prior to the appearance of Islam in the Arabian Peninsula.[21]

Sayyid Qutb gives new and modern meaning to the concept of Jahilliya and applies its meaning to all of human history.[22] "Today's world lives in Jahilliya, from which life's principles and order have stemmed.... The Jahilliya does not apply to a period of time, but rather to a situation out of all of the situations that exist as long as society has turned away from the ways of Islam in the past, at present, and in the future, all combined."[23]

Qutb defines the Jahilliya as follows:

> The Jahilliyan society refers to any society that is not Islamic, and if I strive to define it objectively, this is a society that does not direct its subjection only to God...a subjugation which is expressed in the perception of faith, ritual commandments and legislation.[24]

All Jahilliyan societies in existence today are included in this definition, as according to Sayyid Qutb's characterization, in any case their main intellectual and material "yield" was Jahilliyan, although they appeared to be respectable and distinguished.

Despite the fact that it is universal, neo-Jahilliya focuses mainly on Western civilization that Qutb lumps into one integrative unit, including Christianity, Communism and Judaism. In second place, and on a secondary level, is the Islamic civilization. Although these cultures represent only a single component in the overall history of human cultures, Qutb regards them as a reflection of everything happening in the entire world and chooses to focus on them.[25]

Qutb claims that Islamic society is divided into two categories: Societies that declare their secularity (almaniya) and lack of religious fervor, and societies that declare that they "respect religion" but remove the actual practice of religion from the context of their societies. Qutb believes that any Muslim society that does not base its laws and lifestyle on divine judgment ("al-hakhamiah al alhaya") and on the Sharia, decrees its place as part of the modern Jahilliya.[26]

Sayyid Qutb and his brethren draw an analogy between the strength of neo-Jahilliya and that of the classical Jahilliya. They argue that no one can contest the "superiority and seniority" of the former, not only from the aspect of geographical deployment, but also from the point of view of the scope and severity of its crimes. "The Jahilliya of the twentieth century in reality is the cruelest Jahilliya in the history of mankind on the face of this earth."[27] Therefore, the efforts required by the Prophet to prevail over his enemies were minor in comparison to the efforts needed in the present and those that will be necessary in the future to eradicate evil. Now and in the future the community of believers will have to fight a double enemy: the external one (mainly the Western culture) and the internal one within the Muslim world.[28]

The principle of *Takfir* means that the society in which the Muslim lives is contaminated with corruption and heresy; thus, it is forbidden to cooperate or form any alliance with its components. The God-fearing Muslim must fight this society and its rulers in order to restore Islamic values within it. The battle against society and its rulers will be waged with the help of an advance guard, the *Taliaa*, which will use any means, including violence, to establish the Islamic religious state.

According to Qutb, it is also possible to utilize the principle of *Hijra* just as the Prophet Muhammad did in the year 622, when he was forced to leave the Jahilliyan Mecca and settle in Medina. This step can be emulated in a modern version, not by emigrating outside of the state boundaries, but rather through a behavioral and conceptual "emigration." Qutb regarded this isolationism as merely the first stage of emotional and spiritual preparation, and he believed in the subsequent transfer to direct action and violent struggle.

Sayyid Qutb's writings indicate not only a desire to present the difficulties and needs of true Islam in its struggle against neo-Jahilliya, but also constitute an attempt to conduct a philosophical and historical study of the basic fundamentals of the Western culture. The study of the West by philosophers like Sayyid Qutb does not claim to be either objective or "fair"; its purpose is to expose the inherent weaknesses and maladies of this culture, and through the negation of Western Civilization bring the reader to the conclusion that there is no alternative other than the Islam.[29]

Sayyid Qutb characterizes the maladies of the Muslim society, analyzes its components and reaches the conclusion that only activism, jihad and revolution, whose banner is raised by "Islamic believers," can create the turning point in the desperate existing reality and bring about the establishment of a state based on Islamic religious law. In his book, *Mualem fi A-Tarik* (Milestones), he stresses that there is a strong conflict between the two images, the two ideologies, the two forms of government and contrasting truths.

The Islam and ignorance (Jahilliya), the belief and heresy, the truth and lies, justice and evil, divine and human rule, the lord and the devil, etc.—one side cannot exist without eradicating the other, and there is no possibility of compromise or mediation between them.

Outb avers that this change can only be achieved by overthrowing the government, annihilating the leaders of the infidels, and replacing them with leaders faithful to Islam.

At the end of the fifties, the Shia also began to awaken, and Shiite Fundamentalism as an ideological-political movement started developing in the religious center of Najef, radiating its influence upon the Shiite populations of Iran and Lebanon. Najef of the sixties and seventies became an intellectual, revolutionary melting pot, in which the radical worldview of Lebanese Shiite religious leaders was fused, the same individuals who later became the leaders of the Hizballah in Lebanon.

The awakening of Shiite Fundamentalism is a part of the general phenomenon of Islamic Fundamentalism, whose origins we have already discussed, but the Shia is unique in its sensation of historical deprivation which is not only the result of its backwardness and discrimination vis-à-vis the West, but is also due to the fact that the Shiites have been an oppressed minority in the Muslim world for hundreds of years.[30]

The feeling of deprivation is rooted in the Shiite "Foundation Myth," which is based on the issue of the historical injustice perpetrated against the House of Ali after the death of the Prophet, when the former was deprived of his right to assume power. This phenomenon fuelled and empowered Shiite Fundamentalism, which awakened and surfaced under Khomeini's leadership. Khomeini's main contribution to the political thinking of the Shiite Islam was the concept of Wilayat Al-Fakiah—the rule of the Muslim religious cleric.[31] Khomeini argued that if the ruler is faithful to Islam, then he must be subordinate to the Fakiah and consult with the Fukaha themselves; control of the state must be placed in their hands.

The new meaning that Khomeini gave to Shia includes the belief in immediate messianic redemption, which can be promoted through political activity. Thus, one must not wait for redemption but rather take action to hasten it. According to the new Shia, the religious doctrines and symbols are to go hand in hand with the political struggle; not only is there no distinction between religion and politics, but even the most ritualistic aspects of Shiite Islam (such as the Ashura) take on political meaning. The Day of Ashura, which commemorates the tragedy of the battle of Karbala, at Khomeini's initiative became a symbol of political activism and self-sacrifice in the Shiite struggle against its foes.

In order to adopt this activism, modern Shia had to shift significantly from its basic concept of Takiya (the external appearance of a non-Shiite), which was characteristic of Shia until the last century. The Takiya was replaced by Khomeini's theory of the jihad in order to rectify the historical injustice carried out against the Shiites and reinstate Islam's former glory.

The various shades of Islamic Fundamentalism thus represent a radical ideology, which negates the existing order and expresses a longing for a more just society. This is a struggle aimed at changing a socioeconomic situation as part of an overall battle to return the Islamic peoples to their authentic culture. Fundamentalism takes up arms against a failing socioeconomic reality and against modernism, which cannot meet the materialistic and social expectations that it raises, and searches for an adequate response to the social maladies at the root of Islamic society, according to authentic and traditional standards, and not according to foreign and modern Western criteria.

The radical Islamic movements exist and act at various levels of intensity and violence in all Muslim countries in order to topple regimes and establish Islamic states according to the spirit of the Sharia, and to achieve independence for Muslim minorities in states identified with other cultures (Russia, China, the Philippines, Serbia, India, and more).

Radical Islam is therefore involved in struggles against foreign cultures on four levels:

- Deposing "secular" regimes and replacing them with Islamic regimes in Muslim states.
- The struggle of Muslim minorities to achieve independence and establish independent Islamic states.
- The struggle against ethnic-cultural minorities demanding autonomy or independence from Muslim states.
- The struggle against foreign cultures, particularly Western culture, at friction and contact points with the Islamic culture.

This reality is also compatible with the basic concept of Islam, according to which the world is divided into the Islamic area (Dar al-Islam) and the heretic area (Dar al-Harb); the goal of Islam is bring the proper faith to all of human civilization.

Islamic Fundamentalism utilizes a variety of means and tools to achieve its goals, from education, information, economic aid and spiritual welfare to political sabotage, terror and war. An analysis of conflict areas indicates that Fundamentalist efforts are primarily directed at changing the political reality within the Muslim world, and to a lesser extent towards other cultures.

Radical Islamic elements count three countries whose regimes can be characterized as Fundamentalist Islamic: Iran, Afghanistan and Sudan, as well as scores of Fundamental Islamic movements and organizations active throughout the Muslim world. The Fundamentalist Islamic states serve as a source of inspiration, encouragement, finance and support for the radical Islamic movements, and they act through their own channels and also via these organizations to export the Islamic revolution, the product of their school of thought, and to wage battle against foreign cultures, particularly the Western culture.

Three events or processes during the past millennium had a decisive impact on the development of Islamic Fundamentalism: (1) Khomeini's revolution in Iran—the turning of Iran into the center of radical Islam, (2) exporting the revolution to the Muslim world, and (3) radical Islam's defiance of the hegemony of the superpowers under the slogan "not east, not west."

The victory of the Islamic Mujahidin in Afghanistan and the Soviet Union's defeat in the theater of war were conceived as an Islamic victory in Islamic circles, not only in the battlefield, but also as a cultural-ethical triumph, which inspired an extensive cadre of volunteers brimming with Islamic fervor and combat experience to continue the dissemination of the Islamic Fundamentalist concepts.

The collapse of the Soviet Union and the disintegration of Communist ideology created an ideological and political vacuum, which opened an historical "window of opportunity" for Islamic circles. Communism and Socialism, which constituted an ideological basis for the majority of secular regimes in Muslim states, crumpled and left an ideological vacuum that radical Islam aspires to fill, so far with only partial success. The disintegration of the Soviet empire brought about the creation of new states with Muslim populations, which constitute a new arena for confrontation in Islamic circles.

For the first time in decades, Europe has experienced a reawakening of the issue of Muslim identity vis-à-vis populations in the Balkan (Bosnia, Kosovo, Albania), and for the first time religious and ethnic conflicts constitute a chance to acquire an ideological foothold for the concepts of extremist Islam. The new geopolitical reality in the era after "the Cold War" is perceived by radical Islamic circles as an expression of their success and places Islam face to face with Western culture in the front line of confrontation, first and foremost against the only superpower, the United States.

One of the most prominent phenomena at the end of the previous millennium and at the beginning of the current one is the appearance of the Afghan "alumni," who constitute the vanguard of the radical Islamic confrontation vis-à-vis rival cultures.

Bin-Laden and Islamic Fundamentalism

In the preceding section dealing with Islamic Fundamentalism we presented the various approaches of the prominent radical Islamic philosophers, who formulated the fundamentals of radical Islam in the twentieth century, concepts which have expressed themselves in the beginning of the present century as well.

All of the Islamic philosophers whose theories were described above played a senior religious role, which gave their opinions and decrees a binding religious validity. Many of them were not satisfied with an intellectual and religious-legal confrontation, but rather sought to implement their worldviews in practical terms, thus becoming shining exemplars and role models for radical Muslims throughout the Islamic world.

Osama Bin-Laden was not raised or educated in religious Islamic seminaries, but actually studied engineering at a prestigious university in Saudi Arabia. His radical worldview was formulated through the perusal and study of the writings of radical Islamic philosophers and took shape mainly during his years in Afghanistan in the framework of the jihad against the Soviets. His outlook was greatly influenced by the worldviews of the radical Egyptian leaders and by Wahabian Islamic concepts from his land of birth, Saudi Arabia. But his main source of influence was the Palestinian Sheikh Abdullah Azzam, the principal ideologist and main formulator of the perception of jihad in Afghanistan, who originated from the village of Silat-al Hartiya in the Jenin district. Azzam, Bin-Laden's partner in Afghanistan, held the ultimate responsibility for formulating the perceptions of the "Global Jihad."[32]

Abdullah Azzam was born in Silat al Khartiya in 1941. At the end of his studies in an agricultural high school, Azzam moved to Jordan where he worked as a teacher. From there he moved to Syria where he studied Islamic law at the University of Damascus and completed his studies in 1966, after which he moved to the West Bank. After Israel's occupation of the West Bank in 1967, he returned to Jordan, where he remained until the end of the sixties. He then moved to Egypt, where he pursued post-graduate studies at the Al-Azar University. After graduating in 1973, he went to Saudi Arabia where he taught at the Jeda University. In the course of his activity, Azzam reached the conclusion that the only way for Islam to succeed in establishing the Islamic community of believers was through armed struggle (jihad) against the foes of Islam.[33]

Abdullah Azzam decided to implement his concept and was one of the first to join the jihad against the Soviet conquest in Afghanistan. In 1979, he arrived in Pakistan where he became a lecturer at the Islamic University in Islamabad, but he left the position after a short time and moved with his family to the city of Peshawar on the Afghan border, which had become the main focal point of the mujahidin organizations in their war against the Soviets. There he established the "House of Supporters" (*Beit ul Ansar*), whose aim was to provide the necessary assistance to the jihad in Afghanistan.

The role of this office was to receive, train and dispatch Islamic volunteers who arrived in Pakistan to join the Afghan mujahidin ranks fighting in Afghanistan.[34] Azzam's work in Peshawar did not satisfy his ambitions, and he eventually joined the ranks of the mujahidin fighting in Afghanistan for a short while.

Azzam toured large areas of Afghanistan and was deeply impressed by the spirit of sacrifice and courage evinced by Islamic circles in their battle against the Soviet conquest. Upon his return to Peshawar, he increased his activities on behalf of the jihad and acted to unite the ranks of the feuding Afghan factions in the city for the common goal of jihad. Due to his activities he rapidly became one of the prominent leaders of the Islamic jihad. Azzam conducted several tours throughout the Arab world to recruit support for the jihad in Afghanistan, including visits to the United States. He wrote several books, in which he recorded his ideas and worldview regarding the jihad and the struggle over the future of Islam.

Undoubtedly, Azzam contributed significantly to the conversion of the war in Afghanistan into a global Islamic issue, a symbol of the Islamic struggle against alien cultures, and to the placing of the jihad in the forefront of Islamic activity against its adversaries. In Azzam's eyes, the jihad was conceived as the main tool with which to achieve victory for Islam and to establish the divine government on this earth. He became a symbol and leader of the jihad organizations and radical Islamic circles worldwide, and his impact on the Global Jihad movement lasted beyond his lifetime.

Azzam also acquired adversaries and enemies inside the Islamic movements, and on November 24, 1989 he and his two sons were assassinated in an explosion on their way to a mosque.[35]

Abdullah Azzam left many books behind him as well as an organized doctrine regarding the concept of jihad that constitutes a theoretical basis for modern jihad organizations. His actions and concepts influenced the development of numerous phenomena and processes in radical Islam:[36]

- The establishment of an Islamic "international" organization on the basis of the recruitment of volunteers from all over the Islamic world on behalf of the jihad in Afghanistan.

- The creation of an international network of Islamic terror cells supported by radical Islámic movements throughout the world.

- The triumph of the mujahidin in Afghanistan created an aura and ethos of bravery around the Muslim fighters and serves as a source of inspiration for Muslims around the globe.

- The creation of an extensive cadre of Islamic fighters imbued with a sense of mission and combat experience was created. These fighters became the vanguard in struggles between the radical Islam and its foes.

In the course of Azzam's years of activity in Peshawar and in Afghanistan, and at the beginning of Bin-Laden's career, the latter filled the role of Azzam's protégé. Bin-Laden adopted Azzam's concepts and ideas regarding the jihad and joined forces with him in the activities of the mujahidin service office. Subsequently, differences arose between the two and Bin-Laden split away from Azzam and launched independent activities involving the recruitment of volunteers, drills, funding, and their activation in the framework of operative activity to promote the jihad.

Bin-Laden's worldview is thus an amalgamation of a belief in an ascetic and puritan lifestyle, in the style of the Wahabians, to which he adheres in practice, alongside a fanatic radicalism which regards the jihad as the only way for Islam to vanquish its internal and external enemies, according to the doctrine of Azzam and his followers.

Bin-Laden, who lacks the authority to issue decrees regarding religious matters, was forced to rely on known, radical Islamic religious clerics who adopted his ideology and provided him with religious approval by issuing Islamic rulings (*fatwas*). His worldview embraced the fundamental principles of radical Islamic thinkers such as Al-Bana, Qutb, Mawdudi, and others who viewed the jihad as the solution for all Islamic maladies in the modern world. However, in contrast to the majority of Islamic jihad movements worldwide, whose top priority was to overthrow secular and corrupt regimes in their own countries, Bin-Laden adopted a different approach. Bin-Laden's outlook is based on the concept of "Global Jihad," which is designated to unite all of the radical Islamic forces and bring about the achievement of a central and supreme goal in the radical Islamic battle. This goal is the annihilation of the United States, which is perceived as the "serpent's head" and, according to Bin-Laden, is the root of every evil in the world.

Bin-Laden believes that the United States can be vanquished, just as the jihad fighters in Afghanistan defeated another superpower—the Soviet Union—and ultimately destroyed it as a political and ideological entity after the latter invaded the territory of an Islamic state. He does not negate the struggles of radical Islamic movements in their own countries, but he maintains that the main effort must be channeled towards the collapse of the United States, symbol of the anti-Islamic, secular Western culture. Bin-Laden focuses his main struggle against the United States because he believes that its collapse will cause the crumbling of all those regimes that in any case enjoy American support and sponsorship, including the "heretic" Islamic regimes and Israel.

Bin-Laden and the Formulation of a Worldview and Ideology of Afghan "Alumni"

The worldview of the Afghan "alumni" was molded during their sojourn and shoulder-to-shoulder combat in Afghanistan with the local mujahidin. Intensive religious and indoctrination lessons accompanied the absorption of the volunteers in Pakistan and Afghanistan. Their prolonged stay in Afghanistan as part of a cohesive religious society involved in a "holy" war against the enemies of Islam influenced their thought patterns and shaped their mode of action.

A central component of the worldview of the Afghan alumni was the waging of a "defensive jihad," believing that Islam must confront a Western offensive headed by the United States and the Jews, the latter of which, it perceived, directed and dictated U.S. policy.

In his combative statements, Osama Bin-Laden–one of the most prominent spokesmen of this conception–declared religious-cultural-historical war between Islam and the conspiratorial Jewish-Crusader alliance, which he believes aspires to vanquish Islam and conquer its holy lands.[37] This perception was expressed in the very first proclamation that Bin-Laden published in 1996 under the name "declaration of war."[38] Two years later, in February 1998, he and his comrades from the Egyptian, Pakistani and Bangladesh terror organizations declared the establishment of the "International Islamic Front for the Jihad Against the Crusaders and Jews."[39] The foundation of the Front served to express the worldview of the Front's members. The Front published a fatwa (religious edict), signed by the leaders of the Islamic organizations, including Osama Bin-Laden, who headed Al-Qaida, Aiman Al-Zawahiri—leader of the Egyptian "Islamic Jihad" faction, Ahmad Rifai Taha—one of the leaders of the Egyptian "Gama'ah a-Islamiyah," Sheikh Mir Hamza—the secretary of the Pakistani "Gamat alal ulma," and Fasslul Rahman—the emir of the "Jihad of Bangladesh" movement.

In this religious edict, the signatories issued a call to all Muslims worldwide to regard the killing of Americans and their allies–both civilians and military personnel–as a personal duty, in order to liberate the "holy temple in Mecca," the al-Aksa mosque, and in its more extensive reference, the Land of Israel in general and Jerusalem in particular, from the hands of the infidels.[40] When relating to this fatwa, Arab commentators noted the fact that the leaders of the Egyptian Islamic Jihad and Gama'ah al-Islamiyah" put aside their differences and agreed to join forces in the interests of their common goal, while establishing a mechanism to implement the decision.[41] These commentators observed that this agreement reflected an appeasement between the positions of the two organizations in light of the fact that this was the first time that the leaders of these organizations had signed a single proclamation and agreed on a strategic issue since the split between the two organizations in 1983. This situation testified to the partners' recognition of the status of the fatwa's initiator, Osama Bin-Laden, which went beyond the common denominator of the declared activity.

In May 1998, Bin-Laden gave his first press interview to a CNN reporter in which he declared his intention to kill Americans everywhere in the world; his justification was that this was his religious duty.[42] Subsequently, this theme arose repeatedly in Bin-Laden's declarations, and he took practical steps to realize his threats. In the framework of his preparations to implement a terror campaign in the United States, Bin-Laden initiated a comprehensive psychological warfare operation, starting with a propaganda film in June 2001, which was aired on the Qatar television network named Al-Jazeera. In the film he appealed to all Muslims to take part in the campaign against the foes of Islam, with the archenemies of the United States and Israel at the head of the list. After the attacks in September 2001 and the launching of the military offensive in Afghanistan on October 7, 2001 Bin-Laden and his followers stepped up their propaganda campaign.

In his series of interviews for Al-Jazeera, Bin-Laden repeatedly pontificated his doctrine against the enemies of Islam, in which he targeted not only the United States and Israel, but also "corrupt" and "sultanate" Arab regimes (the Gulf States headed by the Saudi monarchy). Subsequently, he expanded his list and included among Islamic foes all those who supported the United Nations in the war against the Taliban (while aiming his disparaging arrows mainly at the Muslim regimes that supported the decision).

From the declarations and interviews granted by Bin-Laden and his comrades among the Afghan alumni, it is possible to glean that according to his worldview, the entire globe in general, and the Middle East in particular, constitute an arena in which a conclusive battle for survival prevails between the three main religions. In this struggle, a Christian "Crusader-Jewish" coalition has been formed, which is expressed in the alliance between the United States and Israel (as well as world Judaism), which has conquered Islam's most sacred lands in Mecca, Medina, and Jerusalem, and aspires to crush it. He maintains that this alliance has methodically and intentionally massacred Muslims. As an example, Bin-Laden offers the "massacre" of the Muslim Iraqi population by the American forces in the Gulf War of 1991, the bombing of Iraq in December 1998, the massacre in Sabra and Shatilla during the War in Lebanon, and the killing of Palestinians in the lands occupied by Israel.[43]

With the aim of recruiting and motivating the community of believers, Bin-Laden relies on religious terminology and the use of terms conveying historical significance and Islamic connotations such as "crusaders" and "jihad." His justification of the extreme violence that he preaches, even against women, the elderly and children, is based on his interpretation, on Islamic rulings, and on historical precedents from the days of the Prophet Muhammad. He justifies the terror activities in terms of actions to protect the sanctity of Islam. Muslims throughout the world wage a defensive battle because they are persecuted and victimized by the tyranny and aggression of the West.

Through violence and terror Bin-Laden aspires to prove to his community of believers that the enemies of Islam, such as the United States, the former Soviet Union, current-day Russia and Israel, are vulnerable because of their lack of belief, although they would appear to be powerful and unbeatable.

In his declarations and interviews Bin-Laden stressed the importance of liberating Islam's sacred soil currently in the hands of infidels who desecrate and defile it. Bin-Laden called for the "purification" of the holy cities, Mecca and Medina, "which are under American conquest" in the Persian Gulf and predicted a similar fate for the "holy land" of Al-Aksa invaded by Israel.

In a press interview,[44] during which Bin-Laden was questioned about his part in the terror attacks of August 1998 against the U.S. Embassies in Kenya and Tanzania, he stated that "if encouragement of the jihad against Jews and Americans is considered a crime, then history will bear testimony to my being a criminal. It is our duty to encourage the jihad, and with God's help we have done so and certain people have responded to this encouragement."

In a subsequent interview at a later date, he elaborated on his dogma:[45]

1. My mission is to incite Muslims to rebel against the American invasion of Saudi Arabia.

2. I combat the Jewish attacks against "the Land of Islam," which include al-Aksa and Mecca.

3. In my eyes every American citizen is an enemy.

In another interview, when asked about his biography, Bin-Laden highlighted several biographical milestones that clarify how he chooses to present himself:[46] "I was born to two Muslim parents in Riad in 1377 according to the Hijeric era. My remaining years were passed in Mecca, Jeda and Al-Medina. My father, the sheikh Muhammad, who was born in Hatsarmavet (Yemen), came to Hijaz over seventy years ago in order to work. He had the honor of building the holy mosque in Mecca, where the ka'aba is located, and simultaneously he also built the mosque erected by the Prophet Muhammad in Al-Medina. Later, when it became known that the Jordanian government published a bid to renovate the Dome of the Rock mosque, he offered a fee lower than cost in order to ensure that he would be the one to renovate the mosque. In a nutshell, that is Osama Bin-Laden."

Replying to the reporter's question regarding his goals and wishes, he stated: "We desire and demand the right of every living being. We demand that our land be liberated from the hands of the enemies and the hands of Americans. Islamic lands have been victimized by this aggression, starting from al-Aksa mosque and subsequently this aggression of the Crusader-Jewish alliance, headed by the United States and Israel, continued until overtaking Saudi Arabia. We seek to stimulate the nation to liberate its land and wage a jihad in order to establish the laws of Allah."

In his interviews to the international media Bin-Laden was careful to cloak and justify his actions with articulate and reasoned Islamic religious rulings, based on religious expressions, while mentioning his affinity for the holy sites. Thus, he aimed at the lowest common denominator and appealed to the hearts of all Muslims throughout the world in order to obtain the widest support possible.

When asked in another interview[47] about his responsibility for and acquaintance with the perpetrators of the terror attacks in the U.S. embassies in Africa, he chose to reply in his customary manner, which included denial of responsibility for the attack, but simultaneously offered his support for the deed: "What I know is that those who endangered their lives to please the Lord, are true men. They have succeeded in saving the Islamic nation from shame."

Similar expressions can be found in his approach to other attacks, such as the one that was perpetrated at the joint headquarters of Saudi Arabia and the United States, where a team of American instructors was stationed in Riad in 1995, as well as to the attack on Dahran in 1996. "These acts were popular and pure responses (…) I admire these men who banished the shame from our nation—those who caused the explosions in Riad and Al Hobar (the attack in Dahran) and our brethren like young lions in Palestine, who are teaching the Jews a bitter lesson, on how a believer must act."[48] In the same interview he related to the fatwa (of February 1998) and stressed: "The target of all Muslims is every American man, because he is our enemy, whether he fights us directly or if he pays taxes…there are two parties to this struggle. One side is the worldwide crusade and its alliance with Jewish Zionism, and the second side is the Islamic world. In this struggle we will not accept that the first side attacks and steals Muslim oil, but when it meets Muslim opposition it claims that they are terrorists. It is our duty according to Islamic law to oppose the invasion by the United States, Britain and Israel, with all our strength."[49]

In a letter carrying his name in bold letters and his signature at its end, Bin-Laden wrote:

> The Jews and the Christians (for the first time he placed the Jews ahead of the Christians) are the prototype of the enemies of Islam. Therefore, it is the common duty of every Muslim to uphold the jihad against Jews and Christians. These efforts will bear fruit only if the enemy is crushed on every front. Thus we need relentless efforts to liberate the holy sites: Kashmir (this time he interpolated the holy war in India in order to enlist the Kashmir underground "Harkat al-Ansar" in the continued war effort against the common enemy), Palestine and other occupied territories.[50]

Bin-Laden portrayed the American units as conquering forces in the Gulf and Saudi Arabian Peninsula, which serve as the forefront of an overall American-Jewish conquest of the entire region, with the aim of stealing its resources and debasing Muslims. In his view, preference should be given to getting rid of the American forces and banishing them from the area. Subsequently, a reform must be introduced within Arab regimes in general and in that region in particular. If reform is not possible, then they must be replaced by religious Islamic regimes. It is his belief that the Islamic Sharia must be appropriately implemented and a just Islamic sovereignty must be established in Muslim countries in general and in the Saudi Arabian Peninsula in particular.

After the war broke out, in several interviews for the Al-Jazeera station, Bin-Laden repeated the main principles of his worldview and listed his adversaries, the enemies of Islam, and his goals, and credited the Lord with the blow dealt to the United States:[51]

> Behold Allah has struck America and caused it casualties. He destroyed its largest buildings, may Allah be glorified and blessed. And so America is full of fear from north to south and from east to west, praise Allah. What America is getting a taste of today is only a drop of what we have experienced for decades. For over eighty years our nation has tasted this humiliation and degradation, its sons are being murdered, their blood flowing, their holy sites are under attack and no one reacts. When Allah put success in the hands of a select Islamic group, the group of Islamic pioneers, they destroyed America. When they responded in the name of their oppressed sons and on behalf of their brothers and sisters in Palestine and in many Islamic countries, the entire world shrieked the cry of the infidels, and then came the hypocrisy.
>
> A million innocent children are being killed this moment, as I speak. They are being killed unjustly in Iraq, and we hear no words of condemnation, nor a religious verdict issued by the rulers of the sultanates. These days Israeli tanks and armored cars are entering Jenin, Ramallah, Rafiah, Beit Jallah and other sites on Islamic lands to wreak havoc, and we do not hear anyone raise their voice or lift a finger. But behold, when the sword is wielded against America 80 years later, hypocrisy lifts its head. Here they express sorrow for these murderers who abused the blood and the holy shrines of the Muslims. The least that can be said about them is that they are corrupt and follow falsehood and support the murderer against the victim, the evildoer against the innocent child, but Allah showed what they deserved.
>
> I say these things clearly and candidly, and every Muslim after this event and after the most senior Americans spoke, starting from the head of the world heresy, Bush

> and his gang, who appealed to the people and their commentators, and united the countries against us, even those who belong to Islam, this gang who set forth to damage this religion and combat Islam and people in the name of terror... [Bin-Laden did not finish the sentence]. A people at the end of the world, in Japan hundreds of thousands of people, large and small, were killed, but this is not a war crime. This is an issue that must be investigated. A million children in Iraq constitute an issue that must be investigated, but when several dozen people were killed in Nairobi and in Dar-a-Salam, they bombed Afghanistan and bombed Iraq, and the entire hypocrisy stood behind the head of world heresy, behind that dolt America and those beside her.
>
> I say that these events divided the world into two parts: The part with faith that has no hypocrisy and the part of heresy, may God protect us from it. Every Muslim must leap to the aid of his religion, because the winds of faith and the winds of change are blowing to banish deception from the island of Muhammad.
>
> To America and its people I have only a few words to say: I swear by Allah's name, who raised up the skies without any premeditation, that America must not dream, and not he who lives in America in safety, before we live in security in the reality in Palestine, and before all of the infidel armies vacate the land of Muhammad.

In the videotape, which was not aired publicly but was distributed among his supporters, for the first time Bin-Laden confessed at the end of October and during November 2001 that he was the one behind the attacks in the United States. For the first time, Bin-Laden used first person singular and first person plural. In the video he explained the terror that his people perpetrated by pointing out that there are two types of terror, good terror and bad terror. "What we implement is good terror. If revenge for the murder of his people (Muslims) is terror, then history will testify to their being terrorists. Yes, we killed their innocent people (the infidels who were in the Twin Towers), and this is legitimate both religiously and logically. Those in the Twin Towers were not civilians, because Islam prohibits the killing of civilians even in a holy war. But because the towers were full of supporters of the American economical power which is exploiting the world–they deserve to die."[52]

Despite the attempt on the part of Bin-Laden and his cohorts in the Global Jihad Movement to present themselves as the representatives of all of Islam, there is a difference, for example, between the worldview of the Muslim Brotherhood (in its "pragmatic" interpretation, which was also exploited through extremist commentary to justify murderous terror and violence) and that of the Afghan alumni.

Admittedly, both schools tend to derive their individual and communal behavioral patterns from religion, according to their interpretation; however the main difference lies in their dissimilar interpretations of Islamic religious ruling. The basic perception of the Muslim Brotherhood defines their ultimate goal as enlisting souls for Islam in peaceful ways (through education, persuasion and preaching according to the principle of the "Dawa"). Active jihad is only an auxiliary means to serve the "Dawa"; Bin-Laden and his followers regard the "warlike jihad" as the sole vision and the ultimate goal.

Bin-Laden and his partners preached in favor of the "presentation" of the jihad as a fight against the "Jews and Crusaders," thus they claimed that

> Americans and their allies must be killed, both civilians and soldiers, and this is the personal religious duty of every Muslim anywhere, until the Mosque of al-Aksa and the mosque of al-Haram in Mecca are liberated from the control of these people. These armies must be banished from the land of Islam, and their power must be paralyzed so that they may never endanger any Muslim. We call on every Muslim who puts his faith in Allah and in the holy duty to obey the word of the Lord to kill the Americans and steal their money every place on earth, and we appeal to the Muslim religious scholars, to the leaders, the youth and the soldiers to attack every individual who aids the Americans. He who forms an alliance with them is comparable to someone who has made a pact with the devil.[53]

Bin-Laden's religious and ideological fundamentals serve as the foundation for the action doctrine that he formulated, and at its nucleus is the aspiration to achieve practical and immediate goals according to his belief. The chain of terror activities initiated by Bin-Laden was designed to deliver a strategic blow of terror that would significantly cripple the status and influence of the United States. The weakening of the United States as a superpower representing and leading Western culture would precipitate the collapse of its protégé, Israel, and the fall of corrupt Arab regimes such as the Saudi throne and other governments that betrayed the Muslim world and made peace with Israel.

Bin-Laden and the Jewish/Israeli Issue

The ideology touted and practiced by Bin-Laden underwent developments and variations in emphasis over the course of the years. Bin-Laden adopted a radical Islamic concept for the use of jihad as the main route to realize the objectives of Islam. The enemies of Islam and their role in his worldview were determined by the circumstances. The Jews, as a bitter adversary threatening the realization of the Islamic caliphate vision, did not claim a high priority on Bin-Laden's list of preferences during the battles against the Soviet forces in Afghanistan (1979-1989). However, as the concepts of the "Global Jihad" crystallized, Bin-Laden began also to focus his preaching against what he called "the conspiratorial alliance between world Jewry and its Christian partner."[54] When he first began advocating a holy war against these two cosmic entities, he focused his attention on the United States as the representative of the "crusader" world Christianity and against Jews residing in the United States whom he regarded as a spearhead for world Jewry.[55] In subsequent stages he added on the "Jewish" political aspect in the form of the State of Israel. His characteristically anti-Semitic preaching, in which he described the Jews as a motivating factor in the U.S. anti-Islamic policy, served to enforce his description of the confrontation between Islam, Judaism and Christianity as an international conspiracy. This perception was based on hundreds of years of anti-Semitic incitement in the Arab and Muslim world.

The confrontation that flared up between Israel and the Palestinian Authority in September 2000, and which was given a name with overt religious connotations–Intifadat al Aksa–represented an exceptional window of opportunity for Bin-Laden and suited his aspirations to shift the Arab-Israeli confrontation from a local national conflict to a religiously oriented confrontation which spreads beyond the borders of the Land of Israel.[56] Bin-Laden and other spokesmen from among the Afghan alumni began to show a growing interest in the Israeli-Palestinian confrontation and exploited it as a lever for promoting the dissemination of radical Islam.

In the framework of his preparations for the terror attack in the United States, Bin-Laden increased the anti-Israel propaganda vis-à-vis the Palestinian issue. In a short propaganda film aired on Al-Jazeera in June 2001, for the first time Bin-Laden personally appealed publicly to his "Muslim Brethren" throughout the world to rise up and join their fighting brothers in Palestine.[57] After the attacks in September 2001, and in light of the war declared against him by the United States, Bin-Laden and the senior members of his organization again raised the matter of the Palestinian issue in order to generate enthusiasm and public support in Islamic and Arab countries. They artfully fanned the anti-Israeli feelings stimulated in Arab and Muslim countries by the photos broadcasted from the confrontation arena in Israel and the territories, in order to win support for their goals, on the basis of their solidarity with the Palestinian cause.

Against the background of the vitriolic rhetoric spewed out by Bin-Laden and his spokesmen against Israel and the Jews, the indisputable and conspicuous fact is that in contrast to the Palestinian and Shiite terror organizations that perpetrated many bloody terror attacks against Israeli and Jewish targets worldwide, the Afghan alumni carried out relatively few attacks against these targets, despite their radical view vis-à-vis the Jews and Israel.[58]

In fact, only in the second half of the nineties did the Afghan alumni perpetrate a few attacks and attempted attacks against Israeli and Jewish targets. And these were carried out by radical terror organizations that were not sponsored by Bin-Laden. Thus, for example, on April 19,1996 (during the "Grapes of Wrath" Campaign in Lebanon), the Gama'a al Islamiya Egyptian organization perpetrated a terror attack against tourists at the Europe Hotel in Cairo, killing seventeen Greek pilgrims. When taking responsibility, the organization stated that the attack was originally targeted at Israeli tourists who usually stay at the Europe Hotel.

The Algerian G.I.A. organization perpetrated three attacks against Jewish targets in France, as part of its overall terror tactics against that state. These attacks included placing two car bombs, one near a synagogue in Lyons in 1994 (which was defused) and another near a Jewish school in Vilerban. Thanks only to a faulty mechanism in the school bell, which caused it to fail to ring at its regular time at the end of the school day and delayed it by several minutes, was the slaughter of large numbers of school children prevented. In addition, a letter bomb was sent to the editor of a Jewish newspaper in France (1996).[59]

In 1995, members of the Biat al-Imam (meaning the pledge of faith to the Imam) group were arrested in Jordan, led by Isam Muhammad Taher (called Abu-Muhammad al-Makdasi), a Palestinian born in Jaffa. Their plan was to attack Israeli targets in Jordan. In July 1997, members of the group who were planning to infiltrate into Israel in order to perpetrate terror attacks were arrested.[60]

Despite its being the most radical of all the organizations and cells active on the "Islamic Front" and regardless of its negative attitude to Jews, the Al-Qaida organization headed by Bin-Laden did not directly attack Israeli or Jewish targets abroad up to the year 2000. There are several reasons for the relatively low number of Sunni terror attacks against Israeli and Jewish targets abroad: Al-Qaida was

1. Focusing their struggle first and foremost against anti-Islamic regimes in their countries of origin in order to replace these administrations with Islamic rule based on the Sharia.

2. "Making do with" the incorporation of only sporadic attacks against these targets as part of their overall terror policy against their non-Islamic adversaries.

3. Concentrating their terror policy on American targets due to their view that the United States was their main and central adversary, which must be attacked to protect Islam.

A Shift in Al-Qaida's Trend of Activity and of Its Affiliated Cells Against Israeli and Jewish Targets

Starting at the beginning of 2000, there was indication of a shift in the trend of activities vis-à-vis Israeli and Jewish targets. This change was to be expressed initially in a large terror attack, which was thwarted by the Jordanian authorities on the eve of the millennium celebrations. The terrorists were members of a terror network who underwent training in Bin-Laden's camps in Afghanistan.

The reason for the decision to accelerate the efforts of Al Qaida and its supporters at this particular time is not clear, but it would be reasonable to assume that it was the result of criticism directed against Bin-Laden suggesting he had neglected the Palestinian struggle in favor of his battle against the United States. It is noteworthy that among the Al-Qaida members and their supporters, and among the religious preachers active in the promotion of the Global Jihad concept, there are many who are of Palestinian origin.

The trend of increasing anti-Israel activities took on added momentum after the start of the U.S. attack in Afghanistan (October 2001) and was further fueled by the Palestinian-Israeli confrontation, which had been christened the Intifadat al Aksa. Bin-Laden's men and the Islamic terror cells trained at Bin-Laden's camps in Afghanistan increased their efforts to perpetrate terror attacks targeted at Israeli and Jewish sites, against the background of the growing hostility in the Muslim world vis-à-vis Israel. Most of the attacks against Jewish and Israeli targets in Israel and abroad were foiled, but the intentions of the Afghan alumni to attack these targets has not abated, and they publicly announce their desire to achieve this goal.

The Arrest of the Terror Network in Jordan (December 1999)

In mid-December 1999, a terror scheme scheduled for the eve of the millennium was thwarted in Jordan. This terror setup was known as "The Millennium Plot." (The network included not only Jordan, but also the terror group in which Ahmed Rassem was active. The latter was apprehended on the Canadian-United States border in mid-December 1999, before he had the opportunity to blow up the Los Angeles Airport, and attempt to detonate the American destroyer, the *USS Sullivan*, at the beginning of the year 2000). The intention of the planners was to carry out several attacks at tourist attractions, causing massive casualties to Israeli and American targets in Jordan. The tourist sites included the site of the baptism of Jesus (the Muatas), the site of Moses' burial (at Nevo Mountain), the Radisson Hotel in Amman, and the border control stations between Jordan and Israel.[61]

The intention of the terror network's planners from Pakistan, Afghanistan and Jordan was to cause multiple American, Israeli and other casualties. It was due only to the alertness of the Jordanian security forces that this scheme was nipped in the bud, without any casualties, leaving no impression on public opinion in Israel and the world.

The Arrest of a Terror Cell of Afghan Alumni in the Area of the Palestinian Authority The episode of Saed Hindawi.[62]

In February 2000, Saed Sitan Mahmid Hindawi, a Palestinian whose family originated from Halhoul and who had resided for many years in Lebanon, was arrested. His family had returned to Hebron upon the establishment of the Palestinian Authority and his father is the Commander of the Hebron Police.

During his questioning, he disclosed that he had gone to Pakistan in 1998 to pursue his studies. In the course of his studies a friend told him about the possibility of undergoing military training in Afghanistan. In June 1998, Hindawi and a friend set out for Afghanistan in order to join the ranks of the trainees. They arrived initially at the city of Jalabad, and from there were transferred to one of Bin-Laden's camps, the Darunte Camp, located near that city. Together with twelve other trainees, the pair underwent training in the use of light arms and explosive materials, and at the end of the training period returned to Pakistan.

In November 1998, Hindawi set out for Afghanistan a second time in order to expand his training to other combat means. This time, as well, the training was conducted at the Darunte Camp. The group of fifteen trainees underwent two months of training. At Darunte, Hindawi was trained in the use of rifles, machine guns, RPGs and handguns. At the end of his military training he returned to the West Bank and together with his friends planned to perpetrate attacks against Israel. At the time of his arrest, diagrams for assembling bombs were found in his possession.

The episode of Muhammad Daka.[63] In March 2000, Basal Rashed Muhammad Daka was arrested. Daka was born in 1975 and resided in Tulkarem. During the year of 1999 he was a student at the Karachi University in Pakistan. In the course of his studies he set out for Afghanistan with a friend in order to undergo military training.

On his way to Afghanistan Daka arrived in Peshawar on the Pakistan-Afghan border, where he joined a group of volunteers from various Arab countries. Together they were sent to the Darunte training camp. For three weeks the group underwent training in the use of various weapons (Kalachnikovs, machine guns, RPGs and grenades). After completing this training, he joined another training series in detonating explosives, and at the end of the second bout of training returned to Israel, where he was arrested.

The episode of Nabil Ukal.[64]In June 2000, a resident of the Jabalya Camp named Nabil Mediras Muhamad Abu-Ukal was arrested. In 1990, Ukal had joined the Hamas and participated in the organization's Dawa activities. During the years 1993-1995 he was a member of the Hamas' security mechanism and dealt with the surveillance of people suspected of collaborating with Israel as well as gathering intelligence about Israel defense forces in the Gaza Strip. In 1997, Ukal set out for Karachi, Pakistan, with a number of other Hamas activists in order to attend a conference on the issue of Dawa. During his visit, Ukal underwent military training at a training camp of the Harkat al-Antsar organization in Kashmir and at a Bin-Laden training camp.

In July 1998, Ukal returned to the Gaza Strip to continue his activities in the framework of the Hamas' Dawa. During 1998, Ukal met with Hamas leader Sheikh Ahmad Yassin, told him about the training he had undergone and requested his blessing to establish a military infrastructure, which would carry out attacks against Israel. Sheikh Yassin gave his blessing to Ukal and even provided him with money to fund his activities. In June 2000, Ukal attempted to set out for additional training in Afghanistan through the Dahania Airport in Rafah, but was arrested by the Israeli security forces. From his interrogation, it appears that he intended to perpetrate the following:

1. Terror attacks in markets and Israeli military facilities through the planting of explosive devices activated by a cellular phone.

2. Kidnapping Israeli soldiers.

3. Launching missiles towards a Jewish settlement in the Gaza Strip.

Ukal attempted to recruit Israeli Arabs to collaborate in perpetrating terror attacks in Israel. His arrest in 2000 prevented the realization of his intentions.

The Arrest of a Terror Cell in Turkey En-Route to Perpetrating a Terror Attack in Israel[65]

On February 15, 2002, three members of the Biat El-Imam organization were arrested in the city of Van, Turkey. During interrogation the three (one Jordanian citizen and two Palestinians) confessed that they had been sent by Abu-Museb, a Jordanian activist and Afghan alumnus, who was cooperating closely with Al-Qaida. The three, who had undergone training in Afghanistan, moved to Iran after the beginning of the American onslaught in Afghanistan. Prior to the planned attack, they crossed the border between Iran and Turkey, where they were to have received documentation from a local liaison. From Turkey they were to have traveled to Jordan, and from there their mission was to infiltrate Israel and perpetrate a simultaneous three-cornered suicide mission in Tel Aviv and Ramat Gan. The arrested terrorists divulged that there were two additional three-member cells in Iran, each of which was planning to act in Israel along the same lines.

This incident, in addition to Richard Reed's arrival in Israel in order to gather intelligence about targets in Israel on behalf of a terror cell cooperating closely with Al-Qaida, constituted additional evidence of Bin-Laden's plans, and those of terror cells supported by him, to carry out massive attacks inside Israel. (Reed was a British citizen who attempted to blow up an American Airlines plane on a flight from Paris to Miami on December 22, 2002, by igniting explosives hidden in his shoe, thus earning himself the moniker of "The Shoe Bomber"—see further information pertaining to this incident in the chapter 3, dealing with terror networks in Europe.)

The Suicide Attack Near the Ancient Synagogue in Djerba, Tunisia

On April 11, 2002, Nizar Nawar, a suicide driver, blew up an oil tanker near the ancient synagogue in Djerba. Nawar, a Tunisian from an emigrant family living in France, drove a fuel truck carrying explosives. He aimed the tanker so that it would hit the synagogue and a group of tourists visiting the site, and detonated the explosives. The attack left seventeen dead: eleven Germans, two Frenchmen, and four Tunisians.

The Organization for the Liberation of the Holy Sites and the Al-Qaida Al-Jihad organization claimed responsibility for the attack in letters sent to the *Al-Hayat* and *Al Quds Al Arabi* newspapers, and stated that the act was an expression of solidarity of Muslims throughout the world with their Palestinian brothers' struggle.[66] As mentioned earlier, the responsibility for the attacks in Kenya and Tanzania was also claimed by the organization, whose foundation was declared by Bin-Laden and his deputy Aiman A-Zuheiri in June 2001, when they announced the de jure consolidation of the Al-Qaida and Egyptian Jihad Organizations.

In an interview with Abd Alatim Al-Mohajar, one of the leading military leaders of the Al-Qaida organization, he confirmed that the attack at the synagogue in Djerba was carried out by Al-Qaida members. Al-Mohajar stated that the perpetrator was Nawar Seif A-Din A-Tunisi, one of Al-Qaida's fighters, and that in the organization he was called "Seif."[67] The investigation of the incident indicated that the suicide terrorist had connections with terror cells in France, Germany, and Canada. The suicide terrorist Nawar was an Afghan alumnus and he began his preparations several months prior to the deed. A search of his apartment yielded telephone numbers of Binalshibh, one of the prominent leaders of the terror cell in Hamburg; other members were among the pilots who perpetrated the terror attack on the United States.[68]

In light of the violent confrontation between Israel and the Palestinians, and bearing in mind the deadly blow that Al-Qaida sustained in Afghanistan, Bin-Laden and his men recognize the potential support for carrying out attacks against Israel and Jews among Muslims worldwide. In view of this situation, massive terror attacks against Israeli and Jewish targets around the world, but mainly in Israel, have become a strategic objective in their eyes. Therefore, a concerted effort to realize these intentions is to be anticipated, alongside attacks against other Western targets, particularly those connected to the United States and her allies.

The Terror Attacks in Kenya against Israeli Targets[69]

On November 28, 2002, terror attacks were simultaneously perpetrated against Israeli targets in Kenya: First, two Strella (SA-7) shoulder missiles were fired at an Arkia airplane immediately after its takeoff from the airport in Mombassa but they missed their target; twenty minutes later a car bomb driven by terrorists exploded at the Paradise Hotel in Mombassa.

Responsibility was claimed shortly after the attacks by an unknown organization called the "Palestine Army." Later, on December 2, 2002, a more authentic claiming of responsibility was published in several Internet sites identified with Al-Qaida under the signature of "Al-Qaidat-El-Jihad," the political office. It would appear that it was Al-Qaida that was claiming responsibility, although the style differed in its characteristics from earlier claims of responsibility issued by that organization.[70]

The announcement also stated that the attacks in Mombassa were aimed at "eradicating all of the dreams of the Jewish-Crusader alliance, meant to preserve their strategic interests in the region. The next mission, meant to deal an additional blow to the Israeli Mossad, will be like the blows that fell upon the synagogue in Djerba in the past." The announcement went on to say that both attacks, the attack at the Paradise Hotel and the attempt to shoot down the Arkia plane, "were meant to clarify to Muslims all over the world that the mujahidin stand by their brethren in Palestine and continue in their path." The announcement also referred to the Jewish-American connection, saying that the attack was retaliation for "the conquest of our holy sites" and Israeli acts in Palestine. "For killing our children, we will kill yours, for our elderly we will kill your elderly, and for our homes your turrets." From the investigation it seems that the same people that had been involved in the attacks against the American Embassies in 1998 took part in the two attacks in Mombassa in 2002.

The firing of missiles at the Arkia plane. At about 7:30 a.m., two shoulder missiles were fired at Arkia flight 582 which took off from the Mombassa Airport in Kenya for Israel. There were 261 passengers on board in addition to ten crewmembers. The missiles missed the aircraft and did not cause any damage. About a minute and a half after takeoff, at a height of about 3,000 feet, the passengers felt a thump against the aircraft's hull. Immediately afterwards, the flash of two missiles was identified near the aircraft. The crewmembers rushed to report to the security team on land, and the latter launched searches in the area in an attempt to locate the missile launchers.

A preliminary investigation launched by security entities in Kenya and Israel indicates that the shoulder missiles fired at the Arkia plane were launched at a point one kilometer away from the takeoff area. The terrorists set up the ambush at a distance of a few hundred meters outside of the perimeter fence surrounding the airport, where they launched the missiles. The spokesperson for the Kenyan Police, Kinori Mawangi, reported that a car, apparently a Pajero jeep, with three or four people of Arab appearance in the car, had been seen in the vicinity of the airport. "Fleeing the area," added the spokesman.

Two missile launchers and two additional SA-7 (Strella) missiles were found hidden among the bushes outside of the airport's perimeter, at a distance of several hundred meters from the fence. According to U.S. sources, the missiles found in Mombassa were from the same series and production line as the missiles fired by Al-Qaida at an American military plane in Saudi Arabia in May 2002.[71]

According to the assessment of Kenya Police, the firing of the missiles and the attack perpetrated with a car bomb at the hotel were coordinated and carefully planned in advance. Searches carried out by police investigators in the area where the missiles were fired indicated that the attack was perpetrated from a hill with an excellent vantage point of the airport and particularly of the takeoff areas. It was fortunate that the missiles missed the plane they were aiming for during a phase of flight that is considered the vulnerable point —takeoff.

The Strella is a relatively outmoded missile that was developed about thirty years ago. Armies and guerrilla organizations use it, and it is known that various entities in Africa also have some in their possession. The missile is considered uncomplicated to operate and in regular circumstances its ability to hit a passenger plane during takeoff—which is considered an easy target—is relatively high.

The Strella homes in on heat. It is usually adjusted according to the heat waves emanating from the plane's engines or its landing and takeoff lights. The missile's effective range is defined at 4 to 6 kilometers; its flight velocity is 580 meters per second, and its warhead's weight ranges between 1 kilogram and 1.2 kilograms.

The attempt to hit the Arkia plane in Mombassa, Kenya, is not the first time that terrorists have tried to fire shoulder missiles at Israeli aircraft, and it is also not the first attempt to be made in Kenya. In

1969, a Palestinian cell was apprehended in Rome with shoulder missiles in its possession and the intention to shoot down an El Al plane. The cell was caught due to prior information obtained in a joint operation of the Italian security forces and the Mossad.

The attack at the Paradise Hotel. On the morning of November 28, 2002, some 200 Israeli tourists landed at the Mombassa Airport, Kenya. They disembarked from an Arkia charter flight and passed through the various checks and border control. They boarded two buses and five minibuses, which took them to the Paradise Mombassa Hotel, some 35 kilometers north of the city, where they were to spend the Hanukkah vacation.

At about 7:50, a jeep with two suicide bombers, also carrying 200 KG of explosives and gas balloons (a Kalachnikov was found in the jeep's wreckage), burst through the hotel's security block and detonated at the entrance of the hotel.[72] Thirteen people were killed in the attack; three Israelis and ten Kenyans, including dancers from a dance troupe that received the Israeli tourists at the entrance to the hotel. According to the various reports, sixty to eighty people were injured in the attack, including some twenty Israelis.

Bin-Laden's Islamic Terror as an Expression of the Confrontation Between Cultures

The end of the twentieth century and the dawning of the twenty-first century are characterized by "the conflict between cultures." Samuel Huntington, one of the initiators of this concept, argues that after the end of the Cold War, the source of conflict in the world is first and foremost "cultural."[73] Huntington lists eight central civilizations in the modern world and denotes Islam as the most militant.[74]

The conflict between cultures can be perceived and examined from a different angle, which classifies cultures into two main categories: the state-oriented, institutional and territorial culture and philosophy, as compared to the nomadic culture and philosophy.

It is possible to analyze Islamic terror according to the model of Al-Qaida and the "war against terror" declared by the United States after the terror attack of September 11, 2001, as a salient expression of the cultural confrontation on two levels:

- A confrontation between nomadic culture and the state-oriented, territorial culture.

- A confrontation between the Islamic culture and Western culture.

Despite the fact that ostensibly these are two different aspects, in actual fact there is considerable symmetry between the two, because the United States represents both the state-oriented and Western culture, while Bin-Laden expresses the radical Islamic culture as well as the nomadic culture.

Jacque Derrida, Gilles Deleuze, Felix Guatterri and other philosophers regard nomadism as a philosophical concept, which is in perpetual conflict with the state-oriented and tyrannical philosophy (in their view).[75]

Nomadic society and the nomadic war machine are in constant motion from the conceptual point of view, even if this does not always involve actual physical movement. The nomadic concept opposes "tyranny," which the state-oriented philosophy imposes in terms of organization, space and time. The philosophical issue always relates to law, institutions and contracts that combine to embody the sovereign character of the state, which as previously noted is regarded by nomadism as tyrannical, or to quote Deleuze, even in the Greek city-state (which is perceived as the pinnacle of democracy) there was a philosophical issue regarding tyranny or conceptual force, or at the very least existence in the shadow of this tyranny.[76]

Nietzsche was one of the first philosophers to raise this complex issue for discussion. According to him, philosophical concept and thought must by nature be nomadic and free of the restraints of bureaucratic and procedural conception. Therefore, Deleuze argues, Nietzsche turned the thought into a war machine and a battering ram, which reflect a counter philosophy that constantly challenges the state-oriented philosophy.[77]

Deleuze and Guatterri point out several essential differences between the state-oriented and nomadic approaches.[78] The state-oriented approach, which is founded on the definition of the state's sovereignty, is constructed in the form of a *vertical hierarchy*. The philosophical and constructive logic are based on this concept of structural and logical dependency arranged layer upon layer. By its very nature, the vertical structure creates a dictatorial pattern, since without the enforcement of conceptual and structural order the vertical structure will collapse.

The nomadic approach does not accept the vertical structure and logic. The nomadic system is a *horizontal system*; on the philosophical and structural level there is no clear hierarchy, and the structural links are amorphous and less structured.

The territory. The concept of territory, permanence and the connection with location constitute the basic foundations of the state entity, which defines itself through the delineation of boundaries. Boundaries represent a basis not only for the physical definition of the state entity, but also address the conceptual dimensions of this entity. The nomadic outlook negates the notion of boundaries as well as the concept of state. Nomadism signifies conceptual and physical de-territorization, which expresses itself in constant movement. The state does its best to settle its components, and to establish and patrol their movement and organization. However, the nomadic concept interprets this attempt in terms of compulsion and tyranny on the part of the state entity, and expresses the essence of its existence by opposing any attempt to settle or regulate it.

Nevertheless, Deleuze and Guatterri point out that there is no "quintessential nomadism," and a paradox exists in the very fact that nomadism defines itself as different than the state entity. Moreover, there is the danger that if the nomadic perception emerges victorious, it will then also turn into a state entity.

The concept of time. The concept of time is perceived differently in the state-oriented entity than in the nomadic culture. In the state-oriented culture, the perception of time is also contingent upon conceptual boundaries of the entity and represents part of the definition of the boundaries. The nomadic culture is in constant flow, in both dimensions of space and time. In the nomadic perception, the concept of time does not serve to delineate boundaries, but rather exists as a point of reference and orientation in the course of history. In the following sentences Deleuze and Guatterri encapsulate the nature of the difference between the state and nomadic entities:[79]

> As a non-disciplinary force, the nomadic war machine names an anarchic presence on the far horizon of the state's field of order. The nomadic movement is based on a fundamental antagonism, which opposes any structured form and flow of normalization and order. To illustrate, it can be compared to the quiet and regular flow of water in a river as opposed to the turbulent churning of water in whirlpools, thus creating a swirling disorder.[80]

As stated earlier, Samuel Huntington believes the source of conflict in the world at the onset of the twenty-first century is not rooted in ideological or economic reasons, but primarily in cultural ones. He claims that until the end of the Cold War the modern world was dominated by Western culture and most of the significant conflicts took place within the framework of this culture or to quote his term of reference, "Western civil wars."[81]

At the end of the era of the Cold War the international political system was released from the framework of Western cultural dominance, and the center of gravity shifted to the reciprocal connections and conflicts between the West and non-Western cultures, and among the non-Western cultures themselves.

From this stage onward, nations and countries belonging to the non-Western civilization ceased being the product and victims of Western colonization, and became active and dominant partners in the impetus and development of history. During the period of the Cold War it was customary to categorize the world according to the political systems, and the technological and economical development of the various countries (developed and underdeveloped countries, first-, second-, and third-world countries, etc.).

Huntington believes that today countries should be classified in terms of cultures or civilizations. His definition of civilization is as follows:[82]

> A civilization is the highest cultural grouping of people, and the broadest level of cultural identity people have short of that which distinguishes humans from others.

Civilization is defined with objective components such as language, history, religion, customs and institutions; and also via subjective components such as self-definition or the solidarity of the individual and a group. Thus, it is possible to say that the civilization with which an individual identifies is the one that to him constitutes the deepest and broadest level of solidarity.

Huntington offers an all-encompassing, blanket approach when he presents all the Islamic states as a single Islamic cultural unit that confronts Western and other cultures. A close examination of most of the governments in Muslim states indicates that the majority of them are either secular, or moderate pragmatic Islamic regimes that are not involved in conflict with the West, and have even jumped on the bandwagon of "the modernization convoy," by adopting Western technologies, values and lifestyles. Huntington also does not distinguish between this main stream in the Muslim world and the Fundamentalist Islamic streams, which have raised their banner against Western culture and still constitute a militant Islamic minority.

Therefore, the Muslim world is involved in a profound and sharp internal, cultural conflict regarding the nature and direction of Islamic society, and the results of this internal struggle currently dictate and will dictate in the future the nature of the ties between Islamic culture, and Western and other cultures. Governments in many

Islamic states have not only adopted Western cultural patterns, but also rely on Western military, political and economic aid in order to sustain their existence.

One of the prominent trends at the end of the previous millennium and at the beginning of the current one, which clearly reflects the perception of the cultural conflict according to Huntington's theory, is the phenomenon of the Afghan alumni who constitute the vanguard of the radical Islamic confrontation with adversarial cultures. Osama Bin-Laden and the Al Qaida organization constitute the most salient expression of the phenomenon of Afghan alumni, as well as the cultural and philosophical perceptions of this phenomenon.

The Al-Qaida Organization and Bin-Laden as an Expression of the Nomadic Concept

Osama Bin-Laden left Saudi Arabia for Pakistan and then traveled to the Afghan front. In the city of Peshawar, Pakistan, he founded an organization that dealt with recruitment, absorption and training of Muslim fighters from all over the world who enlisted for the jihad against the Soviet Union in Afghanistan. Already at the beginning of his career Bin-Laden had adopted radical Islamic conceptions, which regard Islam as caught up in an existential struggle against the stronger forces of a superpower and against secular, corrupt Arab regimes that function according to the interests of their superpower allies.

According to Bin-Laden's beliefs, radical Islam is involved in a battle to remove corrupt leaders in the Muslim world and establish a utopian, Islamic group of faithful believers; the "nation." Bin-Laden's view is that Islam has no boundaries, and that the national Muslim states are the artificial creations of colonialism and imperialism, designed to create false schisms in the Muslim world and perpetuate the control and involvement of the Western powers.

Consequently, radical Islam represents a nomadic concept that negates political entity and views it as an expression of conceptual and physical tyranny of Western culture, the representative of state-oriented culture. Bin-Laden adheres to the slogan "not east, not west," which was offered to the radical Islamic believers when in 1979 he first focused his struggle against the Soviet Union, and for this purpose availed himself of aid from the United States, Saudi Arabia and other "corrupt" Arab regimes. But even then he did not conceal his opinion that after triumphing in this struggle against the USSR, the West's "turn" would soon come.

The war in Afghanistan saliently reflects the confrontation between the concept and state-oriented war machine on the one hand, and the concept and nomadic war machine on the other. The Soviet Union and the Communist regime in Kabul were expressions of the hierarchical, vertical perception on the philosophical; conceptual level as well as on the practical level.

The Afghan mujahidin, who availed themselves of the assistance of an "internacionale" of volunteers from all over the Muslim world, similar to Bin-Laden, expressed the concept of the nomadic war machine. This machine, which was structured horizontally, was composed of dozens of organizations and groups lacking an ordered, permanent structure and defined procedures for cooperation, with only a loose bond between them, mainly the joint goal—that of overcoming the communist regime and banishing the USSR forces from Afghanistan.

The nomadic war machine of the mujahidin was in constant motion on various levels:

- Managing a chaotic campaign without any definition of clear boundaries: outside of Afghanistan, inside Afghanistan in areas outside of Soviet control, within the area of Afghanistan but behind the Soviet lines, and even inside the government centers in Kabul and other cities. The aim of the management of this chaotic campaign was to undermine the structural, institutional and operative logic of the state-oriented order.
- A perpetual flow and movement of concepts and ideas combined to undermine the hierarchical and state-oriented doctrines and ideology prevalent in Kabul while creating new subversive concepts (mainly Islamic ones) free of the shackles of state-oriented conceptual tyranny.

The Mujahidin movements served as a salient model for the "nomadic war machine" which is in perpetual motion, acting to undermine the physical and conceptual boundaries of the Afghan state. This motion generates ideas and conceptions unfettered by the conceptual, state-oriented tyranny while realizing a chaotic system that neutralizes the advantages of state-oriented power and offers them to the nomadic machine.

In 1990, the nomadic "war machine" defeated the USSR, which was forced to pull its army out of Afghanistan, and two years later, in 1992, the communist regime collapsed in Kabul and the government was handed over to the mujahidin.

Deleuze and Guatterri had noted the inherent paradox in turning a nomadic system into a state-oriented system. The Afghan circumstances serve as an interesting example of the opposite phenomenon–the mujahidin movements, even after their triumph over the communist regime and the USSR, continued to preserve the nomadic action pattern. Thus, in the years 1992–1996, Afghanistan was left in a chaotic state, and the attempt to create a vertical hierarchical system that would generate a state-oriented government in Afghanistan failed. In practice, Afghanistan was "ruled" by a "nomadic war machine" which perpetuated itself via a complex system of powerful entities battling against each other and preserving the chaotic and unregulated reality characteristic of the nomadic system as an extra-state system.

The ascent to power of the Taliban government during the years 1996–2001 brought about little change in the system's structure, because the internal power struggles in the arena continued. Nevertheless, during these years two systems existed simultaneously but in constant conflict; one was the semi-state of the Taliban regime, and the other was a nomadic system struggling against this regime in the form of a coalition called "the northern alliance." However, for the purposes of our discussion the developments in Afghanistan after the victory of the nomadic system are of secondary importance.

At the end of the war, an even more salient nomadic war machine was designed and took shape in the form of the Afghan alumni, whose most prominent representative was Osama Bin-Laden. The Afghan alumni are not identified or associated with any particular movement or state, but rather express a radical cultural, religious stream that believes in an uncompromising Islamic struggle against heretic Muslim regimes and adversarial cultures.

It is possible to note four main channels of activity vis-à-vis the Afghan "alumni":[83]

- Incorporating activities and leadership of radical Islamic organizations in their lands of origin (Egypt, Western countries, Jordan, etc.).
- Establishing new terror organizations such as the Al-Qaida organization headed by Bin-Laden.
- Establishing "independent" terror cells without any defined organizational affiliation or identity while cooperating with other established terror organizations.
- Joining the fighting at Muslim population focal points such as the Balkan, Chechnya, Kashmir, Tajikistan and others.

As stated above, the Al-Qaida organization and its leader, Osama Bin-Laden, most conspicuously reflect the nomadic concept.

After the end of the war in Afghanistan, Osama Bin-Laden decided to perpetuate the jihad against Islam's enemies when he selected the United States as the main target of the campaign. During the years 1992 to 2002 he "wandered" back and forth between Afghanistan, Saudi Arabia, Sudan and back to Afghanistan, until his "disappearance" as the result of the American attack in Afghanistan launched in October 2001.

Bin-Laden represents the nomadic concept of the roamer, who does not settle down and strike roots within a state-oriented framework, but rather is in perpetual motion. Territory has essential significance as a means to promote his objectives, but there is no permanent affiliation with any given territory, and the latter merely expresses a functional and temporary need.

The Al-Qaida organization is based on the nomadic concept and takes the form of an organization without a clear hierarchical structure. It is composed of cells and groups deployed throughout the world which share conceptual and organizational affiliations with countries that support terror (such as Sudan, Iran and more), as well as Islamic organizations that adhere to similar worldviews. The organization's goal is to wage an uncompromising war against the United States, the West and Zionism, all of which can also be defined as entities that reflect the state-oriented concept.

The organization disputes Western cultural concepts on every level; on the ideological-religious level it calls for the annihilation of the Western adversary and the establishment of an alternative Islamic culture. On the economic level it exploits the economic foundations of the Western world for its own purposes with the aim of undermining its infrastructure, in the full knowledge that the main strength of the West lies in its economy. On the military level, the "nomad war machine" confronts the superior power of the Western, state-oriented war machine by challenging it in such a way that this machine becomes vulnerable and irrelevant. The organization acts according to the nomadic concept at any place and at any time, and creates a "turbulent" reality that shakes the foundations of the state-oriented establishment.

The agility, flexibility and independence of the various components of the nomadic war machine create a serious problem for the Western, state-oriented war machine, which operates according to

Figure 1.1
The "Nomadic" System in Contrast to the "State-Oriented" System

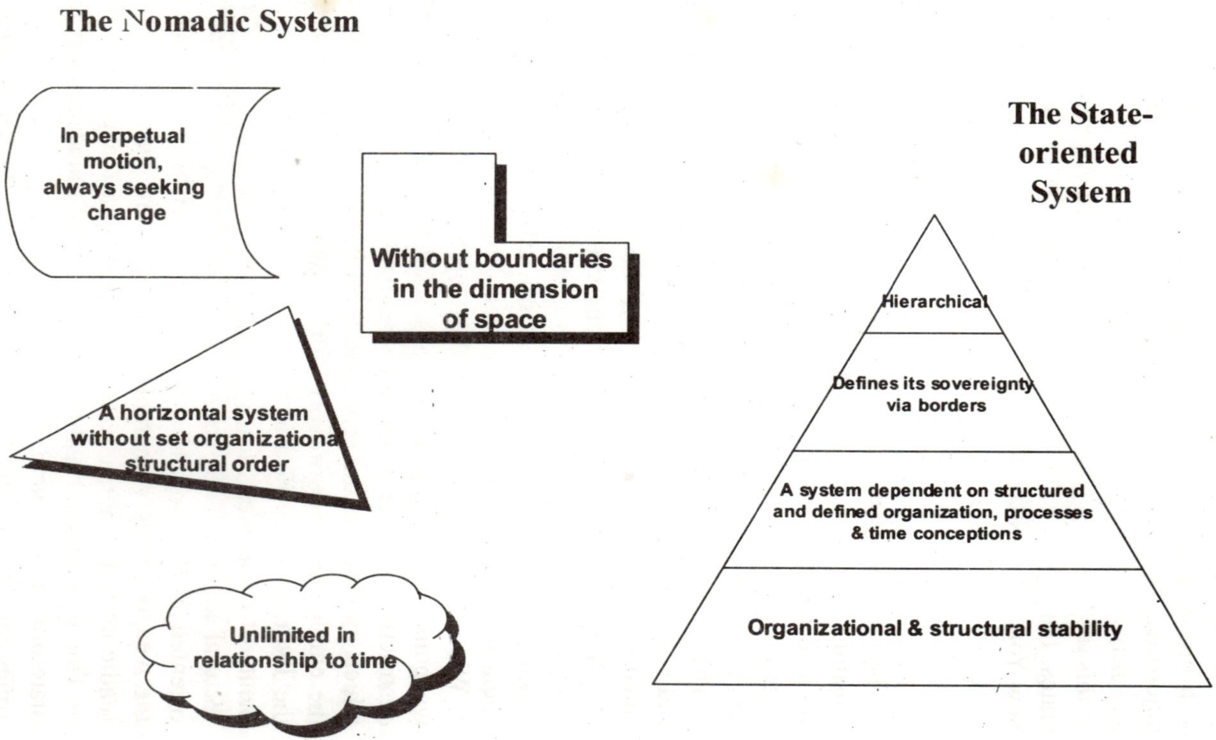

the limitations and checks that the hierarchical, state-oriented order enforces upon itself.

The terror attack of September 11, 2001, manifestly expresses both the confrontation between the nomadic war machine and the state-oriented war machine on the one hand, and the cultural conflict between Islam and Western culture, on the other. In the course of this attack four passenger planes were hijacked within the United States: two of the hijacked planes rammed into the Twin Towers in New York City, causing their collapse, a third airplane plowed into the Pentagon in Washington, while the fourth crashed in a wooded area in Pennsylvania, though the assessment is that its target was the presidential facility at Camp David.

The targets of the terror attack, which were painstakingly selected, constituted salient symbols of Western culture and the United States, the leader and representative of this culture. The Twin Towers represented economic power (the World Trade Center), and the Pentagon the symbol of U.S. and Western military power.

The terror attack expressed the asymmetry and the deep cultural and conceptual schism between the United States and its state-oriented concepts on the one hand, and Bin-Laden with his nomadic concepts, on the other. The attack was perpetrated by several small groups of terrorists (nomads) that came from different places in the world. The terrorists themselves originated from different Muslim countries (Egypt, Saudi Arabia, Algeria, and more).

While overpowering the aircraft without guns and even without weapons they converted the planes into the attack's instrument of destruction. The use of an aeronautical medium of transportation, which epitomizes ultimate mobility, symbolizes the destruction of the emblems of the "state-oriented war machine." As stated above, the Twin Towers are architectural symbols that represent the achievements of the state-oriented Western culture. These two static architectural monuments, which concentrate the epitome of the state-oriented tyranny within them, were destroyed through the use of the weapons that symbolize the mobility and dynamics of the nomadic culture.

This terror attack exposed the weakness and vulnerability of the state-oriented system despite its absolute power, which is so many times more forceful than the might of the nomadic war machine. The "war against terror" declared by the United States in response to the terror attack of September 2001 serves also as convincing testimony to the difficulties inherent to a confrontation between a nomadic system and a state-oriented one.

In its war against terror, the United States declared its first goal was to destroy the Al-Qaida organization and the Taliban regime in Afghanistan, which had given Bin-Laden a haven. With little effort, the American "state-oriented" war machine crushed the "state-oriented war machine" of the Taliban as well as the components of Al-Qaida that were dispersed there. The infrastructure of Al-Qaida in Afghanistan was damaged, and some of its fighters were killed or taken prisoner, but Bin-Laden and most of the senior members of the organization have so far eluded capture by the Americans. Moreover, the "horizontal," decentralized organizational infrastructure was barely affected. While the infrastructure of a state-oriented war machine like that of the Taliban can be annihilated through the use of the tools, technology and doctrine at the disposal of the "Western war machine," it is clear that the nomadic infrastructure requires totally different handling.

The concepts of space, time and organizational narrative of the nomadic culture create a threat against the state-oriented logic and undermine its foundations through its very existence, even before the operational capabilities of the nomadic terror infrastructure have been translated into actual attacks.

Notes

1. Bernard Lewis, Islam and Liberal Democracy, *The Atlantic Monthly*, February 1993, pp. 10-14.
2. Lawrence Kaplan (ed.), *Fundamentalism in Comparative Perspective,* University of Massachusetts Press, Amherst, 1992, pp. 4-5. Emanuel Sivan, *Islamic Extremists*, Sifriat Ofakim, Am Oved, Tel Aviv, 1986, pp. 192-195.
3. Lawrence Kaplan (ed.), *Fundamentalism in Comparative Perspective*, pp. 6-7. David Manshari, *Iran in a Revolution*, Hakibbutz Hameuad, Tel Aviv, 1988, pp. 202-205.
4. Martin Kramer, *Protest and Revolution in the Shiite Islam*, Hakibbutz Hameuhad, Tel Aviv, 1985, pp. 11-15.
5. A. B. Lughud, *Arab Rediscovery of Europe*, Princeton University Press, Princeton, NJ, 1963, pp. 69-158. A. Horani, *Arab Thought in the Liberal Ages 1939-1978,* Oxford University Press, 1962, pp. 34-102.
6. J. Waardenburg, World Religions as Seen in the Light of Islam in A. Walch and P. Cachia (eds.), *Islam Past Influence and Present Challenge*, Edinburgh University Press, 1979, pp. 255-265.
7. Sayyad Qutb, Mualem Fi Al-Tarik, Alkahara, Dar Alshruk, undated, pp. 124-126.
8. Cris Khouri and Peter Chippendale, *Islam, What is It?* Ahiasaf Publications Ltd., Tel Aviv, 1991, pp. 92-93.
9. Hava Latsarus Yaffe, *More Discussions about the Islamic Religion*, The Hebrew University, Jerusalem, The Ministry of Defense Publications, pp. 92-97.
10. Cris Khouri and Peter Chippendale, *Islam, What is It?* pp. 93-94.

11. Emanuel Sivan, *Islamic Extremists*, Sifriat Ifahim Am Oved, Tel Aviv, 1986.pp. 94-95, 103-114.
12. Ilan Pepeh (ed.), *Islam and Peace-Islamic Approaches to Peace in the Arab World of Our Day*, The Institute for the Peace Research, Girat Haviva, 1992, pp.
13. Fuad Ajami, *The Arab Predicament*, Cambridge University Press, New York, pp. 63-67.
14. Hassan Al-Banah, "An Epistle to the Fifth Conference."
15. Jabar Razek, Alamam Al Shahid Hassan Al-Baneh, by his followers and peers, Dar Alifa, Egypt, 1987, p. 12.
16. Ibid., 16-17.
17. Hassan Al-Banah, "An Epistle to the Fifth Conference," p. 63.
18. Emanuel Sivan, *Islamic Extremists*, pp. 95-110.
19. Sayyad Qutb, *Mualem Fi Al-Tarik*, Alkahera, Dar Alsharuk, Egypt, undated, pp. 13-60.
20. Ibid., pp. 9, 224, 204.
21. Ibid., p. 120.
22. Ibid., pp. 141-153.
23. Sayyad Qutb, Al Adalah, seventh edition, p. 258.
24. Sayyad Qutb, Jahallia, p.9.
25. Ibid.
26. Ibid.
27. Emanuel Sivan, *Islamic Extremists*, pp. 94-100.
28. Martin Kramer, *Protest and Revolution in the Shiite Islam*, Hakibbutz Hameuhad, Tel Aviv, 1986, pp. 141-143.
29. Sayyad Qutb is among the founders of the study of the West by Islamic researchers.
30. Martin Kramer, *Protest and Revolution in the Shiite Islam*, pp. 144.
31. Ibid.
32. Shaul Shay, *The Endless Jihad, the Mujahidin, the Taliban and Bin-Laden*, Mifalot Interdisciplinary Publishing, the Interdisciplinary Center, Herzliya, 2002, p. 131.
33. Sheikh Abdullah Azzam, Bin-Laden's Spiritual Mentor, in Internet site, www.ict.org.il/articles.
34. Yossef Bodansky, *Bin-Laden, The Man Who Declared War on America*, Forum, Roseville, CA, 1999, pp. 49-50.
35. Sheikh Abdullah Azzam, Ibid.
36. Ibid.
37. Magnus Ranstorp, Interpreting the Broader Context and Meaning of Bin-Laden's Fatwa, *Studies in Conflict Terrorism*, Vol. 21, October-December 1998.
38. Ely Karmon, Terrorism a la Bin-Laden is not a Peace Process Problem, Policy Watch, Washington Institute for Near East Policy, No. 347, October 28, 1998.
39. American Soldiers are Paper Tigers, Interview, *Middle East Quarterly*, Vol. V, No. 4, December 1998.
40. Ibid.
41. *Al-Hayat*, United Kingdom, May 25, 1998.
42. *Time*, January 22, 1998. *Newsweek*, January 22, 1998.
43. American Soldiers are Paper Tigers, Interview, *Middle East Quarterly*, Vol. V, No. 4, December 1998.
44. *Time*, January 4, 1999.
45. Reuters, June 10, 1999.
46. *Al-Jazeera*, June 10, 1999.
47. *Time*, January 22, 1998.
48. *Newsweek*, December 22, 1998.
49. *Al-Jazeera*, June 10, 1999.

50. Ibid.
51. Abd El Beeri Atuwan, editor of the newspaper *Al Quds Al Arabi*, from a television show on *Al-Jazeera*, June 1999.
52. *Daily Telegraph* Internet, November 11, 2001.
53. *Al-Jazeera*, October 7, 2001.
54. *Al Quds Al Arabi*, London, February 23, 1998.
55. Yoram Schweitzer, Does Bin-Laden Constitute a Threat to Israel? *Maarchot*, Issue 373, November 2000, p. 39.
56. Shaul Shay, *The Endless Jihad, the Mujahidin, the Taliban and Bin-Laden*, pp. 126-128.
57. Ibid., pp. 127-128.
58. Ibid., pp. 127-128.
59. Ibid., p. 126.
60. Ibid., p. 127.
61. N. Tal, *Confrontation from Within—Egypt and Jordan's Handling of Radical Islam*, Papyrus Publication, Tel Aviv University, 1999, p. 208.
62. The charge sheet against Saad Hindawi, in Osama Bin-Laden and the Al-Qaida Organization, a special collection of information, Malam Intelligence Corp, Herzliya, Israel.
63. Ibid., charge sheet against Muhamad Dakah.
64. Ibid., charge sheet against Nabil Ukal.
65. *Maariv*, Tel Aviv, February 16, 2002.
66. *Al-Quds Al Arabi*, April 18, 2002.
67. *A-Sharq Al-Awsat* Internet, May 18, 2002.
68. *Liberacion*, Internet, April 18, 2002, and Reuters from Berlin, April 18, 2002.
69. Samuel Huntington, The Clash of Civilizations and the Remaking of World Order, *Foreign Affairs*, summer 1993.
70. Ibid.
71. John Lechte, *Fifty Key Contemporary Thinkers*, Routledge, London, 1994.
72. Gilles Deleuze, Nomad Thought, in David B. Allison (ed.), *The New Nietzsche*, MIT Press, Cambridge, MA, 1988.
73. Ibid., p. 149.
74. Ibid., p. 148.
75. Ibid.
76. In the introduction to the book by Gilles Deleuze and Felix Guatterri, *A Thousand Plateaus: Capitalism and Schizophrenia*. Trans. Brian Massumi, University of Minnesota Press, Minneapolis, 1987.
77. Samuel Huntington, *The Clash of the Civilizations and the Remaking of World Order*, Simon and Schuster, New York, 1996, p. 9.
78. Ibid., p. 23.
79. Yoram Schweitzer, Middle East Terrorism: The Afghan Alumni, in Shlomo Brom and Yiftah Shafir (eds.), *The Middle East Military Balance, 1999-2000*, J.C.C.S., Tel Aviv, and M.I.T. Press, Cambridge, MA, 2000, p. 122.

2

The Terror of Afghan "Alumni" in the International Arena

Introduction

Bin-Laden's uniqueness in the world of terror lies in his being a man of action, and not necessarily a spiritual leader or philosopher. The prominent and exceptional characteristic of Bin-Laden's activities lies in his decision to realize the vision of the foundation of an Islamic caliphate. To achieve this goal, Bin-Laden was not satisfied only with the religious backup and legitimacy provided by senior Islamic clerics, but rather he concentrated on the establishment of a unique organizational structure that would facilitate the attainment of his vision and bring his ideological concepts to fruition in a reality where the West is conceived as categorically powerful vis-à-vis the Muslim world.

Bin-Laden based his activity on the Afghan "alumni." He acted to fortify the solidarity and support of established radical Islamic terror organizations founded by Afghan alumni, which concentrated their activity in Islamic countries in order to seize control from existing regimes. He reinforced the Al-Qaida organization, which abided by his direct commands and instructions, and was composed of hundreds of his followers who had accompanied him since the days of his Jihad war in Afghanistan and remained with him even after it ended. This entity was designated to supervise and channel all of the activities of the Islamic radicals towards the realization of Bin-Laden's ultimate goals. Simultaneously, Bin-Laden concentrated on the training of many thousands of fighters who were attracted to Afghanistan. At the end of the training, he made them pledge their total allegiance to the beliefs of the Global Jihad and dispersed them throughout the world as terror cells and networks faithful to the road that he had paved. Bin-Laden made efforts to bolster support in Islamic areas, mainly in places where there is political instability and a large Muslim minority, which constitute an important potential to facilitate his global objectives. Since 1998, Bin-Laden has established an umbrella organization under the symbolic name of "the Islamic Front for Jihad Against the Jews and Crusaders," which was to serve as a global organization for Muslim terror organizations worldwide. This unique structure was designated to assist him in realizing his dream to renew the Islamic caliphate through the use of terror, which he regarded as "propaganda through practice."

During the eighties, Afghanistan served as a lodestone for Muslim volunteers from various Islamic and Arab countries that joined the ranks of the Afghani mujahidin in their struggle against the pro-Soviet regime in Kabul and the invading Soviet forces. There are no exact data regarding the number of volunteers, but it would appear that their ranks swelled to several thousand and rose to the challenge of the Afghani jihad mainly out of a sense of religious solidarity, or else were motivated by a spirit of adventure. During their sojourn in Afghanistan, the volunteers underwent military training and acquired intensive experience in guerrilla warfare.[1]

The training of the mujahidin usually took place in Pakistan; the city of Peshawar (near the Afghani border) and its general vicinity in Afghanistan served as a center and focus for mujahidin activity. Pakistani instructors and experts from Arab countries conducted the training; for a short period Western experts also performed part of the training, particularly Americans. In addition to the training camps in Pakistan, volunteers from Arab countries underwent training in camps in Sudan, Yemen and Iran.

We lack information as to the distribution of volunteers according to their affiliation with the various Afghani revolutionary organizations, but the Pakistani intelligence commander, Hamid Gol, reported that between 16,000 and 20,000 Islamic fighters arrived in Pakistan and Afghanistan during the jihad. From the little that is known, it appears that the radical organization of Hekmatyar (Hezb-e-Islami) absorbed many of the volunteers (several reports indicate approximately 3,500 individuals), some of whom also continued to serve in its ranks in the framework of its struggle against the Rabbani regime in Kabul. After the collapse of the pro-Soviet regime in Afghanistan (May 1992), the role of the volunteers had in effect come to an end and most of them started to return to their lands of origin.[2]

Figure 2.1
Establishment of the International Front for Bin-Laden's Jihad, February 1998

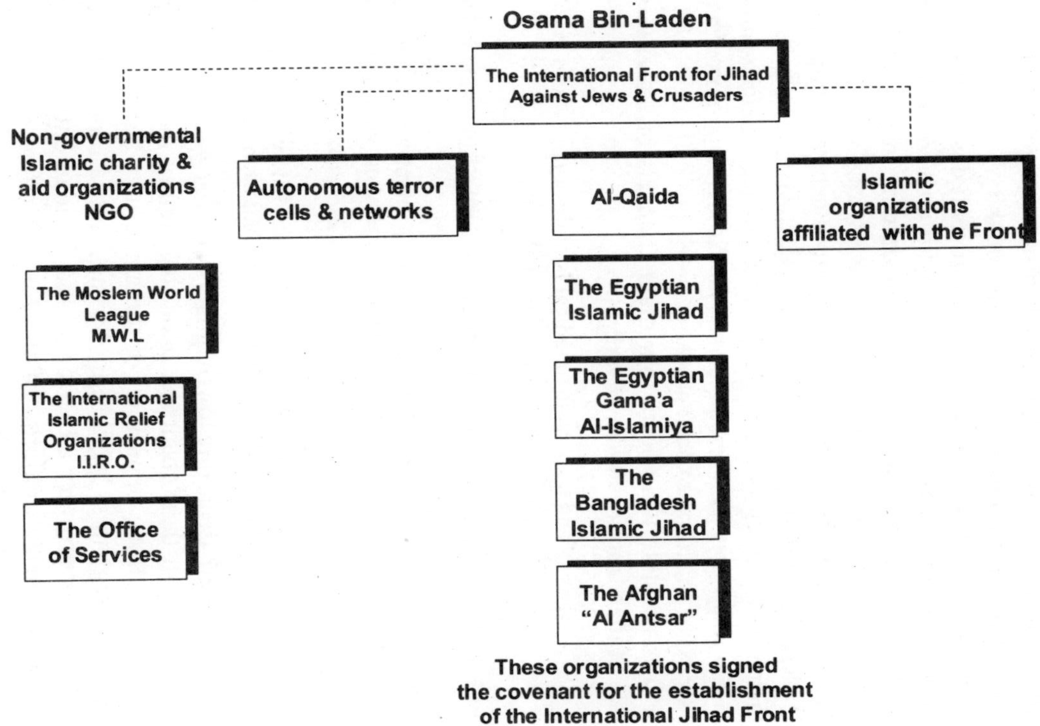

Regardless of the January 1993 declaration of the Pakistani government, according to which it intended to close down the offices of the Afghani associations and deport all of those residing illegally within its boundaries, no practical steps were taken to realize this decision and many of the mujahidin remained at the camps in Peshawar or at other locations in the country.

Another category of Afghan alumni includes hundreds of members of Islamic terror organizations who arrived in Afghanistan after the end of the war and underwent training in guerrilla and terror combat under the sponsorship of the various mujahidin factions. The Afghan alumni currently constitute a central component of the leadership of Fundamentalist Islamic terror organizations thanks to their status, which is based on the ethos of their heroic participation in the jihad and their triumph over the Soviet superpower as well as extensive military experience.[3]

It is possible to indicate four main channels of activity in which the Afghan alumni are involved:

1. Activity and leadership in radical Islamic organizations in Arab countries (Egypt, the Magreb, Jordan, and more).
2. Establishing new terror organizations like the Bin-Laden-led Al-Qaida.
3. Creating "independent" terror cells without any defined organizational affiliation or ties, through cooperation with other established terror organizations.
4. Joining centers of Muslim populations where fighting is going on such as Bosnia, Kosovo, Chechnya, Tajikistan, and Kashmir.[4]

While their departure for Afghanistan was generally blessed by the regimes in their countries, upon their return the alumni came up against the strong opposition of the authorities because they feared that the "Afghanis" would rapidly turn into a threat against them, due to their military experience and Fundamentalist worldview. Therefore, in the majority of the Magreb countries, as well as in Egypt and Jordan, the authorities took steps to prevent the return of the volunteers and the joining of the ranks of radical Islamic opposition in their lands. One of the prominent leaders of the Arab Afghanis is Ahmad Shawki al-Islambuli, brother of the assassin of President Saadat. In interviews he and other radical leaders reject the definition of their activity as terror and claim that their steps to topple the "corrupt" regimes in Egypt, Algeria, Tunisia and other places are part of the jihad, whose aim is to change the types of governments in these countries.[5] Afghanistan, Sudan and even Yemen were focal points and served as both asylum and transitional countries for the Afghan alumni on their way back to their lands of origin in order to join the ranks of the radical Islamic movements.

Despite Iran's ideological and religious dispute with Taliban-ruled Afghanistan, the former hosted leaders of organizations linked to the Afghan alumni, supported several groups identified with them in Lebanon, and enabled the passage of activists and weaponry to the mujahidin lines battling in Chechnya. Nevertheless, it is important to note the cautious and qualified position adopted by Iran vis-à-vis its relationship with the Afghan alumni against the background of tension that characterizes its ties with Afghanistan.[6]

Since the beginning of the nineties, mainly after the end of the fighting in Afghanistan against the Soviet forces, there has been a marked increase in activity by terror organizations that have accumulated considerable strength since the return of the Afghan alumni to their own countries. Their impact on the increased level of violence in their own countries was significant, and they quickly took over leadership positions and directed the terror setup of their organizations. The terror attacks were mainly aimed at replacing the infidel regimes in Islamic countries. However, some of the organizations also dealt in international terror both in their own countries and others.

Al-Qaida[7]

Al-Qaida is the most important and central organization connected to the activity of the "Islamic front" and the Afghan alumni, whose main influence has been felt in recent years in the international arena. Osama Bin-Laden founded the organization in Afghanistan in 1988. From the "office of services" (Maktab al-hidamat), which was one of the non-governmental Islamic welfare organizations (NGO), he dealt in the recruitment, absorption and placement of thousands of Islamic volunteers from fifty countries all over the world in mujahidin camps in Pakistan and Afghanistan.

During the first years after the end of the war against the Soviets in Afghanistan, his main activity was run from Sudan and Afghanistan through a network of offices spread throughout the world, including the United States (mainly the Al-Kifah center in Brooklyn) and the Philippines. Al-Qaida provided assistance to other terror organizations with which it maintains contacts and acted to enhance the radicalization of Islamic movements active in Chechnya, Bosnia, Tajikistan, Somalia, Kashmir, Yemen and Kosovo. At the same time, there is evidence of his link to terror attacks planned and perpetrated by terror cells supported by Al-Qaida such as the one acting under the leadership of Ramzi Yusuf in New York (1993) and in the Philippines (1994), and the terror cell that acted against an American target in Riad in November 1995, claiming six casualties (five of whom were American soldiers). As to the last two incidents, the Saudis claimed that Bin-Laden did not have any direct connection to them, but it is possible that the perpetrators were influenced by his preaching to combat American imperialism.

Subsequently, Al-Qaida itself perpetrated the terror attacks against the U.S. embassies in Kenya and Tanzania, and against the American destroyer *USS Cole* in Aden. The "crowning glory" of the Al-Qaida terror campaign was the attacks of September 11, 2001, perpetrated in the United States. (For further elaboration of Al-Qaida activity, see chapter 3).

Egypt

Al Gamaa al Islamiya

This organization grew and developed mainly in Upper Egypt against the background of the great economic distress and the population's hostility against the Coptic (Christian) minority and the central government in Cairo. Al Gamaa al Islamiya believes in the use of terror to achieve its goals, the first of which is to establish a religious Islamic state in Egypt. It has a military faction that oversees the violent activities as well as a civilian faction that acts to promote the organization's aims through preaching at mosques as well as offering medical and welfare services to the needy.

At the beginning of the eighties a short-lived effort was made to consolidate the organization with the Egyptian Islamic Jihad under the leadership of Sheikh Omar Abd al-Rahman, but this alliance did not endure and disintegrated when the leader of the Jihad Faraj was executed and Omar Abd al-Rahman was sent into exile after the assassination of Egyptian President Saadat.[8]

Al Gamaa al Islamiya was the leading terror organization in Egypt and its members perpetrated attacks on a wide scope, including at-

Figure 2.2

The Islamic Front and Bin-Laden's Global Terror Network

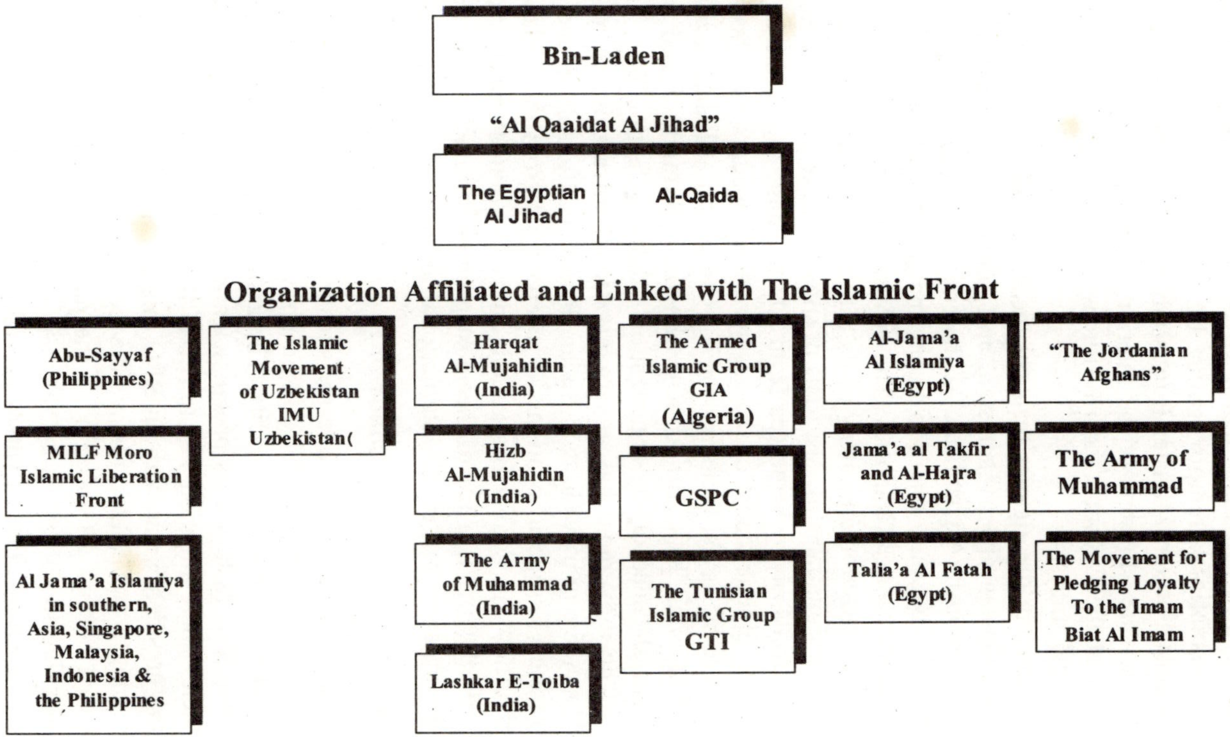

tempts to assassinate senior government members in Egypt (two assassination attempts against Egyptian President Mubarak, one against Foreign Minister Butrus Ghali and another two attempts to assassinate Ministers of the Interior).[9] Additional targets were members of the Egyptian security forces, members of the Coptic minority and tourists.

Early in the eighties many of the organization's activists departed for Pakistan and Afghanistan, and joined the jihad against the Soviet Union in Afghanistan. At the end of the war in Afghanistan the activists began to return to Egypt and spearheaded the organization's anti-government activities. The government acted ruthlessly against the organization and many of its activists were either killed, arrested or fled Egyptian soil. The trials of some of those arrested were termed "the trials of the returnees from Afghanistan." Since the beginning of the nineties most of the organization's leaders have been living outside of Egypt, including Sheikh Omar Abd al-Rahman, Rifat Teh, Tlaat Fuad Kassem, Ahmad Shawki al-Islambuli and Mustafa Hamzah, head of the organization's military faction.

The movement has an organizational infrastructure mainly in Upper Egypt as well as in Sudan, Pakistan, Afghanistan and cells in various European locations. It received aid from the Sudanese authorities and Osama Bin-Laden, and was granted Iranian funding.

Following is a list of the most prominent attacks perpetrated by the organization in the international arena.

The Attempted Assassination of President Mubarak[10]

On June 26, 1995, a terror squad attacked a convoy of vehicles escorting President Mubarak on his way from the airport in Addis Ababa to a hotel in the city. The assailants trailed the convoy and attempted to block its progress while isolating the president's vehicle. Their intention was to fire at the bodyguards' vehicles, attack the president's car with an RPG missile, and place a suitcase containing a powerful explosive device on the car's roof. The assault failed because of an error on the part of the advance guard when blocking the bodyguards' vehicles, which caused the entire attempt to go wrong. The Egyptian president emerged unscathed. This attack had been in the planning for almost two years prior to the event, and included the preparation of an operational and logistical infrastructure, rental of safe houses, smuggling and concealing weaponry, the purchase of vehicles, methodical gathering of intelligence regarding access roads and planning of the blocking, assault and escape routes. The organization sent agents to Addis Ababa so that they would become assimilated in the area, and one of the cell members even married a local woman and served as a collaborator for the terror cell.

All nine of the members were Egyptian citizens born in Lower Egypt, who had undergone training in the Afghan camps and had combat experience. The organization demonstrated a high level of sophistication and daring in the preparations for the attack to be conducted outside of its geographical home base, and the perpetrators were also well trained despite their ultimate failure due to a marginal but fatal error in one of the operational stages. The two leading Egyptian organizations claimed responsibility for the attack–the Al Gamaa al Islamiya and "The Pioneers of Conquest" (Talia'a al-Fatah).

Attacks against Tourist Attractions in Egypt[11]

Attack against Greek tourists in Cairo. On April 16, 1996, a cell of Gamaa al Islamiya attacked a group of tourists, Greek Orthodox pilgrims, with light weapons as it was about to leave the Europe Hotel for a tour of the city. Seventeen Greek tourists lay dead after the attack. Subsequently, the organization published an announcement claiming responsibility for the attack, but stated that its target had actually been Israeli tourists that usually stayed at the Europe Hotel in Cairo, to avenge the attacks of the Israel Defense Forces in Lebanon.

Attack against German tourists in Egypt.[12] On September 19, 1996, a Molotov cocktail was thrown at a tour bus carrying German tourists in Cairo. There were ten casualties, including nine German tourists and one Egyptian citizen, the bus driver. The attack was carried out by two brothers who independently initiated the attack out of religious Islamic motives, that is, they targeted infidels who were defiling Egyptian society.

The massacre of tourists in Luxor.[13] On November 17, 1997, a three-member team of the Gamaa al Islamiya attacked a group of tourists touring a temple in Luxor. The attackers killed 58 tourists and 4 Egyptians, and injured 24 tourists. The perpetrators used Kalachnikov assault rifles and knives. All of the attackers were ultimately killed by Egyptian security forces.

The cell members, some of whom were students, were all in their twenties and most of them were from the A-Siut region in Upper

Egypt. The cell's leader had previously been involved in terror activity in Egypt and was an Afghanistan alumnus, who had returned from abroad to serve as commander of the attack.

The organization chose to attack the tourists to deal a blow to the recovering Egyptian tourism during the height of the tourist season. The attack was well planned and was carried out with murderous detachment; three separate teams attacked the guards and tourists, leaving them with little chance to evade the crossfire. Those they had missed were butchered with knives. The cell members left behind leaflets bearing the headline "Gamaa al Islamiya—the devastation and destruction regiments." The cell members wore headbands bearing the slogan: "Mustafa Hamza–we are at your command," naming the head of the organization's military branch. The heavy criticism prompted by the murderous nature of the attack aroused conflict and condemnations even within the leadership of the organization, and there were attempts to deny its involvement in the attack..

The suicide attack at the police station in Rijeka, Croatia.[14] On October 16, 1995, a suicide driver detonated himself at the police station in Rijeka, Croatia. The apparent aim of the attack was to issue a warning to the Croatian authorities that had ostensibly been involved in the capture of a senior military commander in the organization named Tlaat Fuad Kassam. The goal was to place pressure on the Croatian government, which was suspected of collaborating with the Egyptian authorities, so that it would release the detainee immediately.

The Egyptian Islamic Jihad Organization[15]

This organization was founded at the end of the seventies by Muhammad Abd Al Salaam Faraj. Faraj adopted the outlook and ways of Sayyid Qutb regarding the need to wage a jihad against secular Muslim regimes and infidels. Faraj's ideas were recorded in his book *The Missing Commandment*.

Several months prior to the assassination of Saadat an attempt had been made to consolidate the Jihad with the Gamaa al Islamiya under the leadership of Sheikh Omar Abd al-Rahman. Faraj was inspired by the blind leader and offered him the leadership of the organization, but the latter refused, claiming that a blemished person is not worthy of this role. Nevertheless, Sheikh Abd al-Rahman remained the spiritual leader of the Jihad organization.

It was Faraj who was behind the planning of the assassination of Saadat on October 6, 1981, while Omar Abd al-Rahman gave the religious sanction (fatwa) to commit the killing. After the president's assassination, most of the members of the Jihad organization were arrested; some were executed (including Faraj), and Omar Abd al-Rahman was put on trial, but was subsequently released. Rahman left Egypt, spent some time in Iran and Sudan, and finally moved to the United States. He settled in New Jersey, where he quickly set up an Islamic terror network.

The death of Faraj and the Sheikh's departure for the United States brought about the dismantling of the alliance due to disputes regarding the choice of an organizational leader (the emir). Members of the Jama'a demanded that Rahman serve as the leader, while members of the Jihad preferred Aboud Zoumour, who had been sentenced to life imprisonment in Egypt.

Subsequently, the Jihad organization underwent additional splits: In 1993 a new organization called The Pioneers of Conquest (Talia'a al Fatah) was founded under the leadership of Aiman A-Zawahiri, who is currently operating under the sponsorship of Bin-Laden, and another faction of the organization led by Ahmad Salah maintains close ties with Iran. Additional factions that split away from the Jihad organization, and which are active mainly in the Egyptian domestic arena, are Ashawkiun an A-Najiun Min A-Nar (the survivors of hellfire), El-Vatikun Min Al-Antsar (those confident of victory) and Al-Haramium, which acted against the Copts.

The Egyptian Islamic Jihad organization focuses its international activity mainly outside of Egypt. Its most prominent attacks include the assassination of an Egyptian diplomat in Switzerland due to his efforts to track down and arrest organization activists in Europe and have them extradited to Egypt, and the bombing of the Egyptian Embassy in Pakistan because of similar circumstances involving the extrication of activists from this state to Egypt.

Recently, the name of one of the Egyptian Islamic Jihad factions has been linked with the attacks on the American embassies in Kenya and Tanzania sponsored by Osama Bin-Laden. The organization's attacks demonstrated impressive logistical and operational capabilities. In Egypt the organization was active mainly in the vicinity of Cairo against senior government targets. In this framework the organization carried out assassination attempts against the Minister of the Interior on August 18, 1992, during which five people were killed (the minister was not hurt), and against Prime Minster Sidki, using a car bomb. The prime minister was not hurt, but a young girl was killed and eighteen people were wounded.

The assault at the Egyptian embassy in Islamabad, Pakistan.[16] On November 19, 1995, the Egyptian Islamic Jihad carried out a two-staged suicide mission at the Egyptian embassy in Pakistan. Primarily, an explosive charge was activated, which burst open the entrance gate, and at the second stage a car bomb driven by a suicide terrorist armed with a charge containing about a half ton of explosives detonated at the center of the embassy compound. As a result of the attack seventeen people were killed and fifty-eight were wounded. The attack was perpetrated at 10:45 a.m., which is one of the busiest public reception times at the embassy. The terror cell was made up of two Egyptian assailants, members of the organization in their twenties. One of them had resided in Pakistan for several years.

Pakistan was chosen as the venue for the attack in order to deter the Pakistani authorities from collaborating with the Egyptian government against members of the Egyptian organizations. The presence of collaborators and sympathizers of the Egyptian organizations in this country facilitated the smuggling of weapons and the terrorists, as well as abetting the escape of the attack's commanders to Afghanistan upon completion of their mission. The "World Justice" organization and the Egyptian Islamic Jihad claimed responsibility for the attack. The Egyptian Islamic Jihad demonstrated considerable skill in enlisting weaponry and suicide attackers to carry out this large-scale attack outside of Egyptian borders.

On the evening of November 14, 1995, the Egyptian attaché in Geneva was murdered by a lone assassin. The World Justice organization claimed responsibility for the shooting, stating that the victim was an agent of the Egyptian secret services.

"Talia'a al Fatah"[17] *(The Pioneers of Conquest)*

The organization was established in 1993 as the successor to the Jihad, which had been relentlessly oppressed by the Egyptian authorities after the assassination of President Saadat (it is sometimes called the New Jihad). There are conflicting versions regarding the organization's founder and leader: according to the first version, Dr. Aiman A-Zawahiri, one of the leaders of the Egyptian Islamic Jihad, is the founder of the organization. This theory claims that he called the organization Talia'a al Fatah in order to differentiate between it and the Jihad organization, thus avoiding confrontation with Aboud Zoumur, the leader of the Jihad incarcerated in an Egyptian jail. According to the second version, Abd Al-Hamoud Haballah, an Afghani alumnus who returned to Egypt, was influenced by the conceptions of Aboud Zoumur, which led to the founding of the organization.

The organization included religious groups from various Egyptian districts, and during its first years concentrated its efforts on terror attacks inside Egypt. The most prominent of them were:

- February 15, 1992—An attempt to take over a weapons warehouse in order to facilitate a plot to invade Cairo.
- August 18, 1993—An assassination attempt against the Egyptian Minister of the Interior Hassan Al-Alfi, who was wounded in the attack.

The authorities also accuse the group of involvement in the suicide attack at the Egyptian embassy in Islamabad, Pakistan.

On December 19, 2001, the Swedish government extradited Ahmad Hussein Agiza to Egypt. The Egyptian authorities regarded him as one of the senior commanders of Talia'a al Fatah. Ajiza had fled Egypt in the beginning of the eighties and was sentenced in absentia to life imprisonment for his involvement in the plot to assassinate President Saadat.

For many years Agiza and his family lived in Pakistan, but due to pressure exerted by the Egyptian government on Pakistan, he moved with his family to Sweden where he resided for two years. As stated earlier, he was recently arrested and extradited to Egypt. The Egyptian authorities claim that Ajiza was one the planners of the attack on the Egyptian embassy in Islamabad.

Jordan

During the eighties, the Fundamentalist Islamic movement became a central opposition to the Hashemite monarchy. Alongside the Muslim Brotherhood, Islamic organizations and movements dealing in subversion and terror started to become active in Jordan in the nineties.

These groups can be divided into two main categories:

1. Factions of the Palestinian Islamic Jihad inspired by Iran and Syria that acted in Jordan (further elaboration will not be supplied about these factions).

2. Fundamentalist Islamic organizations and associations established in the beginning of the eighties under the influence of the Khomeini revolution and the wave of Islamic radicalism that swept over the Muslim world.

The goal of these organizations was to overthrow the Hashemite monarchy in Jordan and perpetrate actions against Israel and secular Western influences.

At the end of the war against the Soviets in Afghanistan scores of Islamic fighters returned to Jordan and joined terror organizations to become the vanguard in the subversive activities. Following is a list of the organizations:

The Jordanian Afghans
The Army of Muhammad (*Jeish Muhammad*)
The Pledge to the Imam Organization (*Harqat Biat Al-Imam*)
The Youths of the Islamic Ram's Horn (*Shabab A-Nafir Al-Imam*)
The Islamic Renewal Organization (*Harqat A-Tajdid al-Islami*)
The Islamic Liberation Party (*Hizb A-Tahrir al-Islami*)

The Jordanian Afghans[18]

In the beginning of 1994 a series of bombings took place in movie theaters in the Jordanian cities of Amman and Zarka. After the attacks, the Jordanian authorities arrested scores of suspects who were found to have large amounts of explosives and other weapons in their possession. Some of the detainees had returned to Jordan in the course of 1993 after having undergone training in the mujahidin camps in Afghanistan. Others to join the Jordanian Afghans were former members of The Army of Muhammad, many of which were Palestinian.

The organization had set itself the goal of banishing the corrupt regime in Jordan through a jihad, as part of the overall war to remedy Islamic society. Weapons and explosives were found in the possession of the organization members. Interrogation revealed that their intention had been to perpetrate extensive terror activities against factors that in their view were identified with the regime's corruption, including public figures, movie theaters and hotels.

Although Osama Bin-Laden provided the main funding for the organization's establishment and activities, it was through contact with Muhammad Jamal Halifa, Bin-Laden's brother-in-law, that members received help setting up the organization and funding its activities. Halifa was arrested in the United States and was extradited to Jordan where he was brought to trial. The court acquitted him of the crime due to a procedural technicality and because of the lack of supportive evidence. Subsequently, Halifa left Jordan.

The trial of the Jordanian Afghans was held in two cycles, in the middle and end of 1994. Eleven of the accused were sentenced to death, and others were given various prison sentences. However, the verdicts of execution were later mitigated to life imprisonment.

The Army of Muhammad—(Jeish Muhammad)[19]

In 1988, Dr. Smiah Muhammad Zidan established the organization called The Army of Muhammad in the wake of the sense of triumph of the Afghan alumni and due to their aspirations to perpetuate the jihad at additional fronts. The idea to establish the organization became a reality during a meeting between Dr. Zidan and Abdallah Azzam while they were serving in Afghanistan. Zidan believed that the establishment of the organization and the launching of an armed battle with its help would constitute the first step in liberating the Middle East from the yoke of Western tyranny. Upon his return to Jordan he began to recruit people from among the Afghani returnees and established clandestine cells. In January of 1991 the organization already had about twenty cells. The organizational structure of The Army of Muhammad contained several branches, including military, training, and religious departments in addition to foreign activities. Three committees acted within the organization: The military, financial, and "western sector" committees (*Al-Kuta'a Al-Gharbi*), the latter of which was responsible for activities in Israel and the territories, and also enlisted candidates from the West Bank.

The organization's goal was to topple the Hashemite monarchy, establish a religious Islamic state and renew the caliphate via revolution and armed jihad. The organization's first two years of existence were dedicated to training and obtaining funding and weapons. Money was collected from worshippers in mosques all over the monarchy under the guise of aid for the ongoing struggle in Afghanistan. In the beginning of 1991, organizational members began launching terror attacks in Jordan. They assassinated a Jordanian intelligence officer involved in exposing the organization by planting an explosive device in his car. They also perpetrated terror attacks at banks in Amman, including "The British Bank," and torched liquor stores and the French cultural center in Amman as well as vehicles belonging to foreign diplomats.

In mid-1991, Jordanian security forces began impeding the organization's activities. Hundreds of suspects were arrested for questioning, but most were subsequently released. Only eighteen were tried in military courts for state security in October 1991. The accused were charged with attempting to repeal the country's constitution in order to reinstate the Islamic caliphate, possessing weapons, carrying out acts of terror, attempted murder and membership in an illegal organization. On November 25, 1995, the court sentenced eight of the accused to death, and the rest received various prison sentences. On December 24, King Hussein mitigated the verdicts of those sentenced to execution to life imprisonment.

In the course of the security campaign against the organization, a large arsenal was found in the possession of its members including dozens of rifles, handguns with silencers, hand grenades, explosives, and homemade bombs. The trial of the organization members was utilized by the regime to send a clear message of warning to the Muslim Brotherhood, while emphasizing the past affiliation of Zidan and others with this organization. Zidan and his followers were eventually released from prison in the framework of a general amnesty granted by King Hussein in November 1992. In the mid-nineties, the organization attempted to rehabilitate itself and some of its members were involved in the founding of the Jordanian Afghans in the beginning of 1994, and in the establishment of the "Biat Al-Imam" at the end of 1995 (see below).

The Pledge to the Imam Organization (Harqat Biat Al-Imam)[20]

In 1995, the Jordanian intelligence arrested twenty-five members of The Pledge to the Imam Organization, many of whom were Palestinian. The organization had adopted the ideology of "A-Takfir and Al-Hijra" which perceives society as heretic, thus necessitating isolation from it and return only after the necessary purification and renewal according to the spirit of Islam. In addition, this organization was affiliated with the Egyptian organization Al Gamaa al Islamiya.

The Pledge to the Imam Organization was headed by a Palestinian from Jaffa, Atsam Muhammad Taher, who was known as Abu-Muhammad Al-Makdasi. During interrogation, the detainees confessed to setting up the organization in the early nineties and admitted that some of them had been trained in Afghanistan. Among the organization's founders were former members of The Army of Muhammad. One of the detainees confessed to sending a mail bomb to the editor of the *Al-Wattan Al-Arabi* periodical in Paris in 1993, to protest the publication of a poem that in his opinion slandered the good name of the Prophet.

Thirteen detainees were tried in a state security court, and eighteen additional detainees were tried in a civil court. The organization's leader, Makdasi, was sentenced to fifteen years imprisonment with hard labor, and the rest were condemned to long prison sentences.

In July 1997, the Jordanian intelligence arrested five young Jordanians of Palestinian origin, who were planning to infiltrate the Israeli border and perpetrate terror attacks against Israelis and senor figures in the Palestinian Authority. During their interrogation the youths stated that they were affiliated with The Pledge to the Imam Organization. Weapons and explosive devices were found in their possession, and they were sentenced to ten to fifteen years of imprisonment by a state security court. Today this group is led by Abu-Musab-el Zarqawi.

Independent Terror Activities in Jordan (December 1999)

In December 1999, an Islamic terror group was exposed by the authorities. The group included Jordanian citizens, one Iraqi citizen, one Algerian citizen, and Palestinians with American passports. The group's leader was Abu-Hushar, who had previously been arrested (in 1993) in Jordan for perpetrating attacks against the monarchy, but, after having been granted amnesty by the King, was released. Abu-Hushar had undergone training in Afghanistan and returned to Jordan. He was among the founders of The Army of Muhammad, which was partially composed of Afghan alumni.[21] The interrogation revealed that they had intended to carry out attacks against Jewish and Israeli tourists staying at the Radisson Hotel in Amman, visitors at the burial site of Moses on Nevo Mountain, at the border check post between Jordan and Israel, and pilgrims visiting the site of Jesus' baptism.[22] (See further elaboration concerning Bin-Laden's terror networks in chapter 3.)

Algeria

The Armed Islamic Front (GIA)

During the eighties many volunteers left Algeria for Afghanistan; their numbers are estimated between several hundreds and three thousand, and they fought alongside the Afghani muhajidin. The Algerian mujahidin in Afghanistan and Pakistan were split during the struggle against the Soviets and are still split between the trend that supports the radical "Islamic Salvation Front," and the trend that supports the more moderate Algerian Hamas led by Mahfud Nahnah.

Some of the Algerian participants fought in the framework of the "Algerian Legion" under the command of Sheikh Ahmad Masoud. It was Sheikh Abdullah Azzam who initiated the contact between the Algerian commanders, headed by Haj Bonua, and Sheikh Masoud.[23]

At the end of the eighties, and particularly after the victory of the mujahidin in Afghanistan, these volunteers began to return to Algeria, taking with them considerable experience in guerrilla warfare and revolutionary Islamic fervor. Upon their return to Algeria these volunteers, dubbed the "Afghans," joined the ranks of radical Islamic movements such as The Armed Islamic Organization and the Al-Hijra and A-Takfir organization.[24]

Ali Belhaj, one of the leaders of the Islamic Front in Algeria, served as the spiritual mentor for most of the radical opposition organizations, and there are those who claim that he paved the way for the incorporation of the "Afghan groups" within the organizational system of the Islamic Front, with the aim of establishing a militant, radical focus that would form resistance against the attempt of some of the organization's leaders to take the path of political compromise and struggle through political means.[25]

The first violent activity of the Afghans was recorded in the town of Gumar on the Algerian-Tunisian border, when a group of fighters attacked the police station causing multiple casualties and injuries.[26] From this point on, as the struggle between the Algerian regime and the Islamic opposition intensified, reports regarding the involvement of the Afghans in terror activity throughout the country steadily increased.

The terror activity of the Islamic organizations that had begun in 1991 with sporadic attacks against military targets and government institutions, gradually expanded to a widespread civil war, which to date has claimed tens of thousands of lives. During this period Islamic terror entities succeeded in taking over many focal points in rural areas and even certain neighborhoods in the large cities.

In 1994, and mainly in the years 1995-1996, the GIA started perpetrating terror attacks abroad. All of these attacks took place in

France or were carried out against French citizens outside of their country, and were supposedly justified by the fact that the French government supports the current regime in Algeria. The acuteness of the confrontation between the GIA and France was also explained by its spokesmen in the context of the historical conflict between Algeria and France during the Algerian war of liberation in the beginning of the sixties.

The GIA's terror campaign abroad included the hijacking of an Air France airplane in December 1994 and two waves of attacks in France (in July to October 1995 and in December 1996), in which some twenty people were killed and scores were wounded.

As an Islamic terror organization, the GIA, like other fundamentalist organizations in Arab countries, believed in the establishment of a religious Islamic state and viewed the United States, Israel and Jews as the enemies of Islam. Nevertheless, the organization did not carry out terror attacks aimed directly against American and Israeli targets, but instead carried out three terror attacks against Jews in France as part of the overall terror campaign against this country. These attacks included the positioning of two car bombs near the synagogue in Lyons (September 1995) and the sending of a letter bomb to the editor of a Jewish newspaper (December 1996).[27]

The GIA terror attacks abroad (all of which took place in France) exposed its infrastructure, which included deployment in several European countries, mainly France, Belgium, Britain, Germany, Italy, Sweden and Spain. Terror cells that were active in these countries included a small number of members, which were mutually linked and cooperated in the sharing of logistic, financial and operational roles. The main role of the European network was to raise funds and combat means, and to smuggle them over to their fighting comrades in Algeria. Enforcement and thwarting efforts of security factors in Europe, which were initiated by France with international cooperation, impaired the Algerian terror network's infrastructure and put an end to the terror attacks initiated by the GIA in the international arena.

In 1998, additional terror cells connected to the GIA were exposed in Europe. The involvement of emigrants and emigrants' children from the countries of the Magreb in the terror attacks in France, and their membership in Algerian terror cells in various European countries, indicates the wide infrastructure for the enlistment of potential volunteers in Islamic terror organizations from among the emigrant population of the lower socioeconomic levels, who feel discriminated against and alienated by their countries of residence. These populations constitute a reservoir for the recruitment of new members, some of which were sent to undergo terror training in Afghanistan in the early nineties, while others volunteered to fight in Bosnia.[28]

Terror Attacks of the Algerian GIA

Hijacking of an Air France aircraft to Marseille (December 24, 1994). On December 24, 1994, an Air France airplane was hijacked in Algeria by a GIA terror unit. The unit, which contained four members, had disguised themselves as maintenance employees, and with the use of fake badges boarded the plane at the Algerian airport prior to its takeoff for Paris. The hijacked plane had 239 passengers and crewmembers on board. The hijackers' demands included the release of several organizational leaders incarcerated in Algerian prisons and a threat to kill hostages if their demands were not met. At the very beginning of the incident, the hijackers killed two hostages, a local policeman and a Vietnamese diplomat. Their bodies remained on board the aircraft throughout the hijacking. Subsequently, the hijackers shot another hostage when their demands were not met. Following negotiations that went on for two days, the plane took off for Marseilles. After a short period of time, a special French counter-terror unit stormed the plane and killed the hijackers. In the course of the incident, there were five casualties and twenty-five were injured. On December 26, 1994, the GIA claimed responsibility for the hijacking via a statement faxed to the French news agency in Paris. In a declaration published by *Al-Hayat* on December 27, 1994, the organization again claimed responsibility. Hijackings of aircraft, which were one of the characteristics of the Palestinian terror organizations and subsequently of the Shiite terror organizations, were rare for the Sunni terror organizations identified with the Afghan phenomenon, although this incident was not completely isolated. For reasons that are unclear, to date these organizations have rarely used this method to seek release of their imprisoned comrades or to achieve political gain.

Terror Attacks in France between July and October 1995. On July 25, 1995, an explosive device exploded on a train in Paris, claiming eight lives and injuring fifty. On August 17, 1995, a bomb that had been placed in a trashcan near the exit from the Etoile Metro station in the eighth arrondissement of Paris exploded, slightly injuring seventeen people. On August 26, 1995, a thirteen-kilo improvised bomb, which had been placed on the rail tracks of the Lyon-Paris line, was discovered and dismantled. The bomb did not explode because of a technical failure in its ignition system.

On September 3, 1995, a bomb exploded under a stand in an open market in the eleventh arrondissement of Paris, causing injury to three bystanders and heavy damage to property.

On September 4, 1995, a bomb was found in a bag placed in public restrooms in the fifteenth arrondissement of Paris. On September 7, 1995, a car bomb exploded near a Jewish school in the town of Villeurbanne near Lyon. Thirteen people were hurt in the explosion, one of them seriously. As previously stated, due to a technical mishap the school bell failed to ring on time and the pupils did not leave the school premises at the anticipated time. Many lives were undoubtedly saved.

On October 6, 1995, a bomb was found in a trashcan near the Maison Blanche Metro station in Paris. The bomb went off before the sappers arrived to dismantle it. Ten individuals were slightly injured in the explosion.

On October 17, 1995, a bomb exploded on a train when it was passing through a tunnel between the stations of the D'Orsay Museum and Saint Michel in Paris. Thirty passengers were injured in the explosion, four of them seriously.

Claiming responsibility for the wave of attacks. The Islamic periodical *Al-Antsar*, which serves as a mouthpiece for GIA activity in Europe, published an article on June 22, 1995, prior to the wave of attacks in France by Rashid Ramada (who was later identified as a central figure in the network that perpetrated the attacks in France), in which the GIA claimed credit in advance for the attacks which were about to take place in the Algerian network's first wave of terror.

On October 7, 1995, in another declaration faxed from Pakistan to the Reuter agency in Cairo and to the daily *Al-Hayat* in London, GIA claimed credit for the terror attacks in Lyon and Paris.

The second terror wave perpetrated in France in December 1996. On December 3, 1996, a bomb went off on a train in Paris. The explosion killed two and wounded thirty-six people.

On December 3, 1996, a booby-trapped video sent to the manager of the Jewish newspaper, *Tribune Juif*, was discovered. The bomb did not go off due to a technical fault.

On December 14, 1996, a bomb was discovered near the Opera House in Paris, but it was dismantled before it could cause any damage.

On December 21, 1996, a bomb went off at the Central Statistics Bureau in Paris. In this case, there were no injuries.

India and Pakistan

Lashkar e-Toiba ("The Army of the Pure")[29]

The LET[30] is one of the largest terror organizations active in the Jammu-Kashmir (J&K). This organization, together with The Army of Muhammad organization, is responsible for the attack on the Parliament building in New Delhi on December 13, 2001, which brought India and Pakistan to the brink of war. The LET was founded at the end of the eighties in the Kunar district of Afghanistan as the military arm of the Fundamentalist Pakistani Islamic movement with Wahabian leanings (*Markaz-ul-Dawa-wal-Irshad*). At the end of the eighties and the beginning of the nineties, the Lashkar e-Toiba organization was involved in the jihad against the Soviets in Afghanistan. Parallel to its involvement on the Afghani front, the organization also started to become active at Jammu-Kashmir, with the aid and under the sponsorship of the Pakistani intelligence. Professor Hafez Muhammad Sa'id heads the organization and also serves as the emir (leader) of LET.

The organization supports the establishment of Islamic rule not only in Jammu and Kashmir, but in all of India, and it has joined the ranks of Muslims fighting throughout the world, in Chechnya and Muslim republics in Central Asia, among other locations. The LET's first attack was carried out in 1993 when a terror cell numbering twelve terrorists of Pakistani and Afghani origins infiltrated the Jammu-Kashmir area, which is under Indian rule.

From 1997 onwards, during the second term of Pakistani Prime Minister Nawaz Sharif, the organization steadily gained strength. At this time the Pakistani intelligence (ISI) sponsored the organization's activities, providing it with funding, training and weapons. An indication of the organization's protected status can be seen in the visit paid by the Pakistani Minister of Information and the Governor of the Panjab region at the organization's headquarters near the city of Murdike and Lahore in 1997.

The increased importance afforded to the organization was linked to a revision in the policy of the Pakistani intelligence, which had decided to shift the center of gravity of the subversive activity from the Kashmir valley to the Jammu region, as part of an overall plan to carry out ethnic cleansing of minorities in the area by escalating terror activities. The organization was an ideal means for this task due to its radical Islamic ideology and its willingness to carry out attacks and massacres against minorities in that area. The fact that most of the members of Lashkar e-Toiba originated from the Pakistani Panjab area helped them to blend in easily with the population of the Jammu region, which speaks the same dialect.

When surrounded by Indian forces, the organization's members generally preferred to die rather than surrender. This became evident in 1997 when the largest number of terrorists killed by Indian forces came from this organization.

The Lashkar e-Toiba organization carried out several terror attacks together with the Hizb Al-Mujahidin organization. Several examples follow:

- The massacre of twenty-three individuals on January 23, 1988, in Wanlhama.
- The massacre of twenty-five people on June 6, 1988, during a wedding in Doda.
- The massacre of thirty-five people on March 20, 2002, at Chattismghpora, which took place during a visit of the U.S. president to India.

Lashkar e-Toiba also carried out a series of suicide attacks against bases of Indian forces:

- An attack against an Indian border guard base in Bandipore, near Srinagar.
- An attack against a border guard base at Handwara on September 4, 1999.
- An attack against the headquarters of the Special Forces on December 27, 1999.

Despite the fact that the head of the organization's suicide unit, Abu Muwain, was killed on December 30, 1999, in a clash with Indian forces, the organization's suicide attacks continued and during the year 2000 another three suicide attacks took place:

- On January 1, 2000, a military base in Surankote was attacked.
- On January 12, 2000, a military base in Anantang was attacked.
- On January 21, 2000, a border guard base was attacked in Srinagar.

The organization's suicide attacks contributed to its consolidation and intensified the level of fear and terror among the Indian security forces and civilians.

After the Hizb-Al-Mujahidin organization signed a truce with the Indian authorities and launched political negotiations, Lashkar e-Toiba continued to serve as the leading terror entity in the jihad against India. Thus, the Pakistani intelligence could simultaneously act vis-à-vis India via the overt political channel but also via the covert channel by allowing the continued terror activity of Lashkar e-Toiba.

Lashkar e-Toïba raises funds from Pakistani populations in the Persian Gulf states through charitable organizations, as well as from Pakistani businessmen and the Pakistani government. It is closely affiliated with Bin-Laden and Al-Qaida and maintains military and religious groups throughout the world from the Philippines, via Chechnya to Bosnia. The organization also offered refuge to Ramzi Yusuf and Mir Imal Kenzi, two terrorists who were apprehended and extradited to the United States.

The Jeish Muhammad (The Army of Muhammad) Organization[31]

This is a relatively new terror organization founded in February 2000. It has been in the limelight mainly thanks to its commander Maulana Masoud Azhar, who has a long record in the area of terror and was released from an Indian prison in December 1999.

Masoud Azhar, a radical Islamic cleric from Karachi, was chosen by the Pakistani intelligence to play a central role in the struggle at Jammu-Kashmir when he served as the secretary-general of the Harqat al Ansar, a dominant terror organization until the mid-nineties. Masoud Azhar was arrested in Srinagar in February 1999, and over time attempts were made to attain his release, but they ended in failure.

In December 1999, members of the organization hijacked an Indian Airlines passenger plane in Kandahar, Afghanistan. In exchange for the release of the passengers, the Indian authorities agreed to release Masoud and two other terrorists from the organization who were incarcerated in an Indian prison.

After his release, many of his supporters expected him to resume his position as head of the organization and lead it to play a central role in the struggle over Kashmir, but the Harqat al Ansar organization had already been weakened after two of its senior leaders, Sayyed Afghani and Nasarullah Langaryal, were killed by India's security forces. Masoud's declarations about the need to persevere in the jihad in Jammu-Kashmir caused the Pakistani authorities some embarrassment, as India already suspected them of being involved in the hijacking of the airliner and the subsequent release of Masoud. Therefore, the Pakistani authorities chose to play down their ties with Masoud and prevented his return to a senior position in the Harqat al Ansar organization, which was largely identified with the Pakistani regime.

In light of these developments, Masoud decided to establish "The Army of Muhammad" organization, vowing to escalate the terror in Jammu-Kashmir. The organization's first attack took place on April 23, 2000, when an organization member detonated himself along with a truck loaded with explosives near the gate of the Indian military headquarters in Srinagar. On June 28, 2000, the organization claimed credit for an attack that included shooting and lobbing hand grenades at a government office building in Srinagar.

On May 18, 2000, rumors spread about the possibility that The Army of Muhammad and Harqat al Ansar had consolidated, but this information has not been verified. In December 2001, members of The Army of Muhammad and Lashkar e-Toiba attacked the Indian Parliament building in New Delhi. The loud Indian and international outcry, and the escalation at the India-Pakistani border, prompted the Pakistani government to take action against the organization by outlawing it and arresting some of its members.

The attack against the Indian Parliament building in New Delhi. On December 12, 2001, five terrorists attacked the Indian Parliament building in New Delhi. They arrived in a vehicle that appeared to be a government car (according to its color and license plates), and passed through the ring of gates and outer barriers surrounding the building.

Four of the terrorists, who were armed with Kalachnikov assault rifles, stormed the VIP entrance of Parliament while shooting and throwing grenades at the policemen guarding the building. A fifth terrorist detonated an explosive belt he was wearing at the entrance to the building. Policemen and the Parliament guard returned fire and a forty-minute gun battle developed between the two sides. At its end, the five terrorists lay dead. Four policemen were also killed and eighteen were wounded. Several government ministers and 300 members of Parliament were present in the building during the attack, but none of them was hurt.

The government of India accused Pakistan of supporting the terror organizations that had perpetrated the attack. An investigation indicated that The Army of Muhammad and Lashkar e-Toiba were responsible. The Pakistani government denied any involvement in the attack, expressed its sympathy, and proposed a joint investigation to discover the responsible parties, but the government of India rejected the Pakistani stance and demanded vociferously that it take immediate steps to put a stop to the terror. As a result of the attack, ominous tension prevailed all along the border between the two countries. Both countries reinforced their troops, and shooting incidents flared up along the boundaries.

The Jammu and Kashmir Liberation Front (JKLF).[32] Two organizations operate under the name JKLF;[33] the first is headed by Amanullah Khan, and the second, which split away from this organization, is led by Yasin Malik. The origin of both organizations is the political movement of the Jammu and Kashmir National Liberation Front (JKNLF), which accepted a peace agreement with India. Radical factions of the organization that did not accept the agreement with India split away and established the JKLF. The JKLF was founded in May 1977 in Britain by Amanullah Khan, after many of his comrades were either killed or arrested by the Indian security forces. The organization's main support was the population of the section of Kashmir that is in Pakistani hands.

In September 1995, a faction led by Yasin Malik split away from the original JKLF organization duc to a conflict related to the desired strategy for realizing the organization's goals-the achievement of the right to self-definition for Jammu-Kashmir and its liberation from Indian control. Yasin Malik favored a violent, uncompromising struggle until achieving that goal, while Khan claimed that action should be taken on three levels:

- A political and informational campaign in India
- An attempt to enlist international support for the organization's stance
- A violent struggle against the Indian security forces in Jammu-Kashmir.

In the seventies and eighties, the JKLF, headed by Amanallah Khan, operated mainly out of London and Pakistani Kashmir, and its main activities involved informational efforts in India, Kashmir, and the international arena. However, already in the seventies terror activities were initiated by the organization, when two of its founders—Altaf and Kuraishi—hijacked an Indian Airlines aircraft in 1971.

Another senior member of the organization, Maqbul Butt, was also involved in the hijacking of the airplane. He had escaped from an Indian jail in December 1968 but returned to that country in 1976 and was arrested that year. In 1980, he was sentenced to death for murdering a policeman, but a stay was placed on his execution.

On February 3, 1984, several JKLF activists kidnapped a senior Indian diplomat in Birmingham and demanded the release of Butt. The Indian authorities refused to accept the terrorists' demand and on February 2, 1984, the kidnappers executed the diplomat. In retaliation, the Indian authorities executed Butt on February 11, 1984. The kidnapping had been carried out apparently without the prior knowledge of the organization's leaders and the kidnappers operated under the cover name of the Kashmir Liberation Front.

The British authorities tried Amanallah Khan, but ultimately decided to deport him from Britain. He arrived in Pakistan, where he enjoyed the patronage of the Pakistani Intelligence (ISI) and set up a network of training camps for recruits from Indian Kashmir, who were willing to cross the border into Pakistani Kashmir to undergo training in guerrilla warfare and terror.

From 1988, the JKLF launched subversive activities and terror operations in the Kashmir region. This organization aspires to establish an independent political entity in Kashmir, while the Pakistani position is that all of Kashmir must be part of Pakistan.

An additional bone of contention between the JKLF and the Pakistan government relates to the Gilghit Baltistan region. The organization argues that this area should also be part of the Jammu-Kashmir autonomy, while the Pakistani authorities regard its annexation to Pakistan as a prerequisite.

These conflicts did not prevent cooperation between the organization and the Pakistani government, but, periodically, the dispute would flare up, leading to the adoption of a tougher policy by the Pakistani authorities vis-à-vis the organization.

In the seventies and eighties, despite the disagreements, Pakistani intelligence relied heavily on the JKLF's ability to enlist young men from Kashmir for subversive activities, but, subsequently, the ISI collaborated in the establishment of terror organizations that were more faithful to the Pakistani line, such as the Hizb-ul-Mujahidin, Harqat al Ansar, and Lashkar e-Toiba. The founding of these organizations, which enjoyed massive Pakistani aid and support, weakened the JKLF and its operational capabilities. The split that occurred within the organization's own ranks in 1995 also contributed to its diminished activity.

In a series of incidents that took place in March 1996, the majority of the central military activists of the Amanallah Khan faction were killed:

- Eleven activists were killed on March 24, 1996.
- Twenty-six activists, including Malik's successor, Samir Tsadki, were killed on March 29, 1996.

After these blows, the JKLF ceased constituting a significant factor in terror activities in Jammu Kashmir and persevered mainly with its political activity, while Yasin Malik's organization continued with its terror campaign, although its operational capabilities and influence remained marginal.

Hizb-ul-Mujahidin[34]

This organization was first founded in 1989 as an extremist faction in the social-political organization Al Jamaa al Islamiya, which was active in Jammu-Kashmir. The organization was initially named Al-Bader but this was quickly changed to Hizb-ul-Mujahidin.

Hizb-ul-Mujahidin was established under the auspices of the Pakistani Intelligence to serve as a counterweight vis-à-vis the JKLF, which had lost the support of the Pakistani authorities. In contrast to the JKLF that believed in autonomy for the Jammu-Kashmir region, the ul-Mujahidin members felt that Jammu-Kashmir should be consolidated with Pakistan. After it was first established, the organization maintained close ties with Afghani mujahidin groups, such as Hizb-e-Islami, which offered aid in the form of training and weapons.

During its years of activities, Hizb-ul-Mujahidin sustained several blows, including the arrest of its leader, Ahsan Dahar, by the Indian authorities in December 1993. Another senior leader, Ghulam Rasool Shah, alias Imran Rahi, withdrew from terror activity and decided that the Jammu-Kashmir problem must be resolved through negotiations.

The Jamaa al Islamiya organization, from which the Hizb-ul-Mujahidin sprang, claimed on November 14, 1998, that it had severed all ties with terror, from which it appeared that the organization was dissolving its connections with the Hizb-ul-Mujahidin and would take only democratic and legal steps to realize its objectives. The organization even claimed that members who had been active in the Hizb-ul-Mujahidin had been banished from its ranks. Nonetheless, there were those in the organization who argued that it must not separate itself from the armed struggle that was going on simultaneously.

Since 1997, Hizb-ul-Mujahidin has been operating in cooperation with Lashkar e-Toiba. Among their joint exploits are the massacres in Wandhama and Chittisinghpora. The organization also cooperated with Harqat al Ansar in an attack on a military base in Nathnusha in the Kupwara region on August 6, 1999, leaving five military personnel dead. The Hizb-ul-Mujahidin was also responsible for the torching of a Muslim house of prayer in Charar-e-Sharif in 1995. Among its most notorious attacks was the detonation of a powerful roadside charge activated against a convoy of Indian security forces near Tral on February 18, 2000, leaving eleven policemen dead.

In order to promote the objectives of the organization and its Pakistani patrons, the former assassinated several moderate Kashmir leaders and attacked a JKLF base in Muzaaffarabad, the capital of the Pakistani Kashmir region. Simultaneously, the Hizb-ul-Mujahidin also suffered from terror attacks perpetrated by activists in rival organizations.

The advantage of the Hizb-ul-Mujahidin was in its being a local organization, whose members were well acquainted with the Kashmir arena and were able to assimilate themselves within its population. This advantage explains the cooperation with other terror organizations like Harqat al Ansar and Lashkar e-Toiba, the majority of whose activists are not natives of Kashmir, thus necessitating the assistance of Hizb-ul-Mujahidin in their operational activities. The latter is the largest of all the terror organizations active in Jammu-Kashmir.

Harqat ul-Mujahidin[35]

This organization was founded in the Penjab district of Pakistan in the beginning of the eighties by radical Islamic parties. Harqat ul-

Mujahidin is a radical Islamic Sunni organization whose worldview is similar to that of the Taliban movement and the Pakistani Daavah Al-Irshad organization. This organization adopted the ascetic Islamic approaches of the Wahabian stream and the Deoband school. It aspires to establish a religious Islamic state that will strictly enforce Islamic lifestyles according to the rules of the Sharia. It is hostile towards alien cultures, particularly Western culture, which it regards as antagonistic to Islam and bent on corrupting and destroying the Islamic religion.

A short time after its establishment, Harqat ul-Mujahidin began recruiting volunteers and sending them to the jihad in Afghanistan against the Soviet forces. In the course of the years of battle in Afghanistan the organization enlisted thousands of volunteers from Pakistan (mainly from areas in Kashmir that are under Pakistani rule), and from other Muslim countries such as Egypt, Algeria, Tunisia, Saudi Arabia, Jordan and Bangladesh, as well as India and the Philippines.

The establishment of camps for the volunteers, and the process of equipping and training them, were financed via donations arriving from Pakistan, Saudi Arabia and Bin-Laden. Some of them underwent training in the camp of the Afghani mujahidin (Hizb e-Islami) led by Yunis Khalis, while others were trained at camps belonging to the organization in Pakistan. There are no exact figures as to the number of volunteers trained by the organization, but estimates place their total at about 5,000 fighters from Pakistan and some 6,000 volunteers from other Islamic states. Following the withdrawal of the Soviets from Afghanistan and the invasion of Kabul in 1992 by the mujahidin movements, the organization decided to perpetuate the Islamic struggle in new battle arenas against secular Muslim regimes and Western countries.

In 1993, the organization consolidated with an additional mujahidin movement, Harqat al-Jihad al-Islami, and began developing terror infrastructures at various focal points worldwide. Harqat ul-Mujahidin joined Bin-Laden's global jihad movement in its struggle against the "Jewish-Crusader alliance," and its leader Fazlur Rahman Halil signed Bin-Laden's fatwa in February 1998 which called for the attack of Western and American interests.

From the mid-nineties, the organization's terror activity focused mainly on the Kashmir region, with the aid and guidance of the Pakistanis, but terror cells affiliated with this organization are also active at many focal points worldwide, including India, Egypt, Tunisia, Algeria, Bosnia, Chechnya, Tajikistan, Burma and the Philippines.

In 1997, the Harqat ul-Mujahidin was added to the U.S. State Department's list of terrorist organizations. Due to U.S. pressure, the Pakistani government withdrew its public support from the organization, but refrained from taking action against it and continued to support its activities in the Kashmir region. Because of the organization's links with Bin-Laden, its camps in Afghanistan were attacked on August 8, 1998, in the framework of the American retaliation after the bombing of the U.S. embassies in Kenya and Tanzania by activists in Bin-Laden's organization. In an attack of American cruise missiles on the organization's camp in the area of Khost, nine members of the organization were killed, and in response the organization's leaders threatened to retaliate in kind against the United States. In the framework of the American offensive in Afghanistan in 2001, facilities and camps of Harqat ul-Mujahidin were also attacked due to its close links with Bin-Laden's organization.

Hijacking of an Indian Airlines airplane (IC-814). A passenger plane of Indian Airlines, with 155 passengers on board, was hijacked on December 24, 1999, by five terrorists from Harqat al Ansar/Harqat ul-Mujahidin. The hijacking went on for eight days and ended on December 31 with the release of three terrorists, including Sheikh Masoud Azhar, the group's ideologist who had been under arrest in India since 1994. One hostage was killed. The hijackers were released in Afghanistan and were transferred to Pakistan following an agreement that the Taliban would not turn them over to India.

During the hijacking, the hijackers made various demands, including the release of thirty-six terrorists and the receipt of 200 million dollars. Ultimately, they were satisfied with the release of the three terrorists.

In the course of the contacts to end the kidnapping peacefully, the Taliban demanded that the hijackers refrain from hurting the hostages and threatened to storm the aircraft if anyone were injured. Nevertheless, the Taliban promised the hijackers that no foreign power would be allowed to act against them in Afghanistan.

Under the leadership of the brother of Sheikh Azhar, the five hijackers planned the operation about two months before it took place. Two of them based themselves in Katmandu, where they organized the logistic and operational infrastructure. Three of the hijackers arrived in Katmandu on a transit flight on the day of the kidnapping and with their comrades' assistance, and possibly also Pakistani diplomatic aid, passed through the security checks at the airport. After the checks, they were handed their weapons and boarded the plane fully armed. At the end of the hijacking, the Taliban enabled the hijackers to leave Afghanistan within ten hours after the incident's end, but refused to offer them asylum. Thus, the hijackers headed for Pakistan.

The "El Faran" group (a cover name for Harqat al Ansar) kidnapped six foreign residents in July 1995. One American hostage succeeded in escaping, while the Norwegian hostage was decapitated. In July 2001, the remains of one of the American hostages was located and identified. The kidnappers are still holding another American, one German and two British citizens (either dead or alive).

Uzbekistan

The Islamic Movement of Uzbekistan (IMU)[36]

The Islamic Movement of Uzbekistan (IMU), which is also named the Islamic Party of Turkistan, constitutes the main threat against the secular regime of Islam Karimov in Uzbekistan. The movement's aim is to undermine Karimov's control and establish an Islamic state in Uzbekistan. In June 2001, the movement changed its name to the Islamic Party of Turkistan and simultaneously revised its goal from founding an Islamic state in Uzbekistan to establishing an Islamic state that would incorporate all of the Islamic states in Central Asia, including Uzbekistan, Tajikistan, Turkmenistan, Kyrgyzstan, and Kazakhstan, as well as the Xingiang Region in China.[37] Most of the members are Uzbeks but its ranks also include Islamic commanders from other countries. Due to its comprehensive and long-term goal, the movement constitutes a threat not only in the Afghani arena, but also represents a danger to the stability of regimes throughout Central Asia.

In the first years of its activity, the movement focused on subversive activity and terror mainly in Uzbekistan, but in recent years (1999 and onwards) it has expanded it activities to nearby countries. Its main focus of activity is at the Fergana Valley, at the junction of the Uzbek, Tajik, and Kyrgyz borders.

On February 16, 1999, five car bombs exploded in Tashkent, the capital of Uzbekistan, killing fifteen and injuring over 150 people.

The government accused the Islamic movement of perpetrating the attacks and claimed that their objective was to kill President Karimov.[38] After the terror attacks, the government adopted a tough stance against the Islamic opposition,[39] and carried out mass arrests. The harsh manner of dealing with the opposition brought down the condemnation of Western human rights organizations on Karimov's government.

In August 1999, 800 members of the Uzbek Islamic movement infiltrated Kyrgyzstan at the junction of the Tajikistan and Uzbekistan borders, took over several villages, seized hostages and engaged Kyrgyz security forces in combat. They subsequently fled to Afghanistan.[40]

In August 2000, another large group of movement members initiated action in the mountainous areas of southern Uzbekistan near the capital Tashkent, as well as in several areas in Kyrgyzstan. The skirmishes left in their wake wounded Uzbek and Kyrgyz military personnel and civilians.[41] In July 2001, movement members attempted to take over a television station in Kyrgyzstan that broadcasts both to Kyrgyzstan and Uzbekistan.[42]

The Uzbek Islamic movement is currently considered one of the most organized and dangerous terror organizations in Central Asia. In the framework of the organization's terror activities foreign citizens were also kidnapped and held as hostages, including four American mountain climbers and a group of Japanese geologists.[43] The Uzbek Islamic Movement enjoyed the support of the Taliban regime in Afghanistan and currently receives aid from radical Islamic organizations in countries in the region. The movement has clandestine, supportive cells in Uzbekistan, Tajikistan, and Kyrgyzstan. Its activities are focused mainly in the Fergana Valley, where the movement has relatively widespread popular support.[44] It also has training bases and infrastructures in Afghanistan that operated with the blessing of the Taliban regime, and it has secret bases mainly in Tajikistan and Kyrgyzstan.

The leader of the movement is Taher Yuldush, whom the authorities consider responsible for the assassination attempt against President Islam Karimov in February 1999.[45] In May 1999, Yuldush visited Afghanistan and, as stated above, received the blessing of the Taliban to open a training facility in northern Afghanistan. It appears that he has chosen to stay there and operates the activities of the movement's members in Uzbekistan and the general vicinity.[46]

Another prominent leader of the IMU is Jumah Nemengani, who serves as its military commander. He fought alongside the Tajik Islamic movement during the civil war in Tajikistan between 1992 and 1997. Following the signing of the peace accords in Tajikistan, he joined the IMU and headed widespread attacks during the years 1999 to 2001, as described above. Nemengani is currently living in Afghanistan, where he trains movement members and plans terror attacks.[47] He is known to have close links with Bin-Laden and his organization, as well as many supporters in Tajikistan. Both Yuldush and Nemengani were sentenced to death in absentia for their involvement in terror activities against the government.[48]

On May 16, 2000, the spokesman of the U.S. State Department announced that the United States had decided to include the Islamic Movement of Uzbekistan in its list of twenty-eight international terror organizations. The significance of this decision is that the movement and its activities are banned according to U.S. law, and sanctions and legal action are to be applied to entities that support or are affiliated with the organization.[49]

To summarize, it appears that the IMU is currently one of the most dangerous Islamic terror organizations in Central Asia, and it constitutes a serious threat to the stability of the Uzbekistan regime and, to a lesser extent, to other Muslim republics in Central Asia.

Southeast Asia

General

During the years of its existence, the Al-Qaida organization headed by Bin-Laden has established a system of infrastructural and operational ties in Southeast Asia through links with Islamic movements and organizations in the region. Al-Qaida has contact with Islamic terror organizations in the Philippines, Indonesia and Malaysia. During and after the jihad in Afghanistan, Al-Qaida assisted with the training of members of these radical Islamic organizations at its facilities and camps in Afghanistan. Al-Qaida also offered these organizations financial aid, supplying weaponry and sometimes even instructors.

The organization's activities in this region expressed themselves through various channels:

- Front organizations appearing as charities and functioning legally in various countries in the region.

- Covert visits of Al-Qaida senior leaders and activists to states in the region.
- Liaison officers of the Islamic organizations who maintain contact with Al-Qaida directly or via messengers.
- Collaboration in the planning and execution of terror attacks such as the attack plans discovered in Singapore.

The reciprocal ties between Al-Qaida and the Islamic organizations are not anchored in regular or structured activity patterns and they vary from state to state and from organization to organization. In any case, widespread and complex reciprocal ties exist, which could lead to the perpetration of terror attacks through local terror organizations, with the active participation or assistance of Al-Qaida.

Radical Islamic Organizations in Indonesia

The Jama'a al Islamiya (JI)[50] was founded in 1995; among its founders is Elias Abu-Bashir, who also became its spiritual mentor. The organization's goal is to establish an Islamic religious state that will include all of the Islamic populations in Southeast Asia. It has branches in Indonesia, Malaysia and Singapore and is linked to radical Islamic organizations worldwide. It is estimated that the organi-

Figure 2.3
Al-Qaida Links in Southeast Asia

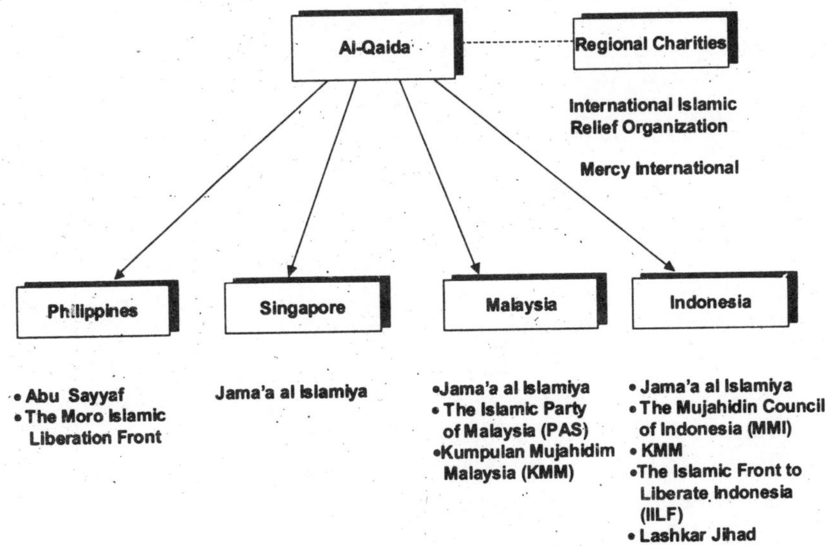

zation has 1,500 members in Solo in central Java, Indonesia as well as 500 additional activists in West Java. Some fifty organization members underwent military training in Afghanistan, and during the past three years Al-Qaida has transferred approximately $240,000 to the movement as financial aid.

The Mujahidin Council of Indonesia (MMI).[51] The MMI constitutes an umbrella organization or coalition of Islamic organizations in Indonesia, and encompasses some 50,000 members. The Council is headed by Elias Bakher Bashir, and is linked to the Jamaa al Islamiya and other radical organizations outside of Indonesia.

Lashkar Jihad.[52] Lashkar Jihad is a radical Islamic organization founded in 2000, which aspires to establish a religious Islamic state through a jihad. The organization has 10,000-15,000 active members and is involved in a violent campaign (jihad) in the Moluka Islands in east Indonesia. The organization receives financial aid from countries like Saudi Arabia and Libya, and maintains active ties with Al-Qaida.

Kompulan Mujahidin Malaysia (KMM). See further details in the section that discusses radical Islamic organizations in Malaysia.

The Islamic Indonesian Liberation Front (IILF).[53] This Islamic terror organization aspires to establish an Islamic religious state in Indonesia and has ongoing ties with Al-Qaida and the Abu-Sayyaf organization. Its members have undergone training in the Mindanao Islands in the Philippines.

Radical Islamic organizations in Malaysia. At the end of the nineties there appeared to be a marked trend indicating the reinforcement of Islamic organizations in Malaysia. The most prominent Islamic party is the Pan Malaysian Islamic Party, whose aim is to establish an Islamic regime that will act according to the Sharia. The party has accumulated power in the Malaysian political system and currently rules two out of thirteen districts in Malaysia.

The Kumpulan Mujahidin Malaysia (KMM).[54] The KMM was founded in 1998 in Malaysia and Indonesia. Its objective is to establish a religious Islamic state in Southeast Asia that will encompass the entire Muslim population in that area: "A Darul Islamia Nusantra." The organization is linked to Islamic organizations like the Jamaa al Islamiya, Al-Qaida, Abu-Sayyaf and more.

The KMM had already made the following declaration in the year 2000: "American soldiers must be killed because the United States oppresses Islamic states." During 1999-2000, organization activists devised several terror attacks, which were, in fact, never executed. Among them were:

- In 1999, they intended to perpetrate an attack in the commercial area of Kuala-Lumpur, but the perpetrators reconsidered when they encountered intensified security means.

- In 2000, they intended to attack a vehicle transporting American sailors, but the attack was never realized because of a fear that the sailors were armed.

Organization activists in Indonesia were involved in ethnic and religious riots against Christians and were also responsible for several attacks that took place in Jakarta (2001-2002).

Following the exposure of the KMM in Malaysia, Malaysia's Deputy Minister of Defense declared that the government would carefully screen all those recruited into the Malaysian security forces in order to prevent members of the KMM or other radical Islamic organizations from infiltrating the armed forces.[55]

*The Jama'a al Islamiya—(*See following elaboration that discusses Indonesia.)

The arrest of Al-Qaida activist Omar al Farouq in Indonesia. At the end of May 2002, security forces in Indonesia arrested Omar el Farouq, a thirty-one-year-old Kuwaiti-born[56] senior activist in Al-Qaida. Al-Farouq had gone to Afghanistan in 1990 and underwent training over a three-year period at Al-Qaida camps where he became close to Al-Qaida leaders, including Abu-Zubeida. In the middle of the nineties, Omar el Farouq went to Southeast Asia to set up an Islamic terror infrastructure and perpetrate attacks against Western targets and regimes identified with the West.

During his interrogation, he divulged that Al-Qaida activity in Southeast Asia was partially financed by charities such as the Saudi al-Harmin, and that there was close cooperation with radical Islamic organizations such as the Jamaa al Islamiya in Indonesia and the MILF in the Philippines, among others.

Throughout the years of his activity in Southeast Asia, Omar el Farouq was involved in the founding of terror infrastructures, the planning of attacks and their actual execution as follows:

In 1995, Omar al Farouq arrived at the MILF camp Abu Baqer in the Philippines. During his stay in the Philippines he made efforts to register at a flight school in the hope of acquiring the capability to fly a commercial aircraft, which he planned to ram into an unspecified target. These plans did not reach fruition.

In 1998, after the collapse of Soharto's regime in Indonesia, el Farouq moved to that country, married Mira, the daughter of a radical Islamic activist, and forged close ties with an Indonesian businessman named Agus Dwikarna, who was active in the MMI.[57] Al Farouq helped Dwikarna to set up the radical organization Lashkar Jundallah, which perpetrated a chain of attacks against Christian villages in the Siluwasi Island in the middle of 1999.

In mid-1999, el Farouq was part of a conspiracy to assassinate Indonesian presidential candidate Magawati Sokarnoputri, but the attempt was aborted due to the failure of the conspirators to deliver the necessary weapons to Indonesia in time.

In August 2001, el Farouq was involved in the planning of an additional assassination attempt against Magawati Sokarnoputri, the Indonesian president. The attackers planned to place a bomb in a hall where the president was scheduled to meet members of her political party. For unknown reasons, the bomb exploded in the hands of the terrorist who was supposed to plant it, seriously injuring him and causing his apprehension, thus exposing the conspiracy.

Omar al Farouq planned an attack against an American naval vessel at the Surabaya port in Indonesia in 2002. The attack was planned along the same lines as the attack against the destroyer *USS Cole* in Aden in 2000. The attack never took place because el Farouq failed to recruit and organize a terror cell at the required time.

Around the time he was arrested, al Farouq was busy preparing a series of attacks against the U.S. embassies in Indonesia, Malaysia, Singapore, the Philippines, Thailand, Vietnam, Cambodia and Taiwan. The attacks were to take place simultaneously through the use of car bombs, utilizing the same modus operandi applied during the attacks on the U.S. embassies in Kenya and Tanzania in 1998.

The arrest of Omar al Farouq constitutes a severe blow to the Al-Qaida infrastructure in Southeast Asia and his apprehension may lead to additional arrests of Al-Qaida activists and radical Islamic factors that cooperated with him in this region.

Al-Qaida's Links with Philippine Terror Organizations

The initial ties between Bin-Laden and the leaders of Islamic terror organizations in the Philippines were first established in the course of the jihad against the Soviets in Afghanistan. The movement's founder Abu-Sayyaf, Janjalani and the founder of the MILF, Hashem Salamaat met Bin-Laden in Afghanistan and at the end of the jihad agreed to continue their cooperation in order to facilitate the jihad in the Philippines.[58]

During the nineties many fighters from the Philippines underwent training at Bin-Laden's camps and returned to serve in their organizations in the Philippines.

The strongest links are between Al-Qiada and the Abu-Sayyaf organization, which actually joined Bin-Laden's Global Jihad Front.

Al-Qaida operates on several levels in the Philippines:[59]

- Direct ties between the Abu-Sayyaf organization and Al-Qaida
- Ties via commercial and business entities
- Links and activities via charitable organizations.

The Abu-Sayyaf organization and MILF continued to avail themselves of the Al-Qaida infrastructures, mainly in Afghanistan, in order to train their members in guerrilla warfare and terror. According to various sources, Al-Qaida assists Abu-Sayyaf through the provision of weapons and instructors who have visited Mindanao and covert hideaways of the organization in the Philippines.

Indirect operational links existed in circumstances where activists of terror networks or organizations there made direct contact with Al-Qaida, and then visited and availed themselves of the Philippine organizations' aid, as in the case of the Ramzi Yusuf network, which was active in the Philippines, or the KMM and JI, which came to the Abiu-Sayyaf organization for training.

On the commercial-business level, Bin-Laden sent his father-in-law Muhammad Jamal Halifa to the Philippines in order to set up the organization's infrastructure under the pretense of conducting commercial activity. Al-Qaida also operates two charitable organizations in this arena: The International Islamic Relief Organization and Mercy International. Thus, it was no coincidence that one of the first American missions after completing the main stages of the campaign offensive leveled against Al-Qaida in Afghanistan was to dispatch American forces and consultants to the Philippines in order to assist the authorities in their struggle against Islamic terror in the country's southern region.

The Abu-Sayyaf Organization.[60] Abu-Sayyaf is a radical Islamic Philippine terror organization active mainly in the southern Philippines. Its aim is to establish an Islamic state in the southern Philippines. In 1991, a split occurred in the ranks of the Moro National Liberation Front (MNLF), when several activists decided to leave the organization because of what they regarded as its conciliatory positions, and set up a new organization. At the root of the controversy stood the willingness of the MNLF to accept an offer of autonomy for Muslim areas under a secular autonomic government. The founders of Abu-Sayyaf opted to struggle until achieving the establishment of an independent religious Islamic state.

Abd Al-Razek Abu-Baker Janjalani was among the organization's founders and led it until his death in a skirmish with Philippine government forces in 1998. Janjalani fought alongside the mujahidin in Afghanistan and after the banishment of the Soviets returned to his homeland. As he rejected the stance of the MNLF, which at that stage was struggling against the Philippine authorities, he decided with several other leaders to establish the Abu-Sayyaf organization.

During the fighting in Afghanistan, Janjalani became closely involved with the leaders of radical Islamic organizations from all over the Muslim world, including Osama Bin-Laden. After establishing the organization, Janjalani accepted the assistance of Afghani organizations and Bin-Laden in the form of training and equipment provided for his people at training camps in Afghanistan.

The Abu-Sayyaf organization apparently has hundreds of fighters active in the Philippine Islands, in Solana, Solos and Bateau, which all have Islamic majorities. The organization has taken an inflexible stance to date and has refused to participate in peace processes between the government and the isolationist organizations of the Moro (the Muslims)—the MNLF and the MILF.

Abu-Sayyaf kidnaps local and foreign hostages in order to collect ransom and wield political extortion. The organization carries out attacks using explosive devices as well as political assassinations, and extorts protection money from rich businessmen. Abu-Sayyaf's first terror attack was perpetrated in 1991 when two women were hit by grenades. Subsequently, the organization became known mainly for its kidnapping of local and foreign hostages, and for its occasionally widespread terror activities against Christian leaders and population in the southern Philippines. In 1993, collaboration between the terrorist Ramzi Yusuf and the Abu-Sayyaf organization in the Philippines was revealed. Ramzi Yusuf had intended to bomb several American passenger planes in the Far East and perpetrated an attack on a Japanese plane as a model and trial run..

Yusuf also intended to assassinate the Pope, who was planning to visit the Philippines. He was subsequently arrested, brought to trial and charged with involvement in the attack on the Twin Towers in New York (see further elaboration in chapter 3). The Abu-Sayyaf organization cooperates with the Islamic Jihad organization founded by Bin-Laden, and following the American offensive against Bin-Laden and the Taliban regime in Afghanistan he declared that he would assist Bin-Laden in any way necessary. Abu-Sayyaf appears on the list of foreign terrorist organizations published by the U.S. State Department.

The Moro Islamic Liberation Front (MILF).[61] The Front was established in 1977, as the result of a split in the ranks of the MNLF (The Moro National Liberation Front), when Hashem Salamaat and his supporters decided to break away from the MNLF and establish their own organization because of differences of opinion with the MNLF leader, Nur Misouari. Misouari was in favor of the establishment of autonomy for the Muslim population in the southern Philippines and was prepared to negotiate with the Philippine authorities, while Salamaat demanded the establishment of a religious Islamic state and a relentless struggle until achieving this objective. During the eighties and the nineties, the MILF waged guerrilla warfare and terror against the Philippine authorities and refused to abide by the Tripoli agreement or the autonomy agreement signed by Nur Misouari with the Philippine government in 1996.

The organization has thousands of armed fighters and, according to its spokesman, they have the widespread support of the Muslim population in the southern Philippines. The MILF ranks are populated by Philippines who participated in the jihad in Afghanistan against the Soviet Union or who were sent to training camps in Pakistan and Afghanistan after the war. The organization has links with other Islamic terror organizations such as Abu-Sayyaf in the Philippines and Bin-Laden's Al-Qaida.

In 2001, the organization agreed to enter peace talks with the Philippine government and even signed a ceasefire agreement. However, this agreement did not endure and the confrontation between the organization and the Philippine government continues.

The Xinjiang Province in Western China

The Xinjiang Province, located in Western China, is inhabited by over 7 million Uighur Muslims who constitute some 50 percent of the province's population (15 million inhabitants). The Uighurs are an ethnic group of Turkish descent that settled in this area during the spread of Islam eastwards in the direction of China. They called the region Eastern Turkestan. China first conquered Eastern Turkestan during the Manchu Dynasty and controlled the area until 1862. During that period over forty uprisings of the Uighurs against the Chinese regime were recorded.

In 1862, a Muslim uprising succeeded in removing the Chinese forces and Eastern Turkestan enjoyed independence up to 1884, when the Chinese reoccupied the area and changed its name to Xinjiang.[62] The area is currently under Chinese control.

Part of northern Xinjiang enjoyed independence for a short time during 1944 when China was involved in a war with Japan. However, in 1949, the forces of Mao Tse Tung overtook the region and restored Chinese control of the area. At that time, the Uighurs constituted about 80 percent of the province's population, but over the years of the Chinese regime, the Beijing authorities encouraged mass relocation of Chinese (Han) in that area. The latter currently constitute over 50 percent of the population and hold all of the senior administrative and economic positions in the region.[63]

The province has natural resources such as oil and other minerals; revenue from these resources, however, is not invested on behalf of the interests of the local residents but rather flows into the national coffers. Since the sixties, this province has served as a focal point for China's nuclear testing at the Lop Nor base. These tests have caused radioactive contamination in large areas of the province as well as severe physical and ecological damage to the population.[64]

Up to the nineties, despite feelings of discrimination and prejudice, quiet reigned in the province. Several processes led to Islamic and nationalist reawakening in the region:

- The defeat of the Soviet Union in the war in Afghanistan; Uighurs participated in this war as volunteers in the Afghan and mujahidin ranks, returning to the province after their triumph.

- The dismantling of the Soviet Union and the establishment of independent Muslim republics bordering on the province (Kazakhstan, Kirgizistan, Tajikistan, Uzbekistan).
- The dissemination of Fundamentalist Islamic concepts and propaganda.
- The "relative openness" of China that enabled the penetration of Islamic ideas and propaganda within its borders.
- Continued suppression by the Chinese authorities that exacerbated the unrest in the province.
- The assistance of radical Islamic entities offered to Muslim isolationists in the form of weapons, money, and ideological support (the Taliban regime up to 2001, radical Islamic organizations including Al-Qaida, and Muslim states such as Saudi Arabia).

From 1996, isolationist Muslim groups began initiating violent activities against the Chinese authorities. This activity included mass demonstrations, physical attacks and even the elimination of Uighurs suspected of collaborating with the authorities, as well as attacks against governmental institutions and Chinese position holders in the province.

The Chinese authorities took immediate and ruthless steps against the Uighur separatists, carried out mass arrests and even executed those charged with subversive activity against the government.[65] The Chinese repressive actions did not snuff out the Islamic nationalist reawakening, and the restlessness and terror activity in the province continued.

In 1977, the Uighur separatists expanded their activities beyond the boundaries of the province and carried out a chain of attacks during which explosives were detonated on buses and trains in Beijing. This was the first time that terror attacks took place in the Chinese capital since the Communist rise to power. The authorities took ruthless action in response to the activities of the Uighur isolationists. Nevertheless, in the following years several terror attacks were perpetrated by isolationist organizations in various areas of the country.

The most prominent of the Muslim isolationist organizations is the Organization for the Liberation of Eastern Turkestan, which operates from within the province but also deals in propaganda, fund-raising activities and support for various Muslim spots in the

Muslim world (Turkey, Kazakhstan, Saudi Arabia, the Gulf States, and more).

China regards the insurrection within this province as a significant risk, endangering the state's stability and security. Its security forces have taken action to repress the uprising, and the government has initiated political contact with neighboring Muslim states in order to persuade them to prevent the provision of financial aid and weapons to the Muslim isolationists in China. To date, Beijing's efforts in this area have met with only partial success.

Chechnya

Terror serves as an important tool in Chechnya's struggle to achieve independence from Russia. Chechen terror simultaneously serves radical separatists' isolationist factors who apply terror against Russia in the framework of their all-out battle to achieve independence, as well as criminal elements whose main goal is to extort ransom money in exchange for releasing hostages. Since the beginning of the war between Chechnya and Russia, these criminal elements have assumed an ideological cloak for their activities.

The Chechen terror, which has been perpetrated since the beginning of the nineties, has been active on several fronts:

- Terror activities in Chechnya targeted against entities identified as collaborators with Russia, and against Russian elements on Chechen soil
- Terror activities in neighboring republics (Dagestan, Ingoshtia) to assist local Islamic organizations in their struggle against the pro-Russian regimes in these republics and against Russian targets
- Terror attacks in Russia (including the heart of Moscow)
- Terror activities in the international arena (hijacking boats and airplanes to other locations).

The Chechen terror utilizes a wide range of activity patterns:

- Kidnapping hostages
- Detonating explosive charges and car bombs
- Hijacking airplanes, boats and buses
- Suicide attacks.

Russian security and information elements stress the link between the Chechen terrorists and international Islamic terror of the Afghan alumni such as Emir Katab and Osama Bin-Laden.[66] The Chechen terror served as the main pretext for the Russian invasion of Chechnya in 1999, a step that won public support in Russia and the understanding of international entities.[67]

The Russian public and Russian decision-makers perceived the Chechen terror in 1999, which ventured outside of the Chechen boundaries, as a threat to Russia's basic security and as a digression from the "rules of the game" that had applied until that time in the struggle between the Chechens and the Russians.[68] In the eyes of Western countries, the wave of terror attacks perpetrated against innocent civilians triggered a process of de-legitimization vis-à-vis the Chechen struggle, and at the very least brought a condemnation of the use of terror.

Thus, one may postulate that the wave or terror attacks in 1999 caused Chechnya serious damage and attributed legitimization to the invasion and to the state's destruction, as well as the loss of all its wartime achievements between 1994 and 1996.

The Russian security authorities are having a difficult time dealing with the Chechen terror for several main reasons:

1. The weakness of the Russian intelligence and counter-terrorism infrastructure due to reforms, revisions and budgetary slashes in the Russian security system (dismantling of the KGB, establishment of the FSB, and more).[69]

2. Coordination problems between the various elements counteracting terror: the FSB, the Ministry of the Interior, the Ministry of Defense, the Russian Army, the police, and more.

3. The vastness of the fighting arena: The terrorists can strike at any spot all over Russia.

4. The Chechen adversary is well acquainted with Russia and its security capabilities, and has considerable experience in waging guerrilla warfare and terror against Russia (the former USSR).

Bombing Attacks against Civil Targets in Russian Cities

During the months of August-September 1999 a wave of severe terror attacks was perpetrated against civilian targets in Russia, with emphasis on the capital, Moscow.[70] According to the Kremlin,

Chechen terrorists detonated powerful explosive charges and car bombs at civilian targets in Russia. The attacks were directed at residential buildings, shopping centers, markets and subway stations in Moscow. Nearly 300 Russian civilians were killed and hundreds were wounded.[71] Russian security forces made a supreme effort to thwart the attacks and apprehend the perpetrators, but despite widespread arrests (about 11,000) there are doubts whether those responsible for the attacks were actually apprehended.[72]

According to Russian military officials, after the failure of the commanders of the Chechen rebels, Shamil Basayev and Emir Katab in Dagestan, about thirty terrorists (divided into four groups) were dispatched on August 10, 1999, to carry out terror attacks at four focal points:[73] Moscow, St. Petersburg, Rostov-on-Don, and Dagestan.

At the end of September 1999, the Russian Security Services (FSB) reported the discovery of a Mercedes truck carrying eleven tons of explosives and the detection of seventy-six backpacks stuffed with explosives in an apartment in Moscow. It was believed that the explosives were designated for additional attacks by the Chechen terror networks. The president of Chechnya Aslan Maskhadov and Emir Katab denied Chechnya's involvement in the wave of attacks.

An unknown terror organization called "The Dagestan Freedom Army" claimed responsibility for two of the attacks, but Russian security forces were skeptical about this organization's very existence and suggested that this was an attempt to conceal the identity of the true perpetrators, the Chechen terrorists.[74]

The Kidnapping of Hostages by the Chechens

The kidnapping of hostages has become a frequent phenomenon in Chechnya. In 1999, 341 people were kidnapped and 484 hostages were released, while in the year 2000, 66 people were taken hostage in Chechnya and 203 were released. Kidnapping victims include thirteen children and foreign residents. The number of released hostages also includes victims taken hostage in previous years.

The director in charge of the war against organized crime in the Russian Ministry of the Interior, Vladimir Kozlov, stated in an interview that as of May 2001 that some 700 hostages are being held by the Chechen terrorists.[75] He averred that at least twelve of them were carrying foreign passports of Turkey, France, Slovakia and Israel.

The kidnapping phenomenon carried out by Chechen elements can be classified according to five main models:

1. Kidnapping hostages for criminal reasons in order to extort ransom money

2. Seizing a facility/site and capturing a large number of hostages (hospitals, government facilities, etc.)

3. Hijacking an airplane

4. Hijacking boats

5. Hijacking buses.

Kidnapping of Victims for Criminal Reasons

For many years, even prior to the Chechen-Russian war, Chechen criminal elements (the Chechen mafia) took hostages in order to extort ransom money. As a rule in these cases, a single individual is kidnapped after information is collected about him and he is found to be a suitable prospect, mainly from the point of view of his relatives' financial ability to pay a ransom for him. Most of the kidnappings in this category ended with the release of the hostage in exchange for ransom money, although during the abductions the kidnappers would treat the hostage violently, even to the extent of amputating fingers and sending them to relatives, in order to force them to surrender to the kidnappers' demands.

After the outbreak of the Chechen-Russian war, the kidnappings of hostages for criminal reasons continued, but in many cases these were ostensibly or truly linked with ideological motivation.

Seizing a Facility/Site and Capturing a Large Number of Hostages

During the war between the Chechen rebels and the Russian forces, there were several incidents where the Chechen rebels seized a facility or a site populated at the time by many civilians. They held them as hostages, generally in order to enable the safe retreat of rebels that had been surrounded and outnumbered by Russian forces. A few prominent examples follow.[76]

> On June 14, 1995, Chechen rebels under the command of Shamil Basayev seized control of a hospital in Budennovsk, in southern Russia. During a botched Russian rescue attempt 150 people were killed. At the end of the negotiations the kidnappers freed the

hostages in exchange for the kidnappers' unimpeded retreat to Chechnya. After the incident in Budennovsk, both sides agreed to a ceasefire until December 1995.

Between January 9 and January 24, 1996, Chechen rebels invaded the Dagestan towns of Kiziliar and Pervomaiska under the command of Shamil Basayev and Emir Katab and held some 2,000 people hostage. After two weeks of siege and combat against the Russian forces, the Chechen rebels withdrew to Chechnya.

Hijacking of Airplanes

Since the beginning of the war between the Chechen rebels and Russia there have been numerous hijacking attempts and several actual hijackings of Russian aircraft by the Chechens. The airplanes were hijacked in Russia or in another country and after taking over the plane, the hijackers generally forced the pilots to land in Muslim countries (Turkey, Saudi Arabia).

After forcing the aircraft to land, negotiations were held between the rebels and the local authorities, and in most cases the aircraft and hostages were released in exchange for political asylum for the hijackers. In instances when the hijacked plane was forced to land in a Russian airport, Russian forces gained control of the hijacked plane and the hijackers were either arrested or killed.

Several examples in this category are:

November 11, 1991[77]—A Tupolev 154 aircraft carrying 178 passengers and crewmembers was hijacked during a domestic flight (from Mineralnyye Vody in Caucasus to Ekaterinburg in the Urals) by several Chechen hijackers. The aircraft was forced to land in Georgia, where the hostages were released, and the airplane continued on with the hijackers to Ankara, where the hijackers surrendered to the Turkish authorities.

October 1994–A Chechen terrorist hijacked a plane carrying twenty-seven passengers and crewmembers in Mahatchkala. When the Russian commando force stormed the plane the kidnapper detonated himself.

March 15, 2001[78]—Three Chechen hijackers hijacked a Tupolev 156 aircraft carrying 162 passengers and twelve crewmembers that was en route from Istanbul to Moscow. The hijackers boarded the plan in Istanbul and took it over a short time after takeoff. They forced the pilot to fly in the direction of Saudi Arabia and land in the city of Medina. For about a day negotiations were held between the Saudi authorities and the hijackers, resulting in the release of fifty hostages. After the second stage of the negotiations with hijackers failed, special Saudi forces burst into the plane and liberated the hostages. The rescue action claimed three casualties (one hijacker, a flight attendant, and one passenger). Due to the kidnapping, President Putin cut short his vacation and returned to Moscow in order to handle the crisis.

The Russians sent two airplanes to Saudi Arabia, one to fly the released hostages back and the other to fly back the hijackers that had been apprehended, but the Saudi authorities refused to turn over the perpetrators.[79]

The Hijacking of Boats

The Chechens have hijacked only one boat to date. On January 16, 1996, a group of Turkish, pro-Chechen terrorists overtook the Auras ferry at a port on the Turkish coast of the Black Sea. The ferry was en route to the Russian port of Sotchi, and it carried 150 passengers on board, the majority of whom were Russian. After three days of negotiations with the hijackers, the hostages were released and the hijackers surrendered to Turkish authorities. In 1997, a Turkish court found the hijackers guilty and sentenced them to nine years of imprisonment.[80]

Hijacking of Buses

The hijacking of buses constitutes one of the most common methods used by Chechen terrorists. This action can be achieved with relative ease because it is impossible to secure every single bus, because a bus stops at many places, and because there is no real supervision over the passengers (as opposed to a flight on an airplane or traveling by boat, which necessitates registration, documentation, supervision and control when boarding the mode of transportation).

A bus can be hijacked almost anywhere, particularly at unexpected locations on Russian soil. The hijacking of a bus provides the hijackers with mobility and the ability to reach a destination or location of their own choice, and even demand transfer to another mode of transportation (for example, an aircraft or helicopter) with some of the hostages. When a bus is full of passengers it provides the hijackers with cover and makes it difficult to carry out an effective rescue action without harming the passengers.

May 1994—Four Chechens hijacked a children's bus in western Russia. The hijackers demanded and received a helicopter, took four hostages with them and flew to Chechnya. In a confrontation with a Russian commando unit one of the kidnappers was killed and three were apprehended. The three kidnappers were tried and sentenced to life imprisonment in Russia.

March 1996—Chechen rebels held 84 hostages in Georgia but ultimately released them.

April 1997—Twenty-six passengers were held as hostages on a bus hijacked at the Dagestan airport. The hijacker was apprehended and the hostages were released.

June 1998—A bus at Ingoshtia was hijacked by Chechen terrorists and all of its passengers were subsequently released.

August 2001—Two Chechen terrorists hijacked a bus with forty-one passengers near the city of Novinomisk in Russia and demanded the release of the Chechen terrorists who had hijacked the children's bus in May 1994 and were serving their sentences in a Russian prison. After over twelve hours, during which time the bus stood outside of the town, Minolanya Wodi, members of the Russian commando unit, gained control of the bus. In the course of the operation, one of the hijackers was killed, his comrade was injured and several hostages were slightly injured.

Suicide Attacks

To the end of 2002 Chechen suicide attacks have taken place only on Chechen soil, and their main targets are the security forces and/or Russian government or military facilities.

These attacks have generally been perpetrated by a single terrorist equipped with a bomb or an explosive belt, or by a car driven by the suicide bomber who detonates himself near the chosen target.

The Attack on the Theater in Moscow, October 23, 2002[81]

On October 23, 2002, about fifty Chechen terrorists took over a theater in Moscow during the performance of a play and held 750 people hostage. The Chechen terrorists, who were armed with grenades, bombs, explosive belts and other weaponry, booby trapped the building and threatened to detonate themselves and the hostages if Russian forces attempted to penetrate the building. In exchange for the hostages' release, the Chechens demanded "a cease of the combat and withdrawal of Soviet forces from Chechnya."

Immediately upon receiving notification regarding the attack, the Russian authorities had the building cordoned by police and security forces that initiated negotiations with the Chechens. The Chechen terrorists classified the hostages and released Muslims and eighteen children.

The group of terrorists was led by Mubarak Barayev, the nephew of one of the most senior Arab Chechen commanders, who had been killed by the Russians a year earlier. Most prominent among the terrorists was the large number of women who were clad in traditional "Islamic clothing" and wore explosive belts. During the attack, a video featuring the terrorists before their departure for the mission was submitted to broadcasting stations. The preliminary filming and the attackers' self-identification as *shahids* bore testimony to their willingness to conduct a suicide attack if their demands were not met and proved their readiness to convert the bargaining attack (i.e., conducting a siege with hostages for the purpose of negotiations) into a suicide attack if the Russians attempted to forcefully liberate the hostages and refused to respond to their requirements.

Initial findings of the investigation of the attack indicate that the attack had been planned over a period of several months. In the framework of the preparations, the terrorists purchased the theater's concession stand and under the camouflage of renovation work being conducted at the theater, were able to smuggle in all of the equipment needed for the operation—explosive belts, explosive charges and light weapons. On the evening of the attack, the terrorists bought tickets for the performance and entered the theater with the regular audience.[82] There was also indication that some of the terrorists were of Arab descent and it is possible that they were in contact with Middle-Eastern entities.[83]

During the three days of the siege on the theater in Moscow, the Chechen terrorists enabled hundreds of hostages to use their cellular phones to placate their loved ones and at the same time to announce the terrorists' demands. Their unconcealed goal was to put psychological pressure on the hostages' families so that the latter, in turn, would turn the screws on the Russian government to give in to their demands without reverting to the military option.

According to security sources in Moscow, which helped to plan the release mission, the relative liberty given to the hostages brought about the terrorists' downfall. A senior security source indicated that agents of the Russian secret service, the FSB, identified scores of telephone calls conducted by the hostages immediately after the attack, and understood that these could be an important source of information about what was happening inside the theater. When calls arrived for family members from the hostages, they first asked if there were any terrorists nearby. If the coast was clear, and there were no terrorists in the vicinity, the relatives would hand over the phone to security officers who asked them to answer "yes" or "no" to various questions pertaining to the terrorists, thus avoiding any suspicion.[84]

Russian Foreign Minister Igor Ivanov described the action as "a link in the chain of terror activities planned and coordinated in one center outside of Russia."[85] After fifty-eight hours of siege and negotiations, approaching the time that the terrorists' ultimatum was about to expire, shooting was heard inside the building. These shots and the fear that the terrorists had started to execute hostages prompted the immediate invasion of the theater by Russian forces. The raid took place at 5:15 a.m., just before dawn.

The Russian forces pumped in a gas from the morphine family called fentanyl (which is 200 times stronger than the substance used in hospitals). This neutralized most of the terrorists and prevented them from realizing their threat to detonate the building with all of the hostages inside it. Scores of terrorists—some of them women wearing explosive belts ready for detonation—were unable to even press the electric switches that they held in their hands.

The commando force poured into the hall from the basement, with a diversionary force attacking through the front door. Already on the first day of the siege workers were observed digging openings into the sewage and heating pipes. Now it appears that these activities were part of the preparation of rapid access points. Scores of Chechens were killed remorselessly; eyewitnesses divulged that some were executed on the spot via a single shot through the forehead.

The fear was that the vast amounts of explosives planted around the room at sensitive points would cause the stage to collapse upon the heads of hundreds of hostages. The Special Forces succeeded in preventing this particular nightmare.[86] "We succeeded in preventing a massacre," Russian Deputy Minister of the Interior Vladimir Vasiliyev subsequently declared. About 119 hostages perished as a result of gas inhalation; almost all of the others were injured and hospitalized with various degrees of injury. The majority of the hostages recovered completely. Most of the terrorists were killed on the spot as the result of gas inhalation, but there are reports that some were captured alive, including a female terrorist who masqueraded as a hostage and was evacuated to the hospital.

"We do not rule out the possibility that next time a group of Chechen rebels may try to take over a nuclear facility," stated the representative of exiled Chechen leader, Aslan Maskhadov. The representative, Ahmed Zakayev, told journalists that while the elected Chechen leaders are willing to reach a political resolution with Moscow, they cannot control desperate extremists. "We cannot promise that another group will not act on Russian territory," he added. Zakayev also stressed that the attack on the theater was executed without Maskharov's knowledge. "What happened is the act of desperate people and the result of the prolonged war," he noted. When addressing the possibility that the next group of rebels may choose to take over a nuclear facility, Zakayev said, "the consequences in this event would be disastrous not only for Russia and Chechnya, but also for all of Europe." He added that the Russian rulers must be held accountable for this attack because they were unable to put an end to the violence in Chechnya.[87]

The bargaining attack in Moscow is one of the mega terror acts based on the dogma of the Afghan alumni to emerge after the attacks on September 11. This attack was unique due to the large number of terrorists taking part, and among them the high percentage of women who were wearing explosive belts, signaling their willingness to carry out a massive suicide attack. However, the existence of male and female suicide bombers among the Chechen terrorists is nothing new, as about a dozen suicide terrorists have already been active, including women. Nevertheless, the use of such a large number is an innovation that may signal a tendency towards the emergence of groups of suicide terrorists from within the Islamic terror organizations, as expressed in the terror campaign of September 11.

Although it is not classified as a prohibited nerve gas, the use of fentanyl by the Russian forces may serve as justification for the Afghan alumni to use non-conventional warfare in the future, based on the claim that their adversaries had already used it. There is no doubt that non-conventional terrorism, which is already in existence, has been afforded additional momentum due to the bargaining attack on the Moscow Theater.

The Balkan Region

Since the dismantling of Yugoslavia and the outbreak of ethnic conflicts, the Balkan region has become a focus for Islamic terror entities, particularly for some of the Afghan alumni. During the civil war in Bosnia, the Muslim world came to the aid of the Muslim minority in Bosnia, and countries like Iran, Libya and Saudi Arabia sent money, humanitarian assistance and weapons to the Muslim side in Bosnia, thus circumventing the UN embargo banning the provision of weaponry to either of the parties to the war. In the framework of the mobilization of the Muslim world on behalf of the struggle of the Muslim minority in Bosnia, thousands of volunteers poured into the country, mostly the "alumni" of the war in Afghanistan, and their numbers were estimated at 3,000 fighters.[88]

Initially, the volunteers joined the various Bosnian militias that were fighting the Serbs, but these fighters were quickly reassigned to a special unit, which received the blessing of Ilya Iztavagovich, the prime minister and leader of the Muslim minority. This unit was called the "Mujahid Brigade," and Iztavagovich appointed himself its honorary commander.[89]

The contribution of the Islamic volunteers to the success of the Bosnian Muslims was significant. They helped raise the morale of the Bosnian fighters, filled them with enthusiasm and the fighting spirit, and increased their awareness and Islamic affiliation. The volunteers fought on the various fronts but were also involved in the training of the Bosnian Muslim fighters.

The headquarters of the Mujahid Brigade was located in Zanitsa, but its forces were active throughout the country and carried out many operations, in which the soldiers demonstrated daring and considerable combat capabilities. The Islamic volunteers were also involved in many brutal massacres against the Serb forces and the Serb civil population, and three of the commanders of the Mujahid Brigade are currently being tried in the Hague for committing crimes against humanity.[90]

In the framework of the mobilization of the Islamic world for the Muslims in Bosnia, some of Bin-Laden's people also arrived in Bosnia and set up infrastructures for Al-Qaida in the Balkan region.

In 1994, Bin-Laden published an article in response to reports about "ethnic cleansing" perpetrated by the Serbs among the Muslim Bosnians. His article states:[91]

> Up until this point the world not only refrained from any response to these evil incidents, but also prevented these helpless people from purchasing the weapons they needed to protect themselves. All of this is part of a public conspiracy between the United States and its allies to protect the heretic UN.

According to information from Serbia, Bin-Laden and his assistant Zawahiri carry Bosnian passports. Another source of information maintains that Bin-Laden also holds an Albanian passport. In any event, the Bosnian government denies these claims and believes that these are Serb leaks aimed at vilifying Bosnia's good name.

In November 1995, the war in Bosnia drew to an end with the signing of the Dayton agreements, and Bosnia became a federation of sorts, composed of Bosnia-Herzegovina with a two-thirds Muslim majority, and the Serbetska Republic with a Serb majority.

At the end of the war, the Bosnian government was asked to disarm the mujahidin and deport them from the state, but from the point of view of the Bosnian authorities exiling the mujahidin would turn into a political fiasco, both because Bosnian law enabled anyone who participated in the fighting to automatically receive Bosnian citizenship, and also due to the moral debt which the Muslim society in Bosnia owed to those who came to its aid during the civil war. Thus, although Bosnia disbanded the Mujahid Brigade, most of the volunteers remained in Bosnia, settled down and established families, and were assimilated into Muslim Bosnian society.[92]

Estimates have it that at least 1,000 mujahidin stayed in Bosnia, settled in the cities and villages, and even set up their own villages, in which they incorporated local supporters and set up autonomous societies ruled by the Sharia and strict Islamic lifestyles that contravene Bosnian laws.[93]

Bosnia currently serves as a haven for the activities of radical Muslims due to the government's weakness and the lack of public security, shaky enforcement of law and order, economic backwardness, institutional corruption, and the presence of a widespread infrastructure for organized crime. These circumstances, combined with the existence of some 400 border-crossing points most of which are not under effective government control, turn Bosnia into a natural focus for terrorist and criminal activity. There is currently no indication of terrorist activity on Bosnian soil, mainly because of the desire of radical Islamic entities to use Bosnia as a haven and safe transit point for terror activists. Nevertheless, several arrests carried out by the Bosnian authorities under American pressure testify to the inherent dangers of Bosnia serving as "a land of refuge" for radical Islamic terror.

In April 2001, the Bosnian authorities arrested Karim Sa'id Autmani in response to an international arrest warrant issued by the Interpol on August 2000.[94] Under the alias of Sa'id Hojich, Autmani was a Bosnian citizen at the time of his arrest. He had acquired Bosnian citizenship by entering into a fictitious marriage with a local woman. The CIA had passed information on to the Bosnian Intelligence regarding Autmani and his links with the Algerian terror organization, the "Islamic Rescue Front."

Autmani was charged in Paris, together with another detainee, Ahmad Rassam, who had intended to perpetrate a series of attacks in the United States on the eve of the millennium celebrations and was apprehended at the U.S.-Canadian border with a container full of explosives. According to the charge sheet against Rassam, Autmani supplied him with forged documents that he used to further the purposes of the planned attack. The investigative French judge appeared as an expert witness at Rassam's trial in Los Angeles and identified Rassam and Autmani as members of the Algerian terror organization, and as contacts of Bin-Laden.

It would appear that several other terrorists affiliated with the Algerian Islamic terror organization, the GIA, are hiding in Bosnia. They apparently fled to this country in the beginning of the nineties after a wave of terror attacks that they had perpetrated in France. Some of the organization members served during the war years in the Mujahid Brigade, moved to France where they carried out a series of terror attacks, and fled back to Bosnia, where they are wanted by the authorities due to extradition requests made by the French government.

Another example of the links between Islamic terrorist elements and Bin-Laden is related to Anwar Shaaban, a friend of Sheikh Tallal, who was sentenced to death in Egypt in the early nineties for perpetrating terror attacks. Purportedly, Shaaban was the manager of an Islamic charitable organization named "The International Islamic Cultural Institution" in Milan, Italy. He fled to Bosnia to avoid a police investigation in Italy and was killed in Bosnia when he ran a police roadblock in 1996. A police investigation revealed that Shaaban had been appointed by Bin-Laden to recruit and send volunteers in Europe to Al-Qaida's training camps in Afghanistan.

Following the attacks of September 11, 2001, and the United States' declaration of war against terror, there was a marked increase in the pressure placed on the Bosnian authorities to take action against Islamic terrorists who had found refuge in the country. The United States and Britain are acting independently (albeit with the knowledge of the authorities) to arrest terror suspects in the framework of the international peacekeeping forces stationed in Bosnia.

On September 17, 2001, the United States and Britain closed down their embassies in Sarajevo for three days for fear of a possible terror attack by entities affiliated with Al-Qaida.

On September 25, 2001, the British elite SAS unit arrested two suspects at the Hollywood Hotel in a northern suburb of Sarajevo. The two–Abd Al-Halim Kafgia (an Egyptian citizen) and Jihad Ahmed Jamalah (a Jordanian citizen)–were suspected of involvement in the preparations for the attacks at the U.S. and British embassies in Sarajevo.

On September 26 and 27, 2001, U.S.-British actions against entities suspected of involvement in terror continued: On September 26, a force raided the offices of a Saudi association called the "Supreme Saudi Commission for Welfare Issues" and confiscated computers, documents, video cassettes and money (about $200,000). On September 27, the force raided the airport northwest of Sarajevo after receiving information from the CIA regarding the presence of crop-dusters prepared for the spraying of dangerous biological substances. During the raid no evidence was found to verify this information, but a variety of weapons was found including rifles, handguns and grenades, as well as two anti-chemical protective suits.

The U.S. authorities have a considerable amount of information linking humanitarian Saudi organizations to terror entities affiliated with Bin-Laden, as well as additional Islamic terror elements. Two

Islamic charitable organizations are currently under investigation by Bosnian authorities:[95]

1. The Supreme Saudi Commission for Welfare Issues (run by the Islamic aid agency and Prince Salman, governor of Riyadh from the Saudi royal family).

2. The Active Islamic Youth (founded in 1996 by veterans of the Bosnian army's Mujahid Brigade).

In nearby Albania, the CIA is investigating suspicions against four Islamic humanitarian organizations operating in that country:

- The local representatives of the Red Crescent
- The coordinating commission of the Islamic associations
- The Islamic World Council
- The Koran Fund.

Along with this activity, lists of wanted individuals were presented to the Bosnian security forces and authorities.

In the course of November-December 2001, Bosnian authorities carried out arrests. Radical Islamic activists from all over the Islamic world (Iran, Iraq, Syria, Pakistan, Afghanistan, Algeria and more) were taken into custody. Most of them were released for lack of evidence, but extradition requests were filed by Egypt and Algeria for several suspects, and they were subsequently turned over to these countries.

It would appear that not only Bosnia, but also additional Muslim focal points in the Balkan region, such as Albania, Kosovo, and Macedonia, have become places of refuge and hothouses for radical Islamic terror entities, and will continue to constitute a threat to the West.

Yemen

Yemen was an important focus for the activities and movements of the Afghan alumni due to the local authorities' "tolerant" approach to this activity. Yemen served as a meeting place for activists and a relatively safe transit station for their worldwide traffic. In December 1998, the Yemenite authorities arrested a radical Islamic group intending to perpetrate attacks against American and British targets in Aden. The group, which was made up of eight British citizens and two Algerians, was led by a London-based Muslim cleric named Abu Hamza, who was known to be affiliated with a radical Islamic group called "Supporters of the Sharia."

The group members entered Yemen with forged French passports and received aid in the form of weapons and training from a local Fundamentalist Islamic organization called "The Islamic Army of Aden." The latter was headed by Al-Midhar, who was executed after he was found guilty of kidnapping sixteen European tourists. During his trial it emerged that under his guidance, the members of the Islamic Army had abducted the European tourists in order to bring about the release of group members who had been arrested in December 1998 (as mentioned earlier). A rescue mission carried out by the Yemenite security forces, during which the abductors and four hostages were killed, put an end to the incident. An investigation of those involved in both of these terror incidents in Yemen revealed that some of them had undergone training in Afghanistan and maintained ties with the Egyptian Islamic Jihad organization supported by Bin-Laden.

In October 2000, the U.S. destroyer, *USS Cole*, which was anchored in Aden, came under attack. A boat bomb navigated by two suicide attackers exploded alongside the destroyer causing casualties, injuries and extensive damage to the vessel. Although the investigation of the incident has not yet been completed due to reluctant cooperation on the part of the Yemenite authorities, it is clear that Bin-Laden was behind the attack.

After the attacks of September 11, 2001, and the U.S. declaration of war against terror, Yemen revised its policy, fearing it too would become an American target. Yemen rethought its policy and announced its participation in the struggle against international terror. In light of the improved relations between the countries, the commanding officer of the U.S. central command and the director of the CIA visited Yemen in order to further explore this cooperation and formulate an American aid infrastructure for Yemen.

During the months of January-February 2002, radical Islamic activists were arrested, and a search is currently on for several Al-Qaida members who have gone into hiding in Yemen.

Osama Bin-Laden and the Campaign in Somalia[96]

From the beginning of the nineties, Osama Bin-Laden resided in Sudan and, under the patronage of the regime of Hassan Al-Turabi and Omar Al-Bashir, built an economic empire and a terror infrastructure with which he planned to launch the jihad against the West. Bin-Laden, who was favored by Hassan Al-Turabli, became an active partner in the provision of aid to various Islamic terror organizations that enjoyed Turabi's support.

Bin-Laden and his organization, Al-Qaida, were among the participants in the formulation of the Iranian-Sudanese strategy to disseminate the Islamic revolution in the Horn of Africa (his main partner vis-à-vis the activity in Somalia was his right-hand man, Aiman Zawahiri). The tasks assigned to Bin-Laden were mainly of a logistic and organizational nature, but they enabled him to acquire valuable experience in organizing the infrastructure that supported the complex campaign against the United States in East Africa, and to become a key player in the decision-making process and the realization of these decisions within the Iranian-Sudanese coalition.

The consolidation of an effective front of Islamic terror organizations in the Somalia arena required the establishment of a financial and logistic infrastructure that would enable the flow of fighters, weapons and funds. As stated above, the task of setting up this infrastructure was assigned to Bin-Laden, who enlisted his economic and organizational experience as well as his world-embracing connections, and within a short period of time succeeded in placing an effective financial and logistic infrastructure at the disposal of Iran and Sudan.

In Ethiopia, Somalia's neighbor, Bin-Laden established several international companies that dealt with agricultural development. In the Ogaden Desert near the Somali border these "companies" set up agricultural farms that served as a cover for Somali terrorist training facilities, storage of military equipment and the flow of funds to finance the activity.

In mid-1993, in the framework of preparations to escalate the struggle against American forces in Somalia, Bin-Laden headed a complex operation supervising the transfer of fighters (Afghan alumni) from Pakistan, Afghanistan and Yemen to Somalia on a fleet of fishing boats, which landed them on unpopulated shores in Somalia. From there, the local infrastructure transferred them to the fighting area of Mogadishu. Other means of transfer were light planes that landed after dark at improvised landing strips in Somalia, and infiltration via the Ethiopian and Kenyan borders.

Bin-Laden visited Somalia several times but did not actively participate in the fighting. However, his chief assistant and partner Aiman Zawahiri and Ali al-Rashidi apparently served as the direct commanders of the forces fighting in Mogadishu. Bin-Laden's main involvement in terror activity connected to the Somalia campaign focused on the organization of the attack against American targets in Aden.

The Attacks of December 29, 1992, in Yemen[97]

In the framework of the Iranian and Sudanese struggle against American involvement in the Horn of Africa, Bin-Laden helped organize a series of attacks in Yemen against American targets. Within a relatively short period of time he had recruited several Afghan alumni to carry out this mission. The original plan included detonating explosives in hotels where American military staff usually stayed in Aden, as well as hitting American targets at the Aden airport and port.

In order to enable perpetration of the attacks within a short time, despite all of the difficulties involved, Bin-Laden recruited his ally Sheikh Tarik Al-Fadli, who was residing in London, and asked him to personally take command of the mission. In mid-November, Bin-Laden enabled Fadli's secret return to Yemen. Sums of money required for the preparation and execution of the attack were transferred to Yemen via bank accounts of companies and businesses owned by Bin-Laden in Yemen. Bin-Laden and Fadli, who planned the attacks, decided to avail themselves of the aid of the Yemen Jihad, whose people were active in the vicinity of Aden. Fadli believed that action should also be taken against local politicians, and not only against the American presence. For the attack mission against local politicians, the Yemen Jihad members were sent reinforcements in the form of demolition experts from among the Afghani graduates.

For preparation of the attacks, a training base was hastily set up in the area of Saadah in north Yemen, near the joint boundary with Saudi Arabia. An expert sapper of Libyan origin was brought in from Afghanistan, and the weapons required for the attack were smuggled in on boats sailing from Sudan via the Red Sea that landed on a deserted beach in Northern Yemen near Al-Khawkhah. The Libyan expert trained several "Yemenite Afghans" in the preparation of explosive charges, and subsequently supervised the preparation of the charges used for the attack. After completing the preparations, the Libyan left Yemen one day prior to the attack.

On December 29, 1992, the terror cell planted explosive charges at the Aden Hotel and at the Golden Moor Hotel in Aden. In the resultant explosions, three were killed and five were wounded. A terrorist cell armed with a launcher and RPG-7 missiles was apprehended near the fence of the Aden airport, as they were about to launch the RPG missiles at American transport planes parked at the airport. Yemenite authorities launched a brisk investigation and a manhunt to locate the perpetrators. On January 8, 1993, Sheikh Tarik Al-Fadli was apprehended along with some of his men.

Despite the failure of the attack on the Aden airport and the arrest of some of the perpetrators, Bin-Laden and Turabi were satisfied with the results, which they felt had conveyed a message issued by the radical Islam to the United States, containing a warning against continued American involvement in the Muslim world in general, and in Somalia in particular.

The Skirmish of October 3-4,1993—The "Nab and Kidnap" Operation[98]

In the framework of the struggle between the United States and UN forces on the one hand, and the forces of General Aidid that as stated earlier had the support of the radical Islamic entities, an operation was launched with the purpose of nabbing two of Aidid's senior assistants, Ossama Salah and Muhammad Hassan Awali, from the Olympic Hotel, in an area dubbed the "Black Sea," General Aidid's stronghold located near the crowded market of Mogadishu, the capital of Somalia.

The operation was based on intelligence information that necessitated quick action of the American force in order to execute the operation before its targets moved on. The Rangers task force, under the command of Major General William P. Grison, had drilled similar operations many times and had accumulated combat experience prior to this one.

What had initially appeared to be a relatively straightforward operation based on precise intelligence quickly evolved into a bitter battle with far-reaching consequences. The American task force was trapped in a meticulously planned ambush by hundreds of Islamic and Somali soldiers. Two Black Hawk choppers were downed during the fighting, and a third was forced to execute an emergency landing at the Mogadishu Airport.

The American task force took over its target and apprehended Aidid's assistants, but they were quickly surrounded and were forced to fight for their lives. A bitter battle ensued and ended only when a land rescue force intervened with the help of assault helicopters. Eighteen U.S. soldiers were killed in action, seventy-three were wounded, and a helicopter pilot was taken captive by the Somalis. The mission of the U.S. task force was accomplished despite the delay and the heavy toll in casualties and injuries. General Grison's men did indeed win the battle, but it was a "Pyrrhic victory" which led to U.S. defeat in the overall war.

Information gleaned from various sources indicates that forces of Islamic volunteers made up of Afghan alumni participated in the October 3, 1993 battle, and not only the forces of the warlord Aidid.[99] According to this version, the entire operation was under the command of Al-Rashidi (an Egyptian Islamic Jihad activist and Afghani alumnus, personal aide to Aiman A-Zawahiri, head of the Jihad organization and Osama Bin-Laden's partner). The main assault force was made up of SIUP fighters and Afghan alumni, who used anti-aircraft 23-mm. artillery and RPG7 launchers to shoot down the helicopters.

Aidid's people, who played a secondary role in the fighting, isolated the battle arena and instigated mass riots of unarmed civilians, which made the American rescue mission even more cumbersome. The consequences of the action were disastrous for the United States. The heavy losses and traumatic film footage aired on television channels worldwide of masses mutilating the bodies of American soldiers aroused strong opposition in American public opinion and in the Congress to American involvement in Somalia. Following the military fiasco in Mogadishu and due to the combined pressure of public opinion and the Congress, President Clinton decided to discontinue the activities of the U.S. task force in Somalia.

As a lesson drawn from the activities of the American forces in Somalia, the Clinton administration established the principle of "involvement without intervention," according to which the United States would refrain from sending soldiers to fight in foreign countries in order to realize goals that do not directly serve American interests.

An inquiry committee was set up in the U.S. Senate, which heard testimony about the action in Somalia. At the end of the hearings, the committee published a paper placing the blame for the debacle on the president and Defense Secretary Les Aspin. Aspin submitted his resignation two months later, and General Grison ended his career earlier than planned.[100]

The American experience in Somalia, in general, and in the October 3 battle, in particular, became a warning sign for the United States in all matters related to the sending of troops to resolve conflicts overseas. This, apparently, was the reason that for the lack of UN and U.S. intervention in the civil wars in Zaire and Rwanda. The American policy was revised in connection to Bosnia and Kosovo when there was a fear that the conflict would spread outside of the Balkan. It also underwent change as a result of the attacks of September 11, 2001, which led to the U.S. declaration of war against terror, the offensive in Afghanistan, the resultant collapse of the Taliban regime (Bin-Laden's sponsor), and the destruction of the Al-Qaida organization's infrastructure in this country.

The heavy casualties suffered by the United States in the fighting in Somalia and its subsequent decision to pull its forces out of that country by March 1, 1994, were perceived by Islamic and Somali entities, including Bin-Laden, as proof of their ability to bring about American defeat and surrender.

In an interview granted to Robert Fisk of theU.K. *Independent*, Bin-Laden declared:[101]

> We believe that God used our holy war in Afghanistan to destroy the Russian army and the Soviet Union, and now we ask God to use us one more time to do the same to America and make it a shadow of itself.
>
> We also believe that our battle against America is much simpler than the war against the Soviet Union, because some of our mujahidin who fought here in Afghanistan also participated in operations against the Americans in Somalia and they were surprised at the collapse of American morale. This convinced us that the Americans are a paper tiger.

Somalia after the Departure of the UN Forces 1995-2002

Following the departure of the UN forces from Somalia in 1994, the civil war continued and ended attempts led by the UN to achieve a ceasefire and rehabilitate the country's political system.

From 1995, mediation efforts were renewed to bring an end to the war in Somalia by several political elements, including:

- Neighboring countries: Kenya, Ethiopia, Djibouti
- International organizations: Islamic organizations, several associations in Africa, and more

- European and Muslim countries
- Various UN committees

Over the years several conference were held that brought about the consolidation of two political blocs and central tribes:[102]

- A Transitional National Government (TNG) that controls most of the quarters in Mogadishu and several state regions.
- A consolidation of parties opposed to the TNG organized under an umbrella association called the Somali Reconciliation and Restoration Council (SRRC). The TNG was recognized by many countries worldwide, particularly Arab and Muslim countries, because of its Islamic orientation, while the SRRC is mainly supported by countries with interests in Somalia that oppose the TNG, such as Ethiopia, Eritrea and more.

The lack of an effective central government brought about the sprouting of autonomous areas that declared their independence and receive aid from the SRRC and countries such as Ethiopia and Kenya.

Although the political and tribal controversies remained, over the years the fighting eased, although it did not cease, and a status quo made up of the rule of rival factions in the various areas prevailed. The terror infrastructures established in Somalia during the nineties by Iran, Sudan and Bin-Laden continued to flourish in the country without interruption under the sponsorship of their local allies, but the activity and interest focal points of Islamic terror were gradually transferred to new destinations. Bin-Laden's expulsion from Sudan due to American and Saudi pressure induced the Sudanese regime to "lower its profile" and slightly diminish its support of terror activities.

Nevertheless, East Africa remained a central arena of activity for Islamic terror, whose prominent attacks included:

- The assassination attempt against Egyptian President Hussni Mubarak in Addis Ababa, Ethiopia (1995)
- The attacks at the U.S. embassies in Kenya and Tanzania (1998)

Surprisingly, the perpetrators did not avail themselves of the aid of existing Islamic terror infrastructures in Somalia, but rather acted on the basis of terror networks established in advance in the target countries.

After the attacks of September 11 and America's declaration of war against terror, Somalia resurfaced as a possible target for U.S. action against Islamic terror focal points. Towards the end of the offensive against the Taliban and Al-Qaida in Afghanistan, the Americans feared that Bin-Laden and his men would flee to Somalia and attempt to reconstruct the organization's infrastructure from there.[103]

Since October 2001, the United States and her allies have been conducting air and sea patrols opposite the shores of Somalia in order to spot any Al-Qaida activity in this arena.

The United States noted two factors in Somalia that it believes are involved in Bin-Laden's terror activity: The Islamic "Al-Itihad" organization included by the U.S. in the list of terror organizations, and an economic concern called "Barkat" which deals in a variety of business activities such as banking, international commerce, cellular phones and more. The United States is suspicious that the company has links with Bin-Laden, and serves to transfer and launder funds for his purposes.[104]

Opposition elements in Somalia that oppose the TRG point to an affiliation and ties between the government and the Al-Itihad organization and Al-Qaida, and call on the United States to act against the government in order to cause its collapse and banish the Islamic terrorists from Somalia.[105] At present it is not clear whether these accusations against the Somali government are based on fact, or if the opposition parties are attempting to enlist the United States in their domestic struggle. Thc president of the transitional government Abd Al-Kassem Salaad Hassan denies any presence of Islamic terror elements and accuses the opposition of spreading false allegations against his government.[106] In any event, the United States has enacted intelligence reconnaissance vis-à-vis Islamic activities in Somalia. It has also maintained contact with various Somali power brokers, including Hussein Aidid, head of the SRRC, who has declared his desire to rehabilitate ties with the United States, as well as with the leaders of the RRA (see elaboration below), in the event of a U.S. need to take action against Islamic terror entities in Somalia.[107]

At the same time, meetings have been held between U.S. military and political entities, and leaders of neighboring countries (Ethiopia, Kenya and Djibouti) in the event that American action is required in the Somali arena.[108] If the United States decides to act in Somalia, the Al-Itihad and the Al-Qaida infrastructures will be the main targets. It is believed that the SRRC and RRA will probably support the American actions.

The Islamic Union—"Al-Itihad al-Islami"

One of the Somali organizations that cooperated with Bin-Laden and Al-Qaida was Al-Itihad al-Islami–the Islamic Union. This organization was founded in the late eighties by Islamic elements that opposed the regime of Ziad Bare, the president of Somalia. Subsequently, the organization opposed the continued UN and U.S. involvement in Somalia and cooperated with various Somali elements that acted against these forces.

The United States claims that the Islamic Union enabled Al-Qaida to use its bases and other infrastructures prior to the latter's attacks at the U.S. embassies in Nairobi and Dar A-Salaam in 1998. Al-Qaida's liaison vis-à-vis the Islamic Union was Bin-Laden's assistant Muhammad Ataf, who was killed in the bombings of Afghanistan.[109]

The Islamic Union continues to operate several training camps for Islamic terrorists including the Ras Kamboni camp near the Kenyan border, which, according to U.S. allegations, served Al-Qaida in the facilitation of terror activities in Africa (particularly in nearby Kenya). The United States believes that the Islamic Union is linked with the Barkat Concern, an enterprise that allegedly laundered funds for Al-Qaida.[110]

Elements in the opposition claim that the Transitional National Government (TNG), which currently rules Mogadishu and several additional areas of Somalia, relies on the support of Islamic leaders and organizations, some of which are identified with the Islamic Union.

The opposition–the Somali Reconciliation and Restoration Council (SRRC)—accuses the regime of maintaining ties with and availing itself of the aid of Al-Qaida, the Islamic Union and other radical Islamic elements. The government emphatically denies these allegations and claims that the Islamic Union has neither bases nor influence in the areas under its control, and has invited the United States to investigate the matter.[111]

The government declared that it has arrested individuals suspected of terror activity in order to prevent an American offensive in Somalia. Neighboring Ethiopia continues to regard the Islamic Union as a threat, after the organization perpetrated a series of attacks, in the course of which terrorists affiliated with the organization infiltrated Ethiopian soil; another reason for Ethiopia's attitude is the Islamic Union's support of the Ethiopian opposition movements.

Ethiopia responded to the terror attacks with military campaigns, which were targeted at the destruction of Islamic Union infrastructures in the area of Gedeo during the years 1996-1997. Ethiopia claimed that in the fighting in the Gedeo vicinity its forces killed twenty-six "non-Somalis," who were apparently members of Al-Qaida. Ethiopia suspects that the Islamic Union also maintains contact with the TNG, and thus aspires to establish a friendlier government in Somalia.

The Tri-Border: Brazil, Argentina, Paraguay

The tri-border Brazil-Argentina-Paraguay has traditionally been a focus for crime and smuggling, and has served as a haven for terror organizations.[112] This is mainly due to the limited supervisory capacity of the countries involved and a difficulty in coordinating regional activities between them. This tri-border area contains a large Muslim population, mainly of Palestinian and Shiite origin from Lebanon, and constitutes a refuge and activity base for Islamic terror organizations such as the Hizballah, the Hamas and Al-Qaida.

Intelligence reports indicate that various Islamic terror organizations are active in the area: Hizballah, the Hamas and two Egyptian organizations, the Jama'a al-Islamiya and the Islamic Jihad, which are known to be closely linked to Al-Qaida.[113] The activity of these Islamic terror organizations focuses on logistic and economic aspects, but in attacks against Israeli and Jewish targets in Buenos Aires, Argentina, in 1992, the Israeli Embassy in 1992, and the Amia Center in 1994 the footsteps of the perpetrators led to the tri-border. Intelligence sources also aver that Ciudad Del Este, the regional capital in Paraguay, serves as a central focus for terror activity, and according to Argentina this is where the preparations were made for the attacks against Israeli and Jewish targets in Argentina.[114]

On September 12, 2001, following the attacks in the United States, the Argentinean news agency reported that security measures had been taken around all of the airports and the roads leading to the tri border.[115] At the same time, urgent meetings took place between FBI representatives and intelligence personnel from the three countries in order to coordinate security steps to prevent activity of terrorists and collaborators of Islamic terror organizations from this area.[116] The work premise was that the tri-border area was home to dormant terror cells that might go into action.

After the attacks on September 11, the Paraguay authorities carried out a series of arrests. Twenty-three individuals, all of whom were suspected of affiliation with Islamic terror groups, were detained. In actual fact, some were released while others were accused of membership in a criminal organization, tax evasion and the use of forged documents. Among the detainees were individuals suspected of being central activists in the Hizballah and Hamas organizations in the region.[117]

The authorities have not yet succeeded in apprehending Assad Ahmad Barkat, against whom an international arrest warrant has been issued by the Interpol, and who is suspected of handling Hizballah activities in the area. The Argentinean prosecution claims that Barkat played a central role in the attacks in Argentina in 1992 and 1994.[118] Barkat is one of the owners of Galeria Page, one of the largest shopping centers in Ciudad Del Este. The investigators be-

Figure 2.4
International Islamic Terror Worldwide—2002

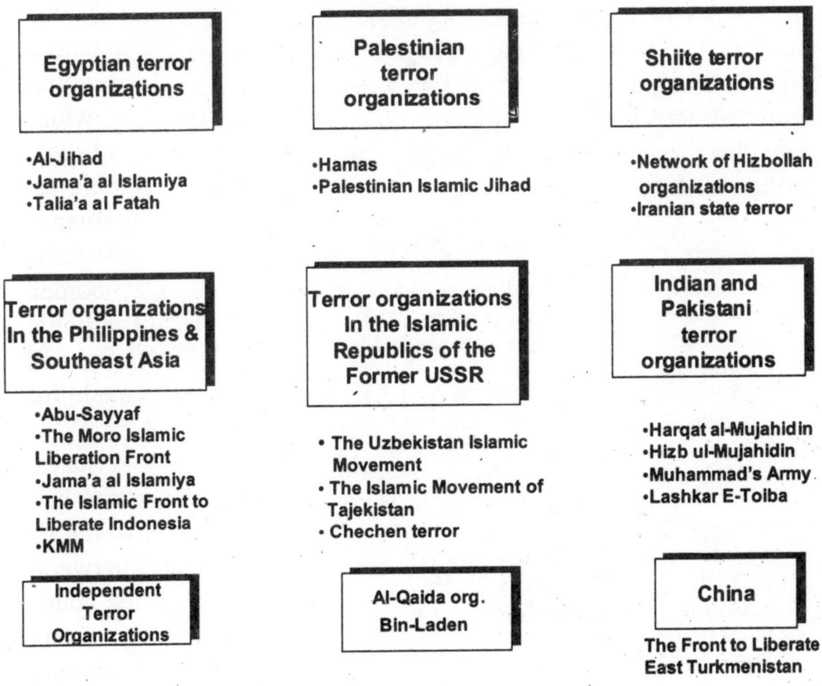

lieve that the commercial activity serves as a cover for his covert activity, and for the raising and transfer of funds to Hizballah.[119]

A raid on his apartment revealed large amounts of incitement material published by Hizballah and information proving that he had laundered funds for the organization. Among other papers, a letter was found from Hassan Nasrallah, thanking Barkat for his fundraising activities on behalf of the organization.[120] The Paraguay authorities are investigating forty-six bank accounts that served the purpose of transferring some $50 million to charitable funds in Iran and Lebanon.[121] According to the investigators, Barkat also has links with Al-Qaida.

In Uruguay, legal procedures are underway to extradite an activist of the Gamaa al Islamiya at Egypt's request. The activist, Sa'id Hassan Muhlis, was arrested in Uruguay under the suspicion of using forged documents. As mentioned earlier, the Gamaa al Islamiya organization is closely affiliated with Al-Qaida. In the "Returnees from Albania" affair, in which Egyptian Islamic Jihad activists were extradited to Egypt from all over the world, one activist was extradited from Ecuador.

It would appear that despite the activity of security forces in the tri-border area, it would continue to serve as an important focus for the activity of Islamic terror organizations. As a result of the tightening ring around Al-Qaida activists in other focal areas of the world, it is reasonable to assume that this area may become a haven and center of activity for the organization's members. Recent arrests of individuals connected to Al-Qaida in the tri-border area may testify to the realization of this trend.

Notes

1. In an article in the weekly *Al-Asbua Al-Arabi*, the number of Moslems who arrived in Afghanistan is estimated at about 12,000 (*Al-Asbua Al-Arabi*, July 1992). In another article, the estimate is between 10,000 and 20,000 volunteers, Conflict International, April 1994.
2. Yossef Bodansky, *Bin-Laden, The Man Who Declared War on America*, Forum, Roseville, CA, 1999, pp. 346–347.
3. Yoram Schweitzer, Middle East Terrorism: The Afghan Alumni, in Shlomo Brom and Yiftah Shapir (eds.), *The Middle East Military Balance 1999-2000*, J.C.C.S., Tel Aviv, and M.I.T. Press, Cambridge, MA, p.121.
4. Ibid., p.122.
5. *Al Wasat* (London), February 15, 1993.
6. *A-Tsabach* (Tunisia), January 22, 1992.
7. Shaul Shay and Yoram Schweitzer, *The Terror of the Afghan Alumni*, The International Policy Institute for Counter-Terrorism, The Interdisciplinary Center, Herzliya, September 2000.

8. Nahman Tal, *Opposition from Within, Egyptian and Jordanian Handling of Radical Islam*, Papyrus Publishing, Tel Aviv University, 1999, p. 45.
9. Yona Alexander, *Middle East Terrorism: Selected Group Profiles*, The Jewish Institute for National Security Affairs, Washington D.C. 1994, pp. 49-50.
10. Nahman Tal, *Opposition from Within, Egyptian and Jordanian Handling of Radical Islam*, p. 45.
11. Ibid., pp. 68-74.
12. Ibid.
13. Ibid.
14. Shaul Shay and Yoram Schweitzer, *The Terror of the Afghan Alumni.*
15. Ibid.
16. Nahman Tal, *Opposition from Within, Egyptian and Jordanian Handling of Radical Islam,* p. 45; Ya'akov Bahat, The Muslim Brotherhood in Egypt.
17. Nahman Tal, *Opposition from Within, Egyptian and Jordanian Handling of Radical Islam*, p. 47-48.
18. Ibid., p. 198.
19. Ibid., pp. 199-200.
20. Ibid., pp. 207-208.
21. *New York Times*, Internet, January 29, 2000.
22. The French News Agency, quoting ABC, January 21, 2000.
23. Shaul Shay and Yoram Schweitzer, *The Terror of the Afghan Alumni.*
24. *Al-Aharam* (Cairo), August 30, 1992.
25. The French News Agency, February 11, 1992.
26. The French News Agency from Algeria, December 8, 1991.
27. Shaul Shay and Yoram Schweitzer, *The Terror of the Afghan Alumni.*
28. Ibid.
29. Lashkar e-Toiba, Terror Organizations' Profile, The International Policy Institute for Counter-Terror, The Interdisciplinary Center, Herzliya, www.ict.org.il; Terrorism Groups: An Overview, SATP, 2001 (Internet site of SATP).
30. LET—Lashkar e-Toiba.
31. Jeish e-Muhammad, Terror Organizations' Profile, The International Policy Institute for Counter-Terror, The Interdisciplinary Center, Herzliya, www.ict.org.il; Terrorism Groups: An Overview, SATP, 2001 (Internet site of SATP).
32. JKLF, Terror Organizations' Profile, The International Policy Institute for Counter-Terror, The Interdisciplinary Center, Herzliya, (Internet site of ICT); Terrorism Groups: An Overview, SATP, 2001 (Internet site of SATP).
33. JKLF—Jammu and Kashmir Liberation Front.
34. Hizb ul Mujahidin, Terror Organizations' Profile, The International Policy Institute for Counter-Terror, The Interdisciplinary Center, Herzliya, (Internet site of ICT).
35. Harqat el Mujahidin, Terror Organizations' Profile, The International Policy Institute for Counter-Terror The Interdisciplinary Center, Herzliya, (Internet site of ICT); Terrorism Groups: An Overview, SATP, 2001 (Internet site of SATP).
36. Islamic Movement of Uzbekistan.
37. "Islamic Party of Turkistan."
38. *Washington Post*, February 17, 1999.
39. AP Moscow, February 19, 1999.
40. Ahmed Rashid, The Taliban Exporting Extremism, *Foreign Affairs*, November/December 1999.
41. Islamic Movement of Uzbekistan (IMU), Center for Nonproliferation Studies, http//cns.ms.edu/research/wtc01/limu.htm.
42. Ibid.

43. Washington File, U.S. Department of State, statement by Richard Boucher, spokesman, September 15, 2000.
44. Arslan Koichev, Skirmishes Suggest IMU is Changing Tactics, EurasiaNet, http//www.eurasianet.org/departments/insight/articles/eua080601.shtm.
45. Ahmed Rashid, The Taliban Exporting Extremism.
46. Ibid.
47. Ibid.
48. The Uzbek Court Sentences Two to Death for Terrorism, *Uzbekistan Daily Digest*, November 20, 2000.
49. Washington File, U.S. Department of State, statement by Richard Boucher, spokesman, September 15, 2000.
50. *The Straits Times* (Singapore), Rohan Gunaratna, Al Qaida, January 2, 2002.
51. Ibid.
52. Ibid.
53. Ibid.
54. A. P. (K. L.) Kuala Lumaur, Jasbant Singh, Malaysia Investigates Terror Groups, December 6, 2001.
55. *The Straits Times* (Singapore), Rene Ahmad, KL Will Tighten Screening of Army Volunteers, January 13, 2002.
56. On June 5, 2002, Omar el Farouq was extradited to the United States and was transferred to a base located at Bagram, Afghanistan, where he was interrogated by CIA agents.
57. Indonesian Mujahidin Council—MMC.
58. *The Straits Times* (Singapore), Rohan Gunaratna, Al Qaida, January 4, 2002.
59. Yossef Badansky, *Bin-Laden, The Man Who Declared War on America*, pp. 112-114.
60. ICT, The International Policy Institute for Counter-Terror, The Interdisciplinary Center, Herzliya, Organization Profile, Abu Sayyaf Group, http://www.ict.org.il.
61. ICT, Organization Profile—MILF.
62. The Chinese word *Xinjiang* means "new front," a name that conveys the Chinese viewpoint that the province is a distant periphery of the Chinese empire.
63. Paul George, Islamic Unrest in the Xinjiang Uighur Autonomous Region, Canadian Security Intelligence Service Publication, *Commentary* no. 73, Spring, 1998.
64. Ibid. The Uighur American Association published the names of 114 Uighurs executed in China during the years 1997-1999.
65. Ibid.
66. Internet, http://Azzam.com, November 20, 1999.
67. *Maariv*, Tel Aviv, February 2, 2001 (quoting an interview given by Putin to the chief editor of the periodical *Nazwisiama Gazette*.
68. Ibid.
69. FBS—Federal Security Bureau, successor to the KGB.
70. Guardian Unlimited, September 19, 1999.
71. Ibid.
72. Ibid.
73. Ibid.
74. Ibid.
75. Russian *Analitica* (Moscow), August 5, 2001
76. AFP, Paris, March 16, 2000.
77. Ibid.
78. AFB, Moscow, March 18, 2000.
79. Ibid.
80. AFB, Paris, March 4, 2000.
81. *Yediot Aharonot*, October 27, 2002.

82. *Maariv*, October 24, 2002.
83. *Yediot Aharonot*, October 24, 2002.
84. *Yediot Aharonot*, October 28, 2002, quotes the French *Les Journal di Dimanche*.
85. Ibid.
86. *Maariv*, October 27, 2002.
87. *Yediot Aharonot*, October 28, 2002.
88. Yossef Bodansky, *Bin-Laden, The Man Who Declared War on America*, p. 100.
89. Ronen Bergman, Afghanistan of Europe, *Yediot Aharonot*, Tel Aviv, December 21, 2001.
90. Ibid.
91. *Yediot Aharonot*, Tel Aviv, December 24, 2001.
92. Shaul Shay, *The Endless Jihad, the Mujahidin, the Taliban and Bin-Laden*, p. 137.
93. Ibid.
94. Ibid.
95. This chapter is based on the book, Yossef Bodansky, *Bin-Laden, The Man who Declared War on America*, Forum, New York, 2001.
96. Ibid.
97. This section is based on the book, Mark Bowden, *Black Hawk Down, A Story of Modern War*, Atlantic Monthly Press, New York, 1999.
98. Yossef Bodansky, *Bin-Laden, The Man Who Declared War on America.*
99. Patrick J. Sloyan, Somalia Mission: Clinton Called the Shots in Failed Policy Targeting Aidid, Newsday Inc., December 5, 1993.
100. *Independent*, March 1, 1994.
101. Mohammad Aden Farkeet, Baidoa Diary: The Political Events Surrounding the Occupation and Liberation of the Somalia City of Bardoa since 1995.
102. Charles Cobb Jr., Hints of Military Action Cause Puzzlement, Worry, allAfrica.com, December 23, 2001.
103. Jeff Koinange, U.S. Seeks Allies against Terror in Somalia, CNN.com, January 13, 2002.
104. Ibid.
105. BBC News, December 21, 2001.
106. Jeff Koinange, U.S. Seeks Allies against Terror in Somalia.
107. allAfrica.com, February 1, 2002: An interview with Hussein Aidid.
108. *The Dawn*, November 26, 2001.
109. Charles Cobb Jr., Hints of Military Action Cause Puzzlement, Worry, allAfrica.com, December 23, 2001.
110. allAfrica.com, February 1, 2002: An interview with Hussein Aidid.
111. *The Dawn*, Pakistan, January 27, 2002; *The Dawn*, Pakistan, December 5, 2001.
112. CNN.com, Harris Whitbeck and Ingrid Arneson, Sources: Terrorists Find Haven in South America.
113. Daniel Sobelman, Israel Takes Special Interest in Triple-Border Area, *Jane's Intelligence Review*, December 2001.
114. Ibid.
115. Patterns of Global Terrorism—2001, Report Cites Terrorist Activity in Colombia, Peru, Tri-Border Area.
116. CNN.com, Harris Whitbeck and Ingrid Arneson, Sources: Terrorists Find Haven in South America.
117. Daniel Sobelman, Israel Takes Special Interest in Triple-Border Area.
118. Ibid.
119. Ibid.
120. Ibid.
121. Patterns of Global Terrorism—2001.

3

Terror Attacks of Al-Qaida and the Islamic Front

Bin-Laden's "Principles"

The terror activity of the Afghan alumni throughout the world since the early nineties influenced the structure of local terror in the Arab countries and in the international arena as well. The return of "war veterans" to their homelands significantly raised the level of violence in these countries; the war veterans became leaders of terrorist organizations and taught their expertise to their subordinates, implementing everything they had learned in Afghanistan on the local level of terror activities. In Egypt, Algeria, Jordan, Tunisia and even in Libya attacks were perpetrated that threatened to undermine the stability of local governments and caused extensive damage. Simultaneously, terror cells deployed worldwide planned to carry out mega attacks against rivals of the Islam. This activity was carried out over a large geographical area and was based on Afghanistan as a focus for training and ideological indoctrination to disseminate the ideas of the Global Jihad. The nationalities of the terrorists were varied: Algerians, Tunisians, Egyptians, Saudis, Libyans, Jordanians, Lebanese, Palestinians and Muslims from Africa, Asia, and other countries.

Bin-Laden formulated an operational pattern that best suited his concept regarding the effective dissemination of the jihad, which on the one hand gave him the ability to control large terror attacks, which he wished to initiate from his headquarters, and on the other hand to nurture cadres of terrorists trained in guerrilla warfare and terror, who would act independently to realize his vision. Bin-Laden's action patterns can best be described in terms of "initiating and impelling."[1]

The Principle of Initiating

This principle is based on the terror activity led, managed and supervised by the command of the Al-Qaida organization. The various stages of the attack, from the original initiative to choosing the target, gathering information and the preparations, and through to implementation are all supervised by the operational command of Al-Qaida from its headquarters in Afghanistan. The attack will be perpetrated by organization members or members of terror cells directly linked with it under the direct supervision of commanders from Al-Qaida.

Thus, complete control is maintained over the operation's management and the choosing of suitable timing; prior arrangements are made for the propaganda and "denial" system that accompanies a mega terror event. All this is done with the aim of squeezing maximum benefit out of it, while minimizing the damages and any possible counter-reactions of Bin-Laden's adversaries.

The Principle of Impelling

This principle is based on the image of Afghanistan as the "Mecca of the Global Jihad"[1] and on Bin-Laden's image as "the modern Salah a-Din,"[2] who is to lead the battle against the infidels all over the world. Bin-Laden's training camps became a lodestone for thousands of young men who were attracted to Afghanistan or were sent there by veteran Afghan alumni, in order to create an ever-growing reservoir of fighters throughout the world. The Muslim youth who were located at different sites worldwide—in mosques and Islamic cultural centers, or those who had already proven themselves through involvement in terror activity in their own countries—generally came to Peshawar on the Pakistan-Afghanistan border. There they were put up in Islamic hostels sponsored by charitable organizations (NGO) such as "Dawa and Tablir," "The Global Islamic Charity Organization," and more. Bin-Laden's men lodged and were active at these places, searching out the most talented and dedicated men among the volunteers in order to offer them military training at the Afghan camps with the aim of teaching them to take a personal part in the Global Jihad. Autonomic and autarchic terror networks arose from this reservoir and were involved in the terror activity of Bin-Laden's Islamic Front.

The Principle of Quality at the Expense of Quantity

The Al-Qaida organization was responsible for a relatively small number of attacks out of the sum total of attacks perpetrated by terror organizations affiliated with the stream of Sunni Islamic Fundamentalism. Al-Qaida, which for years was active behind the scenes lending support to a long line of organizations and terror cells, initiated direct action only following the formal declaration regarding the establishment of an umbrella organization called "The International Islamic Front for Jihad against the Jews and Crusaders" (February 1998). Al-Qaida assumed the leading role in the perpetration of terror attacks, though previously it had been satisfied with providing training, logistical and operational support, and serving as an inspiration for terror activity conducted independently by Islamic terror organizations worldwide.

The first operations by Al-Qaida members were the suicide attacks at the U.S. embassies in Kenya and Tanzania in August 1998. While these attacks were planned over a five-year period prior to their actual execution, the timing was chosen by the Al-Qaida command in Afghanistan and was meant to demonstrate the "Islamic Front's" intention to realize its declarations and lead the jihad assault undertaken by Bin-Laden at the time of its establishment and the announcement of the fatwa (the religious ruling) of February 1998. The next Al-Qaida attack was also a direct assault carried out by two suicide sailors upon a boat loaded with explosives that hit an American destroyer, the *USS Cole*, while the latter was anchored at the port of Aden in Yemen for the purpose of refueling. The pinnacle of the Al-Qaida attacks was the combined terror attack in the United States against the Twin Towers and the Pentagon, whose aim was to deal a heavy blow to the very heart of the United States and the symbols of American power, and incite a global battle between Islam and the West.

Al-Qaida's Attacks

Attacks in Kenya and Tanzania

On August 7, 1998, at 10:00 a.m., a car bomb carrying about three quarters of a ton of explosives was detonated next to the United States Embassy in Nairobi. Two suicide terrorists manned the car (one, Al-Owali, survived because he had gotten out of the vehicle to pursue the embassy's guard who was fleeing). As a result of the explosion, 213 people were killed, the majority of whom were Kenyans, as well as a dozen American citizens who were embassy employees. Over 4,000 people were injured. Simultaneously, an additional suicide attack was perpetrated by the same organization near the U.S. Embassy in Dar A-Salaam in Tanzania. Eleven people were killed and scores were injured. These attacks signaled the organization's intention to perpetrate indiscriminate mass slaughter in attacks against American targets throughout the world, and reflected its characteristic modus operandi, as it was to be expressed sThe apprehension of a number of key activists in the terror network responsible for the planning and execution of the attacks led to a string of arrests and the preparation of a detailed charge sheet, which clearly indicated the direct responsibility of the organization headed by Bin-Laden for the terror campaign in east Africa. The investigation's findings offered a unique preliminary opportunity to closely observe the organization, thus providing in-depth knowledge of its modus operandi.

The Attack in Kenya. The terror cell that perpetrated the attack in Nairobi was composed of a small nucleus of 6-8 local activists under the command of Harun Al-Fazul, an Al-Qaida member born in the Comoro Islands.[3] Their original plan had been to drive a car bomb into the embassy's underground parking, detonate it with the help of suicide drivers and bring the building down upon its inhabitants.[4]

The terror team included three people who drove to their destination in two vehicles. The first car was driven by the mission commander Fazul Abdallah, known as Harun al-Fazul, which served as an escort vehicle for the car bomb. The second carried the two suicide bombers, the driver who committed suicide and his escort Rashed Daoud Al-Owali, who survived the attack, and after being apprehended was extradited by Kenya to the United States to stand trial. The car bomb driver, an Egyptian by origin, tried to enter the embassy's underground parking facility, but was unable to do so because of the Kenyan guard's refusal to open the embassy's gates. His attempt to circumvent the barrier was prevented by a car driving up from the underground parking area that blocked his way. Awali (the surviving driver) threatened the guard and demanded that he open the gate, but when the latter refused, he lobbed a stun grenade at the guard and proceeded to run after him, moving away from the vehicle. The driver detonated the bomb in a compound containing three buildings, about ten meters away from the embassy wall. The explosion resulted in a large number of casualties and the collapse of several buildings near the embassy. The embassy building itself, the attack's main target, did not collapse, although it was damaged.

Preliminary preparations for the attack had begun in 1993.[5] Senior Al-Qaida personnel, including Bin-Laden and his assistant, the military commander Abu-Hafez, participated in the planning. The team contained eight members. Preparations for the attack were divided into several stages: As noted, the first stage was in 1993 when Bin-Laden conceived the idea and sent his representatives to Kenya. One of them was Muhammad Ali—a former sergeant in the U.S. military who subsequently served as a state's-witness in the trials of the attack perpetrators in Kenya and Tanzania held in New York—who confessed that he had met with Bin-Laden and given him photographs of the embassy in Nairobi. Bin-Laden sent several emissaries to Kenya with the aim of learning the lay of the land. They married local women and took work enabling them to gather qualitative information about the potential targets, mainly the U.S. and Israeli embassies.

The second, more advanced stage of preparations in anticipation of the attack was launched in May-June 1998 (about two months before the attack). The decision was made following Bin-Laden's public declaration in an interview with ABC in which he threatened to perpetrate mega attacks against U.S. targets in retribution for the U.S.'s anti-Islamic policy. The practical preparations for the attack were administered from the network headquarters in the target country, the Top-Hill Hotel in Nairobi. The network members also rented a house in Nairobi where they hid the weapons, explosives, stun grenades and handguns smuggled into Nairobi from the Middle East via the Cameroon Islands. A short time prior to the attack, three cell members gathered intelligence about the U.S. Embassy in Nairobi, and when all the preparations were in place, the date for the attack was set.

Several days prior to the attack date most of the network members left Nairobi, with the exception of Harun Fazul, the team's commander, who escorted the car bomb with the suicide terrorists to the target in order to personally supervise the operation. After the explosion, Harun returned to the safe house to cover their tracks and then disappeared.

The Attack in Tanzania. On August 7, 1998, a car bomb exploded near the U.S. Embassy in Tanzania. Eleven people were killed in the explosion and about eight-five were wounded, all local residents. The Tanzanian cell contained six members and additional individuals who assisted in the preparations for the attack in various stages of the planning.

Members of the team, composed of a variety of nationalities including Kenyans, Tanzanians and Egyptians, underwent training in Afghanistan throughout the course of 1994.[6]

With the help of local collaborators, the team members rented a private safe house a few months before the attack. The house was outside of the city and it was used for storage of the car bomb (a van) and the purchased weapons. The van had been bought two months earlier and was rigged as a car bomb a short time before the attack.

The cell members collected preliminary information about the routine procedure for cars delivering water to the embassies, and took advantage of the information to infiltrate a car bomb into the embassy. The suicide bomber arrived separately in Dar-A-Salaam and was kept at a safe house.

On the day of the attack, the suicide driver of the car bomb drove to the embassy building and followed the water truck that arrived at its entrance. When the water truck was about to enter the premises, the car bomb drew up close and the suicide driver detonated the van that was loaded with a quarter ton of explosives.[7]

The African continent was chosen for these attacks because it was deemed a relatively easy site for terror activity due to the limited capabilities of local security forces to perform surveillance of the preparations and to the Al-Qaida activists who had already arrived on the continent at the end of 1993. The slack local security and the ease of traveling to and from Africa were perceived as advantages. In addition, security at the U.S. embassies was problematic, which made the execution of the attack fairly straightforward.

The Attack on the USS Cole

On October 12, 2000, the destroyer *USS Cole* was attacked by a boat bomb containing over a half ton of explosives. The boat bomb was navigated by two suicide attackers from the Al-Qaida organization. Seventeen American sailors perished in the explosion and thirty-five were wounded. The boat bomb was disguised as a service boat on its way to handle technical repairs on the American destroyer. The two suicide terrorists were dressed in white coveralls and therefore did not arouse suspicion. They tried to draw up alongside the vessel's stern in order to wreak as much damage as possible, but were unable to do so and finally detonated the boat near the destroyer's center.

On April 2, 2001, Yemen's Minister of Interior announced that local security forces had apprehended six terrorists, who would be brought to trial; three of them had been directly involved in the attack and another three had served as collaborators. As stated above, two additional members were killed in the attack (the suicide bombers), and another two are still at large.[8] It appears that preparations for this attack were launched about eighteen months prior to its execution. Initially, the chosen target was the *USS Sullivan* that docked in the Aden port on January 3, 2000. Preparations for the attack started in mid-1999, but due to a miscalculation in regard to the boat's load capacity the vessel sank because of an overload of explosives. Therefore, the attack was postponed for nine months.

Two central activists supervised preparations for the two attacks, both the one in January 2000 and the one in October 2000. The commander of the first attack, a man of Saudi origin who had many aliases, including Abd Al Rahaman al-Nashiri, also known as Muhammad Omar Al-Harazi, escaped, while the second, Jamal Badawi Al-Nashiri, the more senior of the two, was arrested in Yemen. Nashiri was eventually arrested in November 2002 and extradited to the United States.

According to an FBI document, Badawi (one of the chief suspects of involvement in the preparations for the attack) confessed that he had traveled to Afghanistan in 1997, undergone training in Bid-Laden's camps and pledged his loyalty oath. Badawi met his future accomplices in the attack, including Yemen-born Tawfik Al-Atash, known by the code name of "Khaled," when in June 1999 Khaled sent two of his men to him. They asked Badawi to travel to Saudi Arabia to purchase the boat that served as the boat bomb. It was bought with false documentation, in order to conceal the identity of the buyers, and the vessel was ultimately presented to the two suicide bombers.[9]

Following the attack, several declarations claiming responsibility were announced in the name of unfamiliar organizations, including the "Islamic Deterrent Forces." According to their announcement, the organization called "the Group of the Al-Aksa's Martyrs" perpetrated the attack in order to defend the honor of the Islamic nation and avenge the blood of the Muslim people subdued in Palestine due to American aid.

The Deterrent Forces stated that the attack was a gift to Al-Aksa and "a means to promote the objective of flying the Palestinian flag over our people in Palestine." The attack was meant "to defend the honor of the Islamic Arab nation so that America will know the cost of its attempt to achieve hegemony on our lands through its warships and military bases on our lands (Yemen). The declaration ended with a warning to the United States not to aid and abet the Zionist entity.[10]

Rifai Taha, one of the most senior members of the Jama'a al-Islamiya, who is currently under arrest in Egypt and was for the first time presented by the newspaper, *A-Zaman,* as Bin-Laden's spokesman,[11] denied that Bin-Laden was involved, but welcomed the attack. Taha stated that this was a great campaign perpetrated against the United States, which is a country

> that harms our lands, our people, our treasures and our honor in Palestine. The lessons to be drawn from this attack are that even the powerful have weaknesses. The practical conclusion is that the United States had to have its destroyer towed in the dead of night and have it moved secretly, as well as raise the alert level in the US navy in the Gulf.[12]

In his announcement to *A-Shark Al-Awsat*, Taha added that the operation had cost $5,000, but the damage caused to the American defense system was in the hundreds of millions of dollars. He added,

> the attack was carried out against a fortified military target, which in contrast to the condemnations we absorbed for action taken against civilian targets, cannot trigger criticism because this is a military target belonging to a hostile country which aids and abets the enemy.[13]

As is their wont, in retrospect the Al-Qaida leaders attempted to attribute this operation as well to their aspiration to aid the Palestinians in their struggle against Israel.[14] It is noteworthy that this attack was perpetrated during a period when Israel and the Palestinians were involved in political negotiations and were cooperating in the framework of the Oslo Accords, before the renewed violence erupted between them in September 2000.

The Assault of September 11, 2001—"The Great Provocation"

The terror assault of September 11 is undoubtedly the most significant and lethal terror operation in the history of modern terror to date. Its repercussions and lessons will likely be studied in the years to come and will serve as a wide field of study for researchers both in the operative areas (secret services, law enforcement agencies), and in the academic research areas of various disciplines.

Even today, it is clear that the action represented the fruition of meticulous planning over several years, and that it was managed and supervised by the Al-Qaida headquarters in Afghanistan. The action pattern chosen by the planners was the development of an earlier concept employed by Afghan alumni terrorists already in the mid-nineties. This fact surfaced in the testimony of Hakim Murad, one of Ramzi Yusuf's men in the Philippines, who confessed to planning a suicide attack in 1995 using an aircraft against the CIA headquarters at Langley. The plan was unable to reach "operational maturity" due to the lack of suicide pilots available to the terror network.[15]

Another link between Ramzi Yusuf's aviation terror campaign in the Philippines and the terror attack of September 11 is Khaled Sheikh Muhammad, the man suspected of filling the role of Al-Qaida's "mission commander" in the assault against the United States. Khaled Sheikh, Kuwaiti born and uncle to Ramzi Yusuf, who was part of the latter's group in the Philippines in 1995, succeeded in evading arrest then and has been on the FBI's wanted list for several years until he was arrested in Pakistan in March 2003.[16]

There is no doubt that in their planning and supervision of the terror attack against the United States, the Al-Qaida commanders demonstrated characteristic patience and thorough long-term planning. This time they concentrated on the training of several pilots, which enabled them to carry out their diabolical scheme.

Various groups doubted the proof of Al-Qaida's responsibility for the attack, but the initial assessment that Bin-Laden was indeed responsible was confirmed by Bin-Laden himself, who confessed to prior knowledge of the attack, but noted that he had preferred to wait for the results.[17] He stated that he, who had been the "optimistic" one among his accomplices in the attack, predicted the collapse of "only" four floors in each of the Twin Towers targeted by the attack, and the consequent death of thousands of victims. He confessed that he had not expected the success to be so "great" and did not foresee that both towers would crumble. The attack against the Pentagon and the Capitol (which apparently was the fourth target) was meant to complete the frontal attack against the United States. He also revealed the fact that Atta was the commander of the team and that most of the suicide attackers did not know about the action plan until immediately prior to its execution.[18]

The Attack Objectives

As is characteristic of many other terror attacks, this September 11 attack was also meant to simultaneously achieve several goals:

Provocation. In Bin-Laden's eyes, this was the primary, concrete and operative goal of the attack against the United States. The multiple deaths and massive damage anticipated by the planners were aimed at dragging the United States into an overall and indiscriminate war against the Muslim world. It was meant to corroborate the concept which Bin-Laden had endeavored to disseminate among the Islamic States and Muslims worldwide regarding the struggle between the West's "evil culture" and the Muslims' "just culture"–the inevitable battle when the American despots and tyranny confronted Islamic purity.[19] Bin-Laden and his people had expected the United States to declare a total war against the entire Muslim world. They hoped that this period would create a dichotomy between two completely rival camps, which would act according to the popular rule of "choose which side you are on." The first camp would be composed of the United States and a handful of Western states that would join her, while the second camp would include the entire Muslim world that would come to Bin-Laden's aid because it felt oppressed or alienated by the antagonistic West.

Bin-Laden believed that in any event the attack perpetrated by his people would expand his small group of supporters to a much larger camp than the one at his disposal prior to the attack. In light of the anticipated counter-attack by his adversaries, this great provocation was designated to "squeeze" from the United States a set of counter-responses that would unmask its true face before the Muslims in particular and world opinion in general, that is, that in contrast to its pretensions and declarations the United Stats is ultimately and fundamentally anti-Muslim, anti-democratic and anti-humane.

Achieving propaganda by the deed.[20] Bin-Laden and his men sought to prove the ability of the "Islamic fighters" to deal American society and its power symbols a mortal blow, thus exposing the weakness and vulnerability of the American superpower before the members of Al-Qaida and his followers in the radical Islamic camp. In a television broadcast on Al-Jazeera in December 2001, Bin-Laden pointed out the achievements of the attacks against the United

States, including the exposure of America's weakness and vulnerability by a handful of Muslim fighters. "The war in Afghanistan has exposed America's weakness. Despite the clear technological advantages of its war machine, it cannot defeat the Muslim mujahidin." The second achievement that he noted was the exposure of what he referred to as "the Crusader hatred for Islam."[21]

Reinforcement of this intention can be found in the videotaped testimony of Al-Hiznawi, one of the nineteen suicide attackers, which was filmed six months prior to the attack, in which Al-Hiznawi read out his will and stated: "America is nothing beyond propaganda and a huge collection of exaggerated and false declarations. The truth is what you see. We have killed them (the Americans) outside of their country, thank God, and we are killing them in their homes."[22]

Accelerating the recruitment of new volunteers to the Global Jihad organization, Bin-Laden stated clearly:

> The acts of these young men in New York and Washington render unimportant all the speeches delivered anywhere else in the world. Their speeches (meaning their deeds) were clearly understood by all the Arabs and non-Arabs as one.... The number of people who embraced the Islamic faith after the campaign was greater than the number that has grasped Islam in the past eleven years.[23]

The killing of as many American citizens as possible. As stated above, the most moderate estimate of the planners was at least several thousand deaths.

Dealing a heavy blow to the American economy.

Damaging the symbols of the American culture, which serves as a role model for members of the Western civilization, their bitter enemy.

The Attack[24]

On September 11, the most deadly terror attack in the annals of international terrorism was perpetrated against targets symbolizing the military and economic power of the United States, and had a dramatic impact on international relations. Three thousand people from eighty different countries were killed in the attack, most of them as a result of the deliberate ramming of two commercial airplanes flown by suicide pilots into the Twin Towers of the World Trade Center in New York. The two tall buildings collapsed, causing the death of more than 2,800 people who were in the buildings at the time or were participating in the rescue efforts to extricate people trapped in the burning buildings.

Another target under attack, which also had symbolic significance, was the Pentagon in Washington, which was severely damaged by a third plane flown by suicide pilots that crashed into the Pentagon. The intention of the hijackers of the fourth plane was apparently to crash into the White House, but their efforts were thwarted thanks to the heroic struggle of the plane's passengers who were informed in telephone calls conducted from the plane with their families, of the fates of the other planes, and of the hijackers' intention to crash into a selected target inside the United States. The decision of the aircraft's passengers to attack the hijackers and prevent them from carrying out their scheme, even at the expense of their own lives, caused the plane to crash in an unpopulated area of Pennsylvania, thus saving many lives.

In all of the four hijacked airplanes, a total of 246 passengers and crewmembers perished. This number does not include the nineteen suicide hijackers. On the ground, more than 2,750 persons died.

The terror attacks in the United States also resulted in heavy direct and indirect economic damages amounting to billions of dollars, and their impact continues to be felt by the American economy in particular, and world economy in general.

Figure 3.1
Management of Terror Attack in the United States

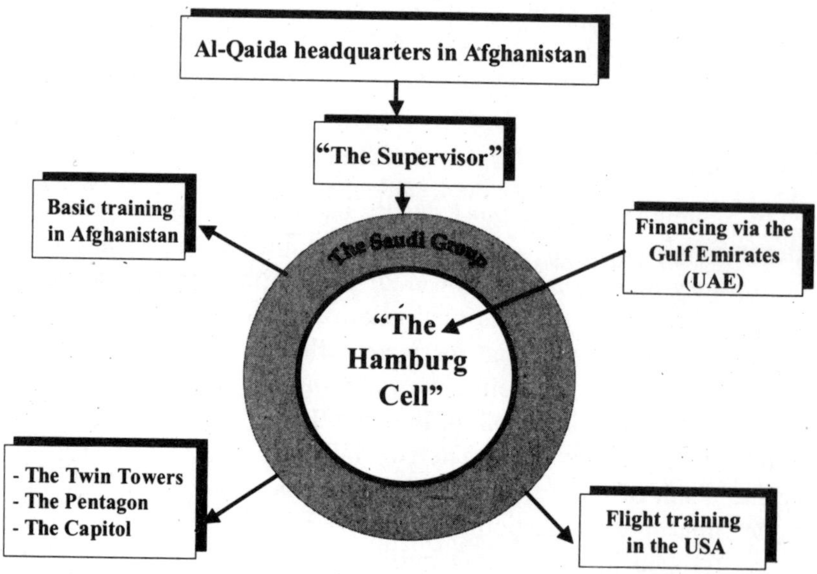

The Hijacked Airplanes

The terror campaign of September 11 started in the early hours of the morning, a short time after the airplanes took off from three different airports on the U.S. East Coast. All of the hijacked aircraft were en route to distant airports on the West Coast. The hijackers intentionally chose long flights in order to ensure that they would be carrying large amounts of fuel and would be less populated. The copious amount of fuel would enhance the effect of the explosion, while the relatively low number of passengers would ensure relative easy in overwhelming them if any opposition were to arise on their part.

The four airplanes that crashed were hijacked by four trained teams of terrorists that were affiliated with the Al-Qaida organization led and commanded by Bin-Laden. The four teams had a total of nineteen men aged 20-33. Fifteen of the assailants were of Saudi origin, one was Egyptian, another was Lebanese and two were from the United Arab Emirates. In each of the teams there was at least one trained and certified pilot.

American Airlines flight 11. The first hijacked plane was a Boeing 767, American Airlines flight number 11, which took off at 8:02 a.m. from Boston for Los Angeles. The hijacked aircraft crashed into the north tower of the World Trade Center Twin Towers at 8:45 a.m. Eighty-seven passengers and crewmembers were killed in the crash. The ramming of the plane into the north tower caused its collapse at 10:29 a.m., New York time, about an hour and forty-five minutes after the initial collision.

Five kidnappers manned the plane: (1) Muhammad Atta, head of the network and commander of the entire operation. Atta, a thirty-three-year-old Egyptian citizen, had arrived in the United States in anticipation of the hijackings on July 29, 2001, and had a pilot's license issued in the United States; (2) Abd Al-Aziz Al-Omri, a twenty-nine-year-old Saudi Arabian (who apparently had a pilot's license); (3) Wa'al A-Shahri, a twenty-eight-year-old Saudi Arabian; (4) Wali A-Shhari, a twenty-five-year-old Saudi Arabian; (5) Stam A-Sukami, a twenty-five-year-old Saudi Arabian.

United Airlines flight 175. The second hijacked plane, a Boeing 767, United Airlines flight 175, left the Boston Airport en route to Los Angeles and crashed into the south tower of the World Trade Center at 9:03 a.m. (New York time), some eighteen minutes after the collision of the first plane. This resulted in the death of fifty-one passengers and nine crewmembers. The south tower collapsed at 9:50 a.m. (New York time), about forty-seven minutes after the aircraft hit the building.

The plane was manned by five hijackers: (1) Marwan Al-Sheikhi, the twenty-three-year-old pilot born in the Gulf Emirates, who arrived in the United States on May 2, 2001, in anticipation of the attack; (2) Hamza al-Ramdi, a twenty-one-year-old Saudi Arabian; (3) Mahnam A-Shahri, a twenty-two-year-old Saudi Arabian; (4) Ahmad Al-Ramdi, a twenty-one-year-old Saudi Arabian; (5) Faiz Ahmad, a twenty-four-year-old native of the Gulf Emirates.

American Airlines flight 77. The third hijacked plane was a Boeing 757, American Airlines flight 77, from Washington to Los Angeles. It crashed into the Pentagon building in Washington at 9:39 a.m. (Washington time), about an hour and twenty-four minutes after takeoff. As a result of the crash, fifty-nine people were killed, including fifty-three passengers and six crewmembers. In addition, 184 people were killed on the ground in the Pentagon building.

There were five hijackers aboard: (1) Hani Hanjur, a twenty-nine-year-old Saudi Arabian and the team's commander. He was a licensed commercial pilot and qualified for his license in the United States. Hanjur had resided in the United States for about ten years prior to the attack. He returned from Saudi Arabia to the United States in December 2000 in anticipation of the attack; (2) Khaled Al-Midkhar, a twenty-six-year-old Saudi Arabian; (3) Salem al-Hazmi, a twenty-year-old Saudi Arabian; (4) Majed Makdad, a twenty-four-year-old Saudi Arabian; (5) Nawaf Al-Hazmi, a twenty-five-year-old Saudi Arabian.

United Airlines flight 93. The fourth hijacked plane was a Boeing 757, United Airlines flight 93, from Newark Airport in New Jersey en route to San Francisco. The plane took off at 8:10 a.m. and crashed at 10:10 in an open field in Pennsylvania, about an hour and twenty-one minutes after takeoff. Apparently, the target was the White House. As a result of the crash forty-four people perished, including thirty-seven passengers and seven crewmembers.

There were four hijackers on board: (1) Ziad Samir Jarah, a twenty-six-year-old Lebanese citizen; (2) Sa'ad Al-Ramdi, a twenty-two-yea-old Saudi Arabian with a pilot's license; (3) Ahmad Al-Hinzawi, a twenty-one-year-old Saudi Arabian; (4) Ahmad Al-Nami, a twenty-four-year-old Saudi Arabian.

Preparations for the Attack

Even now there are still many details connected to the preparations that are unclear or classified. However, in light of past experience, particularly when dealing with highly fatal mega terror attacks (like the detonating of the Pan American flight 103 over Lockerbie perpetrated under Libyan sponsorship, and the attacks in Kenya and Tanzania under Bin-Laden's command), most of the facts related to the perpetrators and their modus operandi do ultimately emerge. The confiscation of many documents and the apprehension of senior Al-Qaida members during the offensive in Afghanistan, as well as the intensive manhunt after the fleeing Al-Qaida leaders, will undoubtedly reveal the planning and implementation details related to this operation.

Despite the existing restrictions connected to the operational planning of a terror attack in the United States, it is possible to sketch a fairly clear overall picture of the preparations for the campaign and its execution. It is evident that the attacks were part of a well-planned and well-orchestrated terror strategy, which was designed and financed by the Al-Qaida command headquarters. The idea of detonating buildings with symbolic significance through the use of suicide pilots was the brainchild of Ramzi Yusuf and his comrade Murad, who had planned to crash into the CIA headquarters in Langley, and also of the members of the Algerian GIA terror cell who hijacked a French plane en route from Algeria to Marseille in December 1994 with the intention of crashing it into the Eiffel Tower in Paris.[25]

Muhammad Attef, Al-Qaida's military commander, embraced this idea, together with Khaled Sheikh, who turned it into a practical plan at the end of the nineties and supervised its execution in September 2001 (Attef was killed in the bombings of the coalition forces in Afghanistan in November 2001). The "Hamburg Group," led by the Egyptian Muhammad Atta, was deemed by Al-Qaida headquarters to be the most suitable team to turn the diabolical idea into an operative plan.

The preparations for the attack in the United States apparently commenced in 1999, after the training of the Hamburg Group, which, upon its return to Germany, became the nuclear terror cell that served as the basis for the activity in the United States. The preparations took two years. Cell members who assembled in Hamburg starting

Figure 3.2
Recruitment Process of a Terror Cell Member Supported by Al-Qaida

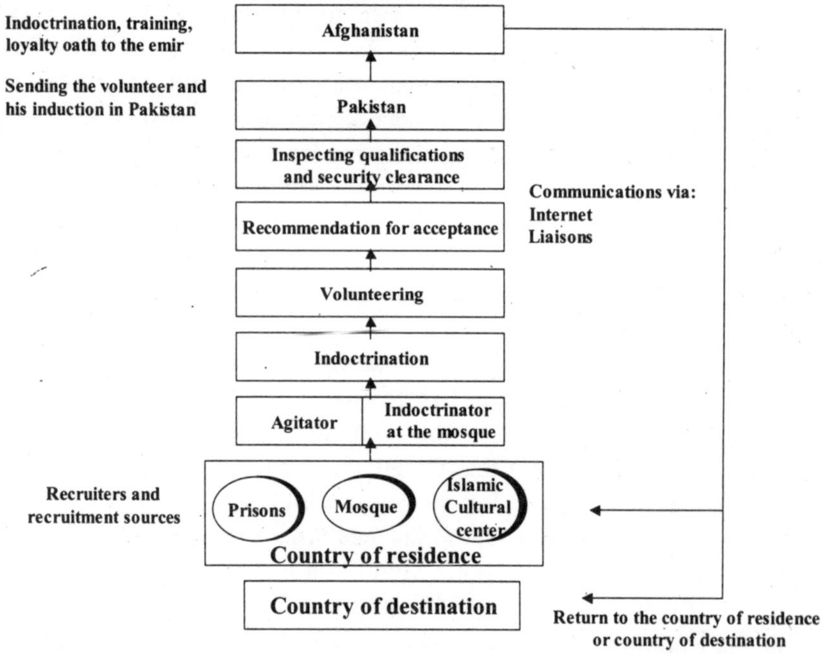

from 1997, dealt with the ideological formulation of their plans to join the Global Jihad and the boosting of their religious faith within a group of Muslim students, which was active at Hamburg's technical college and at the city's local mosque.

Hamburg, which is located in northern Germany, was chosen to serve as the base point for the preparations prior to departure for the country of destination, the United States. The "Hamburg Group" was recruited from among the worshippers at the "Al-Quds" mosque in Hamburg, which, like other central mosques located in various capitals throughout Europe, served as an enlistment site for Muslim youths with radical leanings in order to mobilize and send them for training to Afghanistan, in preparation for an active role in the Global Jihad.

The nuclear cell of the Hamburg Group included six activists, some of whom studied at the technical college in the city. All of them lived in one apartment house in Hamburg; some even shared the same apartment.[26] Three of the six cell members ultimately took part in the suicide operation and actually piloted three of the four hijacked airplanes. The three other members of the cell served as collaborators, as two of them, who were apparently supposed to be part of the group of suicide pilots, were refused entry visas to the United States. This fact induced the attack planners to expand the circle of pilots and to use one pilot who was not initially a member of the Hamburg Group. The three collaborators left Germany for Pakistan about a week before D-day, and from there continued on to Afghanistan where all traces of them were lost. All three are fugitives from justice.

The second group to take part in the attack in the United States was based on the "Saudi Group," which contained sixteen activists (fifteen of whom were of Saudi origins). Their training was conducted separately from the German Group. The two groups were strictly compartmentalized and neither was aware of the existence of the other. The role of the Saudi Group (with the exception of the pilot Hanjur), was to serve as "musclemen" and the bodyguards of the hijacking pilots during the mission. The Saudi Group, whose members were aged 20-29, was completely compartmentalized from the objectives of the assault, and its exact details were provided (it is not clear if this applies to all of them or what the level of information was) only immediately before its execution.[27] Nevertheless, it appears that at least some of the members, although not all of them, knew about and consented to take part in the suicide mission on behalf of the Global Jihad.[28]

The Hamburg Group

Muhammad Atta. Muhammad Atta was the thirty-three-year-old leader of the German Group. Born in Kafar A-Sheikh in Egypt's Nile Valley, he grew up in an educated and prosperous family. His father was a lawyer and two of his sisters had successful academic careers, one as a doctor and the other as a professor of zoology.

Atta arrived in Hamburg, Germany in 1992 to pursue a master's degree in architecture. He had a BA degree from Cairo University and studied at Hamburg University until 1999, when he submitted his final project and completed his studies with honors. During the period of his studies, Atta traveled abroad several times. On one of his trips, he returned to his country of origin for several months. It was apparently then that he became involved with Fundamentalist Egyptian elements that influenced his way of thinking. It became

Figure 3.3
The Hamburg Cell

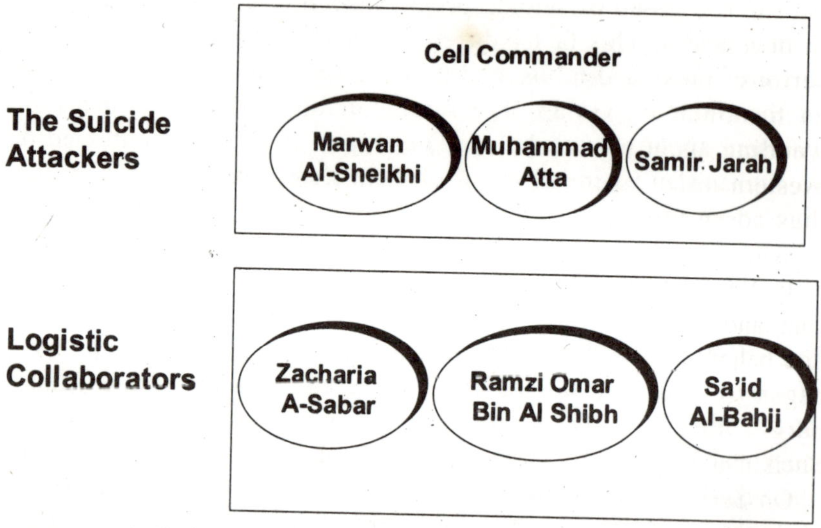

evident upon his return to Germany that a drastic change had taken place, which expressed itself in his lifestyle, clothing and speech. He began to lead an observant Islamic life and visited the El-Aksa mosque in Hamburg, which served as a hothouse for radical Islamic elements in Germany. Atta asked the University's board to allow him and his friends to lead a religious lifestyle on campus as well. The introverted loner Atta gradually but inevitably became an extreme Fundamentalist who embraced the militant jihad route and became the leader of a terror group.[29]

The period of training in 1998 in Afghanistan changed Atta from a quiet, reserved, introverted, and serious young man (although a highly argumentative one who was irritated when his opinions were ignored) into a charismatic leader and the commander of a terror cell that caused mass killings in the name of religion.[30]

Ziad Jarah. In contrast to Atta, Ziad Jarah, a twenty-six-year-old man from Lebanon, was an open, extroverted, friendly playboy. Jarah arrived in Germany in 1996, studied German in the city of Bonn, and a year later registered for aeronautical engineering classes in Hamburg. During that year he joined Atta's group. According to Jarah's cousin Salim, who also lived in Germany, Ziad came from a respectable family and knew that his home in Lebanon offered him a promising and safe future. Ziad preferred disco dancing and alcoholic beverages to women in veils.[31] In Bonn he met a medical student of Turkish origin, fell in love with her and lived with her without the benefit of marriage vows, in contrast to customary practice in devout Muslim society. The relationship between the two was serious, and they were apparently compatible and in love with each other. Jarah visited Lebanon and participated in a family wedding. At the wedding, he was seen dancing with women in Western dress and appeared to be acting completely in character, thus adeptly disguising his enlistment to Al-Qaida and his future mission.[32]

In 1998, he traveled with Atta and Marwan Al-Sheikhi to Afghanistan, and upon their return a major change was evident in his lifestyle and behavior. He started to grow a beard and pray in his room. He began to spend most of his time at the Al-Kuds mosque in Hamburg, together with his travel companions Atta and Marwan Al-Sheikhi, and at the same time cut himself off from his German friends.

On September 10, a short time before setting out on his journey of death, he sent a farewell letter to his Turkish fiancée, in which he stated that he would not return from the United States, and that she should take pride in his deeds. His message averred that he did what needed to be done, this is true honor, and she would ultimately see that everyone would rejoice.[33]

Marwan Al-Sheikhi. Born in the United Arab Emirates, Marwan Al-Sheikhi was the son of a local imam. He spent his childhood as a devout Muslim. His father, whom he adored and to whom he was very attached, died when he was a teenager. Two years after his father's death, he severed all ties with his family and at the age of eighteen moved to Germany to pursue his studies. The army of the Emirates covered his tuition. His landlady described him as a cheerful and calm young man who was popular and participated in social activities with his German friends. He moved from Bonn to Hamburg, apparently in 1997, and from there his leap to membership in the terror cell was short. The impressionable, young Al-Sheikhi was bowled over by Muhammad Atta, whom he regarded as an older brother figure and yearned for his leadership. An expression of this relationship can be found in a description provided by one of the participants in the flight course attended by Atta and Marwan Al-Sheikhi. They were depicted as constantly in each other's company, and Al-Sheikhi's behavior near Atta was compared to that of a student near his mentor.[34]

Figure 3.4
The Four Suicide Pilots

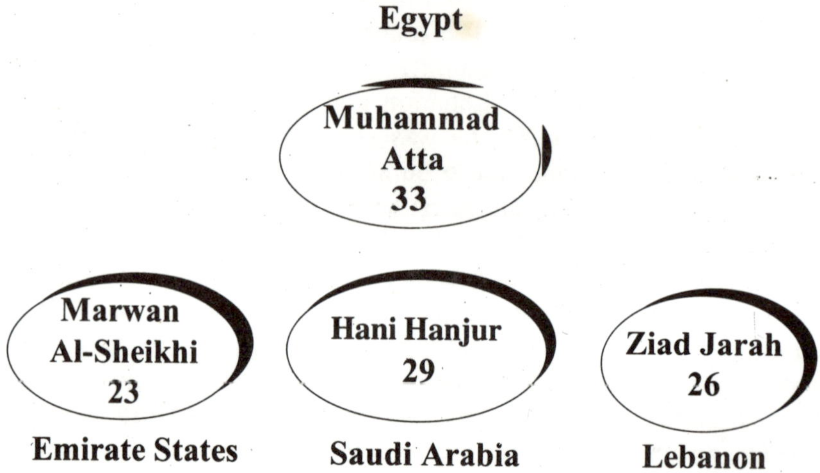

The Logistic Assistants

Sa'id Al-Bahaji. Twenty-six-year-old Sa'id Al-Bahaji was a German citizen and son to a Moroccan father and a German mother. When he was a boy, his family returned to Morocco. At the age of twenty, he returned to Germany where he studied electrical and electronic engineering. Bahaji, who was married and father to a six-month-old baby, fled Germany about a week before the attack on Turkish Airlines flight 1056 from Hamburg via Istanbul to Karachi. From there he continued on to Kuwita near the Afghanistan border and disappeared on September 9. Bahaji sent an e-mail to his wife from Pakistan to tell her that he had arrived safely and that he was well.[35]

Ramzi Bin Al-Shibh. A student of Yemenite origin, Al-Shibh was apparently the most dominant and important individual among the group of collaborators. He was supposed to be a member of the group of suicide pilots but all his attempts to obtain a visa and be accepted to the flight school in Venice, Florida, at the recommendation of his friend Muhammad Atta, failed.[36] Al-Shibh played an active logistical role and served as a channel for the transfer of funds to Atta and Zakaria Musawi, who is also suspected of attending flight lessons in Minnesota (where he was arrested in August 2001 in connection with a terror attack in the air). Al-Shibh was also affiliated with another suicide group that intended to perpetrate additional mega attacks against the United States.[37] Al-Shibh was eventually arrested in Karachi on September 11, 2002, with other Al-Qaida members. His arrest was one of the most significant achievements of the pursuit of Al-Qaida members and his interrogation will undoubtedly shed light on the preparatory period prior to the attacks.

Zakaria A-Saber. According to reports, Zakaria A-Saber (a twenty-four-year-old man of Moroccan origin) was also supposed to take part in the operation as a suicide pilot. He intended to attend flight school in Florida during February 2000 when Atta and Al-Sheikhi were there, but his request for a U.S. visa was turned down. His photographs with the Hamburg Group were found when the German security forces confiscated the video film of the wedding of his friend Sa'id Al-Bahaji. A-Saber fled from Germany to Pakistan with his two friends, Al-Shibh and Al-Bahaji, about a week prior to the terror attack in the United States.[38] Al-Shibh was arrested in September 2002 in Pakistan.

Other Activists Suspected of Connections with the Hamburg Terror Cell

Muhammad Haider Zamar. A forty-one-year-old German citizen of Syrian origin, Zamar has resided in Germany since the age of ten. He is suspected of recruiting Atta and assisting the Hamburg cell, although he initially denied these allegations. Zamar was a regular visitor at Atta's apartment in Hamburg and is considered an advocator of jihad. Despite the suspicions against him, no legal grounds were found for his arrest. In October, Zamar traveled from Germany to Morocco, where he was arrested, apparently at the request of the United States government, and was extradited to Syria. In his interrogation in Syria, he confessed to being the recruiter of Atta and his group within the Al-Qaida ranks.[39] It was also discovered that Zamar is a cousin of Khaled Al-Midhar's wife. Al-Midhar was one of the hijackers of the plane that rammed into the Pentagon.[40]

Munir Al-Mutasadek. German authorities suspect Munir Al-Mutasadek, twenty-seven, of serving as logistical coordinator for the Hamburg Group. He spent much of his time with Muhammad Atta and Marwan Al-Sheikhi, and was a witness to Muhammad Atta's will in 1996. He also had power of attorney for Atta's bank account and had a joint bank account with A-Sheikhi. Large sums of cash were transferred from this account to the United States between the months of May and November 2000, and it is probable that part of the money was used to finance Marwan Al-Sheikhi's stay and flight lessons in the United States. In an interview with Mutasadek in October 2001, he defined his relationship with Atta as an ordinary friendship, and his assistance as the routine aid one Muslim offers to another. He denied the allegations regarding the transfer of funds as well as the charges that he was involved in his friends' terror activities.[41]

Zakaria Musawi. Although Musawi was not linked to the Hamburg group, he is suspected of being the twentieth suicide terrorist, who was supposed to make up the missing number in the four-member cell that hijacked the American Airlines plane that crashed in Pennsylvania. Musawi was arrested in Minnesota in August 2001, about three weeks prior to the big attack, due to his suspicious behavior during a flight course. It appears that he demonstrated great interest in flying and even greater interest in maneuvering aircraft in the air, but showed no interest in landing them. The claim that he was the twentieth suicide pilot in the hijackers' teams has not yet been proven. There is no doubt that Musawi was connected to radical elements in Britain and France, who, in turn, were linked with Al-Qaida, and that he underwent training in Bin-Laden's camps. During his trial he admitted to his membership in Al-Qaida.

Musawi was born in southwest France in 1968 to a family of Moroccan origin. In 1981, his family moved to the city of Ninbonne. Musawi began studying business administration in Montpelier, but in 1993 he left his university studies and moved to London, where he prayed at the mosque in Brinkstone. He began to embrace a devout Islamic lifestyle, which expressed itself in his clothing and manner of speech. He started spending his time in radical Islamic circles, which gravitated around Abu-Katada, one of the most extreme and venomous Islamic leaders in England. His relatives reported that during the seven years he spent in London he visited Turkey, Pakistan and Afghanistan. In February 2001, he arrived in Oklahoma in order to train as a pilot. On August 17, 2001, a little less than a month before the attack, Musawi was arrested by FBI agents due to his strange behavior and exaggerated interest in tilting the aircraft and his lack of interest in takeoff and landing.[42]

The Financing

The cost of the most destructive mega attack in the history of international terrorism is yet unknown. Various figures have been thrown out, ranging between $250,000[43] and $500,000, which appears to be more accurate.[44] The calculation of expenses includes the cost of the many flights (some First Class) that the cell members took during the preparation period in order to gather information in Europe, the United States and Afghanistan, their living expenses in Europe (the students and the others did not work), the flight courses for the suicide pilots, and other related expenses.

The financial mastermind representing Al-Qaida headquarters who was responsible for financing the operation was Al Khazawi, a Saudi Arabian citizen, known as the organization's senior financial director. Investigators of the September 11 attack claim they have proof of money transfers between Al Khazawi and Muhammad Atta. This fact provides additional proof that Atta was indeed the commander of the network and its central axis in managing and commanding the hijacking operation, although he was not the only person to receive funds in his account. Financing was transferred to the hijackers from banks in the Persian Gulf, mainly the United Arab Emirates' Council and from Pakistan.[45] On the day of the attack, September 11, Al Khazawi left the United Emirates for Pakistan and continued on to Afghanistan. He was arrested along with Khaled Sheikh Muhammad in Pakistan in March 2003. His apprehension would undoubtedly facilitate a deeper understanding of the preparations for the attack.[46]

It also became evident that several of the hijackers transferred some $10,000 back from their accounts into Ahmed's account hours before boarding the death flights.[47] The return of funds to Al-Qaida testifies to the great personal discipline, orderliness, and duty of the Muslim suicide attacker to "cleanse" himself of any debt in this world, so that he will be pure when he meets his maker in Paradise.

Another person suspected of regularly transferring funds to the Hamburg Group is Mamoun Derkzaneli, a businessman of Syrian origin, who is believed to have served as a channel through which the cell's activities were financed. Derkzaneli represented Mamduah Salem, a businessman who served as Bin-Laden's financial advisor, and was arrested in Germany in October 1998. Salem was extradited subsequently to the United States for trial.[48]

Claiming Responsibility for the Mega Attack in the United States

The question regarding who is truly responsible for the terror attack on the United States, and whether damning evidence exists against the main suspect, Bin-Laden, engaged the international media for a long time after the attack. The media controversy revolved around the existence of concrete legal evidence pointing to Bin-Laden's direct responsibility for the attack. On his part, Bin-Laden maintained silence during the first days after the attack, and enjoyed the media exposure and powerful image accredited to his capabilities and worldview by world media, although he had not claimed credit for the operation.

The obscurity surrounding the identity of the perpetrators, including in mega and lethal terror attacks, is not a new phenomenon in the annals of modern terrorism. Terror organizations' refraining from claiming credit (particularly in their patron countries) under the organization's real name is fairly common. The organizations generally claim credit under "borrowed" names, which clearly allude to their true identity, ideas and motivation. For example, the Lebanese terror organization Hizballah, that has perpetrated many international mega attacks, took responsibility for the kidnapping of hostages and hijacking of aircraft under the names of "The Organization of the Oppressed on Earth" and "The Lebanese Islamic Jihad." The Abu-Nidal Palestinian terror organization, the most murderous terror movement during the eighties, claimed responsibility under various names including "Fatah—Revolutionary Council" and "The Arab Socialist Revolutionary Army." Arafat's Fatah organization "camouflaged" itself when carrying out infamous attacks in the international arena under the name "Black September," while Al-Qaida adopted the name "The Organization for the Liberation of the Holy Sites."

Cover names enable terror organizations to perpetrate their deadly mega attacks without assuming incriminating responsibility, and to deny that their organization was involved or that they initiated the operation, while still enabling them to bask in the glory of their heinous deeds. Most readers or TV audiences are aware that the attacks were carried out by certain organizations, and their involvement is certainly clear to the target audiences among their supporters.[49]

Bin-Laden and his men also maintained ambiguity for almost two months vis-à-vis their responsibility for the U.S. attacks. On the one hand, they expressed their support for the perpetrators' "noble deed of sacrifice" and their enthusiasm for the blow dealt to their American adversaries, while on the other hand refrained from claiming clear-cut responsibility. Upon the commencement of the American offensive, Al-Qaida spokesmen began dropping hints regarding their responsibility, but even in these instances they did so in such a way that would enable them to deny any clear responsibility for the attack if and when they were put on trial. For example, in the video featuring the Al-Qaida spokesman Sliman Abu Al-Eit (Al Gheit), he confessed, "We carried out Allah's wish...we implemented and executed what Allah taught us, to support the oppressed and strike fear in the hearts of the infidels, and this we did...we responded to the cry of the oppressed in Palestine and the oppressed in Chechnya, and the cry of the oppressed everywhere...we succeeded in dealing a mortal blow to the chief infidel."[50] The incrimination of Al-Qaida is clear, but in the future he could claim that "we" refers to the broader "Islamic" sense of the word.

Even the videotape shot when Bin-Laden hosted the Saudi sheikh in the presence of his men, in which the two gloated about the operation's success, enables interested parties, mainly in Muslim countries, to maintain that there is no clear assuming of responsibility.[51]

The United States and the coalition countries that acted against the Taliban and Al-Qaida in Afghanistan gathered as much evidence as possible to prove that Bin-Laden's organization was responsible for the assault. When they had accumulated enough circumstantial evidence, they initiated the attack on the terror infrastructure in Afghanistan. Today it is completely clear, without an element of doubt, that the terror attack on the United States was perpetrated by a terror network, guided, trained and financed by Al-Qaida, and any attempts to deny this are doomed to fail.

The Terror Attack in the United States and the Phenomenon of Suicide Terror

The terror attack in the United States was first and foremost an operation performed by suicide terrorists. As such, it was based on the willingness of the participants to take part in a collective act of suicide. Although the Al-Qaida organization and other Islamic terror organizations that identify with the Global Jihad had already perpetrated suicide attacks beforehand, the September 11 attacks constituted a precedent from the point of view of the scope of participants and the method of operation. This capability is clearly a product of Bin-Laden's terror industry in Afghanistan, which invested considerable efforts in the development of a "reservoir" of fighters willing to carry out suicide attacks in the name of Islam. Admittedly, according to Bin-Laden, most of the participants in the operation were informed of the details of the operation just a short time before its execution,[52] but it is evident that this was based on their early preparation and willingness to take part in a suicide mission whatever the nature.

This fact is confirmed by a videotape that features Hiznawi about six months prior to the suicide attacks in which he expresses his fierce aspiration to participate in a suicide operation and die the death of a holy martyr.[53]

Despite the unprecedented and remarkable scope of the number of suicide terrorists who took part in this operation, and in spite of the unique characteristics of the attack against the United States, this must also be examined against the background of the general spreading of the suicide terror phenomenon all over the world, and the phenomenon of Muslim suicide terrorists in particular.

Historical Background

Suicide terrorists do not constitute a new phenomenon in the history of mankind.[54] Many have proven their willingness to perish when carrying out attacks on behalf of their political goals while evincing the ultimate sacrifice culminating in death of their own free will. However, the "modern" expressions of the suicide terror phenomenon surfaced with the appearance of the first suicide terrorists in Lebanon about twenty years ago. Modern suicide terror has certain unique characteristics that distinguish it from those of suicide terror in earlier periods. From the early eighties of the twentieth century, terror organizations began to carry out suicide attacks while using one or more individuals who constituted a "guided human missile." The suicide bomber carries explosives on his body or on a platform that he is driving, and out of his own conscious choice moves towards a predetermined target and executes an act of self-killing. The suicide bomber determines the site and timing of the attack, and he can navigate himself and decide on the spot, in keeping with the surrounding environment and circumstances of the execution of the attack so that it will cause maximum damage to the chosen target.

Therefore, a "modern suicide terror attack" can be defined as "a violent, politically motivated action executed consciously, actively and with prior intent by a single individual (or individuals) who kills himself in the course of the operation together with his chosen target. The guaranteed and preplanned death of the perpetrator is a prerequisite for the operation's success."[55]

The choice of the suicide weapon as an instrument in the hands of the terrorists derives from the fact that it is available and "cheap," and the damage caused to the morale of the rival population is grave. A suicide attack, like all other terror attacks in the modern era, is meant to magnify "a powerful self-image."

Suicide attacks in the modern era began in Lebanon in 1983, at the instigation of the Lebanese-Shiite terror organization, Hizballah. During the eighties, Lebanon served as a central arena for the development of the suicide attack method. These attacks continued into the nineties, but with less frequency. Today suicide attacks in Lebanon are rare. A total of about fifty terror attacks were carried out in Lebanon by six organizations. About half of the suicide attacks were perpetrated by Hizballah and Amal (a Lebanese Shiite organization) and the rest were executed by secular organizations, some communist and others nationalist, including the Lebanese Communist Party, the Socialist Nazarist Organization, the PPS—"The Syrian Social Nationalist Party."[56]

The use of suicide attackers stimulated considerable prestige for the Hizballah and turned it into a symbol of sacrifice and a source of inspiration for terror organizations worldwide, such as the movements in Sri Lanka, Turkey, Egypt, Chechnya and more, that adopted and even "refined" the suicide attacks.

Among organizations in the world that adopted this method, the most prominent is the isolationist Tamil organization, The Tamil Tigers (LTTE), which is involved in a struggle for independence of the Tamil minority from the Singhalese majority. This organization began perpetrating terror attacks in 1987, and since then has initiated terror attacks carried out by over 200 suicide attackers; in several of the incidents, more than one suicide terrorist participated in the attacks. These attacks were particularly vicious and caused many hundreds of deaths. This organization, which focused its suicide attacks on senior leaders in Sri Lanka's political and military establishment, is the only one in the world to succeed in assassinating two heads of state. The first, former prime minister of India, Rajiv Gandhi, who at that time was involved in a reelection campaign in Madras, was assassinated in an attack that claimed the lives of a total of eighteen people (May 21, 1991); and the second, Sri Lanka

President Primadasa was assassinated in an attack in which twenty-two additional victims met their deaths (May 1993). On December 17, 1999 the organization made an assassination attempt against Sri Lanka's President Chandrika Kumaratunga, via a female suicide terrorist who detonated herself at the president's front door. The president lost one eye in the attack, but survived.

The organization also acted against politicians affiliated with the Singhalese majority as well as pragmatic politicians from the Tamil minority, senior military personnel, boats, command headquarters and economic facilities such as oil centers. In the attacks, the LTTE demonstrated indifference to the killing of innocent bystanders and had no compassion for anyone who happened to be in the vicinity of their target. The main motivating factors behind the Tamil suicide attackers were an aspiration for national independence, blind obedience to the charismatic leadership of the organization's leader Prabhakaran, and strong peer and social pressures.

The Palestinian terror organizations, the Hamas and the Palestinian Islamic Jihad, adopted suicide attacks at the inspiration and active support of the Hizballah as well as Iran. Palestinian terrorists began perpetrating terror attacks in 1993. Between 1993 and March 2000 they executed about forty attacks. Since the incitement of violence in September 2000 by the Palestinian Authority, dubbed the Intifadat al Aksa, over eighty suicide terror attacks have been perpetrated.

Statistics released by Israeli officials at the end of September 2002 indicate that, according to the daily newspaper *Ha'aretz* (September 29, 2002), since 1993, 206 perpetrators were sent to carry out suicide attacks; sixty-one of them in the first intifada and 145 in the Intifadat al Aksa. Fifty-two were affiliated with the Hamas, thirty-five were from the Palestinian Islamic Jihad, and forty were Fatah members. Five were from The Popular Front for the Liberation of Palestine (P.F.L.P) and thirteen others were from other organizations or were unaffiliated. Close to fifty-five suicide bombers were arrested in Israel.

The number of suicide terrorists is higher than the actual count of attacks because more than one suicide terrorist participated in some of the attacks. (This number does not take into account dozens of attacks involving "self sacrifice" through shootings and lobbing grenades, acts that are not included in our definition of suicide attacks although the perpetrators published their wills and planned to die during the attack.)[57]

For the main part, these activities were carried out by the "religious" Palestinian terror organizations such as the Hamas and the Islamic Jihad. During the past year, "secular" terror organizations like the Fatah/Tanzim have begun to take part in this type of activity under the cover name of "The Martyrs of Al-Aksa" and the "Popular Front for the Liberation of Palestine." Worthy of mention is the fact that in the last year four female Palestinians participated in terror attacks, and several more women were apprehended while planning an attack or on their way to one. All of these women were affiliated with the Fatah's Tanzim/The Martyrs of Al-Aksa.

Another secular organization that perpetrated suicide attacks in Turkey is the Marxist, Isolationist Kurd PKK, though its members are Muslims. The organization was active mainly during the years 1996-99 and carried out sixteen suicide attacks, which caused about twenty casualties and scores of wounded victims.[58] PKK's suicide campaign did not induce the Turkish government to allow a Kurdish autonomy. The PKK suicide operations of male and female terrorists were carried out under the command and inspiration of the charismatic and central leader Oçelan, who was perceived by the members of his organization as a "sun onto the nations." Following his arrest and the death sentence passed in 1999, the suicide attacks of his members ceased. A member of a left-wing Turkish terror organization carried out a suicide attack in 2002 in protest against the treatment of her friends in prison.

Egyptian organizations, the Al Gama'a al Islamiya and the Egyptian Islamic Jihad, which were affiliated with Bin-Laden's "Islamic Front," carried out two suicide attacks, in Croatia (October 1995) and in the Egyptian Embassy in Karachi, Pakistan (November 1995).

Under Bin-Laden's direct command, Al-Qaida has carried out three suicide attacks to date and has been involved in the perpetration of eight additional attacks. Suicide drivers who detonated car bombs in Kenya and Tanzania (September 7, 1998), killing 214 and wounding 5,000, carried out the first attack. The second attack was against the *USS Cole* at the Aden port (October 12, 2000) in which seventeen American sailors were killed and thirty-five wounded. The terror attacks perpetrated in the United States on September 11, 2001, obviously constituted the apex of suicide attack operations in the annals of terror in general, and suicide terrorism, in particular.

Eight additional suicide operations[59] carried out by terror cells supported by Al-Qaida were:

1. The assassination of Massoud Sh'ah, leader of the "Northern Alliance" in Afghanistan, which presented the main opposition to the Taliban regime in Afghanistan. Sh'ah was terminated two days before the terror attack in the United States by a team that was apparently affiliated with the Algerian GSPC (the Salafi Group for Propaganda and Combat), acting according to the instructions of the Al-Qaida headquarters. The attack was meant to neutralize the Taliban's main adversary prior to perpetration of the terror attack in the United States. It was carried out by two terrorists masquerading as press photographers who asked to interview Sh'ah. One of the two detonated himself, killing Sh'ah in the process, and the second was terminated by Sh'ah's bodyguards.

2. The attempt by Richard Reed to cause an explosion on the American Airlines flight from Paris to Miami on December 22, 2001. Reed had placed explosive in his shoes (see elaboration in the section dealing with the activity of Bin-Laden's terror networks).

3. The detonation of the oil tanker near the synagogue in Djerba, Tunisia, by a suicide driver, causing nineteen deaths, including thirteen German terrorists, two French nationalists and four Tunisians who were inside or near the synagogue.

4. A suicide driver detonated his car and hit a bus driving foreign workers to the Karachi shipyards. The death toll was fourteen, including eleven French workers.

5. An attack by suicide terrorists who rammed a boat into a French oil tanker near Yemen on October 6, 2002.

6. A combined attack, which included a suicide bomber in a tourist resort area in Bali, Indonesia, was carried out by a cell of the Jama'a al Islamiya and resulted almost 200 fatalities, most of them tourists.

7. An armed attack on the theater in Moscow led to a barricade and hostage situation with 650 hostages. The Chechen perpetrators wore explosive belts and threatened to blow themselves up and the entire building with the hostages if their demands were not met. During the rescue operation most of the terrorists were killed and about 120 hostages died.

8. A combined attack in Mombassa, Kenya, against Israeli targets included a suicide car bomb against an Israeli-owned hotel, and resulted in thirteen fatalities.

In recent years, the circle of suicide attackers has been expanded by Chechen and Indian terrorists. The Chechen organizations executed over twelve suicide attacks starting from the year 2000, while the Indian organizations carried out three suicide attacks in car bombs driven by suicide bombers, and at least one more attack as part of the joint assault of the Jeish Muhammad and Lashkar e-Toiba organizations on the Indian Parliament in December 2001.

The phenomenon of suicide attacks is inspired by a wide range of motives both on the organizational and on individual levels. As a rule, it is possible to state that the Islamic Fundamentalist terror organizations such as the Shiite Hizballah or the Hamas, the Palestinian Islamic Jihad, the Jama'a al Islamiya, the Sunni Egyptian Islamic Jihad and Al-Qaida motivate their people to carry out these attacks mainly "in the name of God" and in a religious-cultural context, which includes the promise of eternal life in heaven for the perpetrators. The members of the secular organizations, such as the Tamil Tigers, the Turkish PKK and the Lebanese PPS were motivated to commit suicide mainly due to the autocratic and centralized leadership and personality of the organization's leader who is perceived by the members as a sort of "secular deity." A strong component in these groups is the nationalist motive and the sensation of group pressure and unity, which often surfaces among members of the religious organizations.

Suicide Terror Characteristics

General Characteristics of Suicide Attacks Worldwide:

- Are aimed at terrifying a far larger group than the target audience.
- Are a central part of the terror organizations' psychological warfare.
- Preparation for a suicide attack always involves more than one person.
- A wide geographical dispersal of the suicide terror activity.
- Suicide terror extends to both "religious" and "secular" individuals.
- An involvement of both men and women.
- A wide range of motives for suicide attacks (in the name of "God," "nationality," the "leader," the "group," and "peer pressure," and also in the name of "revenge" and "deterrence."
- There is no single profile of a suicide terrorist.

An Analysis of the General Characteristics of the Suicide Team in the United States

Firstly, it is important to note that the suicide group that perpetrated the terror attack in the United States was made up of several teams that acted independently of each other and apparently underwent separate integration processes without any contact between them, under the supervision of the Afghanistan headquarters.[60] Also noteworthy is the fact that we have far greater information about the Hamburg Group suicide members, which acted as a separate unit and bonded around the dominant personality of Muhammad Atta, the Egyptian who was the oldest member of the group and was chosen by Al-Qaida to command the entire mission.

Most of the details that we have about the preparations of the group are based on written or filmed wills of several of the participants, the testimony of the acquaintances of the suicide attackers, and information revealed in the media as a result of journalistic investigation. Also worthy of mention is the fact that there is limited information regarding the biographical details of most of the hijackers, particularly those who were affiliated with the Saudi Group. The age range of the suicide attackers in the United States was between twenty and thirty-three.

The suicide attackers from the Hamburg Group were students, educated individuals from prosperous families, who had lived in the West for several years and appeared to have a promising future. It is clear that the participants differed from each other from a personal aspect as well as from the point of view of background. The Saudi Group was made up of fifteen young men, some of them in their early twenties, and it, too, was not a homogeneous group.

The suicide attackers in the Hamburg Group shared an apartment and a residential building for a long period of time and acted jointly as a separate, cohesive group that trained itself for the attack from the operational aspect, and apparently focused on mental preparations including the embracing of a religious Islamic lifestyle: joint prayers at the local mosque, in their apartment and at the university, and mutual support. This characteristic of mutual influence among suicide attackers is also evident among suicide attackers in Israel, for example, when three Hamas members sharing an apartment carried out suicide attacks one after the other.

It is reasonable to assume that the significant difference in age between the Egyptian Muhammad Atta, head of the Hamburg Group on the one hand, and the twenty-three-year old Marwan Al-Sheikhi and twenty-six-year old Ziad Jarah on the other, aided Atta in leading his team members along the route he had navigated, thanks to his dominant personality and the support he received from the Al-Qaida headquarters in Afghanistan.

Stages in the Preparation of a Suicide Attacker:

- Identification
- Recruitment
- Persuasion to commit suicide
- Mental preparation and "maintenance"
- Training regarding the operation of the explosive charge
- Final preparations (prayer, purification, returning debts, preparation of a written or videotaped will [in secular organizations: sometimes a photograph with the "leader" or a "final meal"]).
- Arrival at the attack site, usually under escort.
- Claiming responsibility by the organization accompanied by propaganda activity.

The Mental Preparation of the Suiciders Immediately before the Attack

Part of the solution to the riddle of how the hijackers were persuaded to take part in the suicide attack is to be found, at least at this stage, in letters found in the bags of three of the nineteen suicide attackers (two from the German Group and one from the Saudi group) on three different airplanes and on a video, in which Saudi Arabian Al-Haznawi reads out his will on film six months prior to the attack. One of the letters was found in the luggage of Muhammad Atta, which was not loaded on the airplane. Similar letters were found at the crash site of United Airlines flight 93 in Pennsylvania and in the luggage of Nawaf Al-Hamzi, who participated in the hijacking of American Airlines flight 77 that rammed the Pentagon. The letters clearly indicate that the hijackers, and certainly the cell leaders and apparently others, were issued detailed guidelines in writing and perhaps orally as well, regarding how to prepare for a suicide operation and how to behave during the attack. In these letters, the suicide attackers asked God to forgive them their transgressions and requested permission to glorify His name in any way possible. The letters specified the exact behavior expected of them the night before their deaths. The hijackers were commanded to engage themselves in prayer, fasting and seeking God's direction, and to continue reading the Koran and purifying themselves in anticipation of their ascent to heaven and meeting their maker.

The suicide attackers were instructed to remain calm, to refrain from showing tension and to internalize the fact that they were going to a better and happier place, and that the life awaiting them after their physical death was eternal life in the Garden of Eden. They were told to draw inspiration from their situations, because if they knew the reward awaiting them after death they would request to die on their own, because the Garden of Eden, which has become even more beautiful in anticipation of their arrival, awaits them...[61]

In addition to the mental preparation, letters included practical instructions regarding reparations for the attack from the operational point of view. For example, they were instructed to prepare the necessary equipment for the mission, to verify that they were not under surveillance, that their box cutters were sharp and that they had their passports on them. The letters included instructions regarding their behavior when boarding the plane, including reciting a prayer to the Prophet Muhammad and to Allah so that they might illuminate their way.[62]

From the video aired on Al-Jazeera in April 2002, in which Haznawi (who, as already noted, participated in the hijacking of the airplane that crashed in Pennsylvania) is taped, it is possible to glean his perception of the act of suicide as an expression of God's will and his envisioning of his role and duty to die in order to promote the world Islamic system and realize God's commandments.[63]

Is There a Profile for Suicide Attackers?

As a rule, suicide terror is a dynamic, broad and growing phenomenon in which various nationalities are involved, and it occurs on various continents and in a wide range of contexts: cultural, social and religious. It is particularly difficult to assess if there is a common denominator among those individuals who choose to respond to the "movement's commandment" and sacrifice their lives for an idea, regardless of whether a religious, nationalist or social principle is involved, because the majority of them did not survive to tell of their motivation, while the wills that they left behind with the sponsoring organization's assistance must be suspected of deliberate disinformation.

The large gap in the ages of the suicide attackers, which ranges from 16-17 to over 40, may possibly indicate a marked difference in the personal maturity of the various attackers. Among the attackers are uneducated individuals alongside individuals with high school educations, and students with a broad education and apparent social skills. Both sexes participate in suicide acts, men (in the Islamic organizations), and both men and women (in secular organizations).

The activity of the female suicide attackers can be explained by a wide range of motives; religion, nationality, for the group or idea's sake, and sometimes to exact revenge and deter the enemy. Male suicide attackers are often influenced by peer pressure or by the supportive public spirit of a society or group involved in a national struggle.

The religious groups often have the support of clerics with leadership or senior religious standing, who issue fatwas justifying the suicide attacks in order to realize God's will among His followers. In the secular groups, the leader, who is often conceived as a "secular deity," fills this role. The religious-cultural-traditional component of a pleasing and pure life as ascribed to the Garden of Eden in the world to come has a significant impact on all of the suicide attackers in all of the Muslim terror organizations. Among the Afghanistan alumni, the loyalty oath (the "biya") to the leader Bin-Laden is also significant in determining the willingness for self-sacrifice.

To summarize, it is likely that the concept of a profile of a suicide terrorist is too broad and varied for definition. It is possible to state that there is a row of profiles or joint characteristics shared by some of the suicide attackers in some of the groups. Even among the Al-Qaida attackers who participated in the attacks in the United States and belonged to the Muslim Fundamentalist stream of the Global Jihad, it is possible to discern several different personality profiles that were channeled within the group's melting pot, into a joint extremist mode of behavior, which led them to the act of collective suicide.

How to Contend with Suicide Terror:

- Identify typical suspicious signs (suspect stands out in the environment due to his behavior, clothing, movements and expression) that may lead to detection.
- Distance suspect from activity in a closed place.
- Create specialized training of manpower to deal with the suicide phenomenon.
- Develop a combat theory to neutralize the suicide bomber
- Develop a specific combat theory for various regions and facilities, according to the type of facility.
- Teach the public greater awareness vis-à-vis suicide attackers.
- Define behavioral procedures for the general public in the event of an incident.
- Supply appropriate communication and information activity following an incident.
- Create comprehensive and systematic international activity against the phenomenon while placing the emphasis on preventing incitement and punishing supporters, in the name of religion, for these terror attacks and those who condone them.

The Attacks of Terror Networks and Cells Affiliated with Bin-Laden's "Islamic Front"

The Terror Networks of Ramzi Yusuf

The terror network headed by Ramzi Yusuf is undoubtedly one of the most dangerous of the many terror networks established by Afghan alumni worldwide. In his activities and plans, Ramzi Yusuf epitomizes the prototype of the "new" international terrorist, one who operates an ad hoc terror network conducting mass indiscriminate killings, with the aim of achieving political gains. His extraordinary sabotage capabilities were given particularly murderous expression.

Academic researchers and writers who wrote about his activities questioned his being a religious Muslim, and some of them, particularly Laurie Mylroie[64] and Simon Reeve,[65] raised doubts in their books as to the identity of his senders.

In any case, Yusuf headed several terror cells, each with three to five members, either Afghan alumni or others, who were affiliated with radical Islamic circles and represented the agenda of Bin-Laden and his followers. Yusuf was both persuasive and charismatic enough to recruit a good number people to aid him in the realization of his plots—the planning and perpetration of terror attacks in various countries including the United States, the Philippines, Pakistan and Iran.[66]

In her profound and methodical book, *The War against America*, Laurie Mylroie raises the theory that Yusuf was activated by Iraq. Other researchers dispute this hypothesis because they regard Yusuf as an Afghan alumnus, who represented the International Islamic Front. Mylroie and Reeve underline his totally secure lifestyle and cast doubt upon his constituting a classic model of the devout Muslim terrorist like those who represented Bin-Laden's Islamic Front.

It appears that during his years of activity in the first half of the nineties, Yusuf enjoyed the logistic support of Bin-Laden's followers, which included training, financing, footing the bill for hosting in safe houses, and assistance in initiating ties. The financing of the extensive terror activities operated by Yusuf required considerable monetary resources. Yusuf, who frequently flew from place to place often via first class, and financed various people who worked for him, had large amounts of cash at his disposal. Despite the lack of clarity that still surrounds his financial sources, it appears that a great deal of it reached him via non-governmental (NGO) Islamic charities such as I.I.R.O. (The International Islamic Relief Organization), the M.W.L. (Muslim World League), and businessmen affiliated with Bin-Laden, including his brother-in-law Jamal Halifa, who had extensive business interests in the Philippines and Saudi Arabia.[67]

Ramzi Yusuf's activity paved the way for the terror attackers in the United States in 2001. His uncle, Khaled Sheikh Muhammad, who assisted him in 1995, served as the "supervisor" of the September 11 attacks in the United States.

Yusuf stood at the head of a terror organization that perpetrated the first attack on the Twin Towers in New York in 1993, which caused a partial collapse upon their occupants. In the beginning of 1995 he also planned to crash an airplane into a chosen target, which included the Pentagon or the CIA headquarters in the United States. Only his apprehension and imprisonment in February of 1995, due to information provided by one of his partners, put an end to his terrorist activities, which had wreaked death and destruction. His arrest prevented the continuation of his plot to kill thousands of people in cold blood as part of a terror campaign designated to promote the Global Jihad ideology.

The murder of Rabbi Kahana in New York. On November 5, 1990, Rabbi Meir Kahana was assassinated by Sa'id Nussair while presenting a lecture in New York. Sa'id Nussair was an Egyptian citizen who arrived in the United States as an emigrant in 1989, married an American citizen, and thus was granted American citizenship. He was part of a radical Islamic group whose members worshipped at the mosque where the blind Egyptian Sheikh Omar Abd Al-Rahman served as spiritual leader and gave his blessing to assassinate Kahana.

The assassin's ties with the group that was involved two years later in the planning and perpetration of several mega attacks in New York, including the attack on the Twin Towers in February 1993, was only discovered after the investigation of the first attack on the Twin Towers. Although Ramzi Yusuf himself was not involved in the murder of Kahana, for his activities in the United States he relied on members of the same Islamic cell.

Three of the seven men accused of perpetrating the 1993 attack on the Twin Towers had connections with Nussair. One, Mahmoud Abu Halima, even served as the driver of Nussair's getaway car; however, due to an error in identifying the waiting place for the latter, his involvement was only discovered years later.[68]

From his prison cell, Nussair continued to plan terror attacks against the judge and prosecutor in his trial, and against Jewish targets with the aid of his friends outside of prison, headed by his cousin Ibrahim Al-Grabawi.[69]

The attacks against the Twin Towers on February 26, 1993. On February 26, 1993, at 12:17 in the afternoon a car bomb loaded with over half a ton of improvised explosives (most of which was composed of uric nitrate agricultural fertilizer and nitroglycerin) detonated at the Twin Towers of the World Trade Center in New York. Yusuf added three balloons of hydrogen gas meant to magnify the power of the explosion. As part of his satanic plan he also added hydrogen cyanide and sulfuric acid. The combination of these two components creates a gas called cyanide hydrogen, which has an effect similar to that of the Zyklon-B gas used by the Nazis to exterminate Jews in the death camps during World War II.[70]

According to Yusuf's plan, the car bomb was supposed to cause the collapse of the north tower onto the south tower at the height of the business day, when the routine number of occupants is tens of thousands of people. Ramzi Yusuf told his interrogators that he had hoped to kill 250,000 people. As a result of the blast six people were killed, and 1,040 were injured, some seriously. The direct financial damage caused by the explosion was half a billion dollars. An unknown organization—until that time, the "Fifth Brigade of the Liberation Army"—claimed responsibility for the attack. All of those responsible for the attack were ultimately arrested and brought to trial, and all received long prison sentences.

Yusuf, who was known to his comrades as Rashid el Iraqi, had arrived in the United States about six months before the attack, and from that time on concentrated on the preparations, along with several collaborators.

Muhammad Salameh served as Yusuf's chief assistant and was the person who rented the car that served to move the charge three days prior to the attack, according to Yusuf's instructions. In addition, he and Yusuf rented storage space at a storage facility in New Jersey, where they kept chemical substances designated for the preparation of additional explosive charges. Salameh was arrested on March 4, 1993, when he arrived at the car rental offices to request a refund for the vehicle he had rented, claiming that it had been stolen. He had planned to use the refund to pay for a flight ticket and flee the United States.

Muhammad Abu-Halima, an Egyptian citizen who took part in the attack, fled the U.S. on a flight from New York to Saudi Arabia four days after the attack. From there he continued on to his parents' home in Egypt until he was extradited to the United States. Halima is a cousin of Sa'id Nussair, Rabbi Kahana's killer in 1990.

Nidal Iyad was involved in the purchase of chemical substances that served as the ingredients of the bomb detonated at the Twin Towers. He was arrested on March 10. Ahmad Ajaj acted as a consultant vis-à-vis the construction of the bomb. He, too, was arrested. Abd Yassin, an Iraqi citizen who collaborated with the group, was interrogated by FBI agents, but succeeded in pulling the wool over their eyes when he pretended to cooperate with them and subse-

Figure 3.5
The Terror Network of Ramzi Yusuf

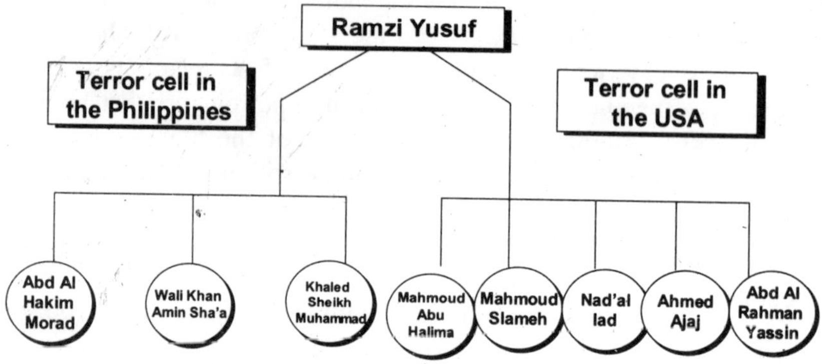

quently succeeded in escaping to Jordan, and from there to Baghdad where he remains at large.

Iyad Ismail, a Jordanian student, was the driver of the car bomb, at Yusuf's request; because of his job as a taxi driver he was well-acquainted with the streets of Manhattan.

Ramzi Yusuf himself succeeded in fleeing from the U.S. on a first class flight to Pakistan. He was carrying a passport under the name of Al-Bassit Karim. Yusuf was ultimately apprehended in February 1995 in Pakistan, due to information provided by a partner who preferred to turn him in for the $2.5 million prize that had been offered for information about his whereabouts. Yusuf stood trial in the United States where he was sentenced to two hundred and forty years of imprisonment and fined $500,000 dollars.

The arrest of an Islamic terror cell in June 1993. In June 1993, nine citizens were arrested in New York, five of whom were of Saudi origins, who belonged to the Islamic terror network active in the United States under the inspiration and permission of the blind Egyptian Sheikh Omar Abd A-Rahman. One of the detainees had served as the sheikh's personal translator. The cell's members were connected to other Islamic activists, who were involved in previous attacks, such as Rabbi Kahana's murder in 1990, and with members of Ramzi Yusuf's terror cell that perpetrated the attack on the Twin Towers in February 1993. One of his friends was the blind sheikh's driver. The cell's members were preparing a series of lethal terror attacks in the greater New York area:

1. Detonating car bombs during rush hour in the Lincoln and Holland Tunnels from the direction of New Jersey.

2. Detonating a car bomb near the UN building.

3. Detonating a bomb at the FBI headquarters.

4. Assassinating senior American politicians and foreign diplomats visiting New York.

The characteristics of Islamic terror networks exposed in the United States in 1993 were that they were made up of young Sunni Muslims originally from the Middle East countries, mostly in their twenties or thirties, some of them Afghan alumni. The cell's members were recruited among the members of the mosque where the Egyptian sheikh ("The Blind Sheikh") served as the main instigator. They were influenced by his militant sermons in which he called for the death of the infidels, enemies of Islam, headed by the Americans. The cell's members acted to realize their mentor's commands through concrete planning to perpetrate a mega terror campaign in the United States. Some of the activists had formal education in the area of chemical and electronics engineering, and they took advantage of this knowledge to put together the bombs that they used.

The activity of Ramzi Yusuf's terror cell in the Philippines. After fleeing the United States and heading for Pakistan, Yusuf apparently moved to Iran where he was suspected of aiding the "Mujahidin Khalk" in perpetrating an attack on the mosque named after the Imam Rizah in Mashed. The blast caused the death of twenty-six worshippers. At the end of 1994 he moved to the Philippines in order to realize his ultimate terror system, which would further glorify his reputation as the man who had succeeded in bombing the Twin Towers, the symbol of American capitalism. Yusuf's choice of the Philippines for his new site of activity was based on his earlier ties with the place and on his acquaintance with activists in the Abu-Sayyaf terror organization, many of whom were Afghan alumni like him. In addition, he agreed to requests made by elements who were affiliated with Bin-Laden's men to train members of Abu-Sayyaf in the specialized sabotage areas in which he was an expert in order to hone their skills and prepare them to participate in the Global Jihad.[71]

Yusuf was also asked by Bin-Laden's emissaries to assassinate President Clinton during his trip to Manila in November 1994, but due to stringent security measures and difficulty in carrying out the mission, Yusuf was forced to relinquish the idea in favor of a far more attractive and murderous terror campaign.[72] This plan would dwarf even the bombing of the Twin Towers and was dubbed the "Bojinka Operation" (in Serbo-Croatian the word means "bomb"). This plan included the assassination of Pope John Paul II during his visit to Manila in mid-January 1995, and the detonation of about a dozen United States commercial airliners in the air within a short period of time. The pope's assassination was aimed to shock the entire Christian world, and the campaign against civil aviation was to cause the deaths of thousands of people, thus dealing a death-blow to the aviation industry and the American economy, and causing tremendous anxiety and chaos all over the world. In order to realize this plan, as was his wont, Yusuf enlisted several collaborators, five of whom were to take an active part in detonating the airplanes, including his childhood friend Wali Khan Amin Shah and Abd Al-Hakim Murad.

To facilitate his plan to assassinate the pope, Yusuf rented an apartment with a view of the route that the pope would follow during his tour of Manila, with the intention of firing a missile at his car. To realize his main plot against American airliners, Yusuf began a series of trial attempts to detonate small bombs "on the ground." On December 1, 1994, he gave Wali Khan Shah a bomb and instructed him to plant it at the Greenbelt movie theater in Manila (the bomb that exploded as scheduled caused minor damage but proved to Yusuf that he was on the right course and that he could move on to the next stage and test the plan to smuggle explosives onto airplanes and detonate them). Yusuf chose to perpetrate the "model attack" against a flight of the Philippine Airline PAL. For this purpose, he purchased a ticket under an Italian passport and the name Armaldo Forlani. Yusuf boarded the plane with the camouflaged components of the bomb. During the flight, Yusuf went to the aircraft's bathroom, where he quickly assembled the bomb, returned to his seat and concealed the compact charge inside the pillow cover belt under his seat. He disembarked at a stopover in the city Sabo and the airplane continued on its route to Narita Airport in Tokyo. Two hours after its departure from Sabo the bomb detonated at a height of 10,000 feet over the Minami Island in Okinawa Prefecture, killing Haruki Ikegami, a twenty-four-year-old Japanese engineer who was sitting in Yusuf's seat, and seriously injuring five other passengers. Fortunately, the pilot succeeded in landing the aircraft safely at the Naha Airport in Okinawa, thus saving the lives of 272 passengers and 20 crewmembers.[73]

Yusuf again succeeded in evading the law and after a short period of time returned to Manila in order to continue pursuing his murderous plans. He was pleased with his trial run. The attack on the PAL airplane had proved the effectiveness of his action plan, his ability to smuggle bomb components onto the aircraft, assemble them quickly and escape at a stopover. He decided to adhere to his plan of action, but at the same time decided to improve the quality of the explosive. For this purpose, he acquired the blueprint of the Boeing 747 aircraft, made calculations, and found the optimal location for planting a bomb, which is at the seat over the main fuel tank near the aircraft's wing, so that the initial explosion and the fire would ensure the complete destruction of the plane in the air.[74]

In the beginning of January 1995, Yusuf and his partner Wali Khan concentrated on purchasing the materials and mixing the substances to prepare the bombs. On January 6, there was a malfunction and a fire broke out their safe house. They were forced to evacuate the apartment when neighbors summoned the police.

When the police entered the apartment they were greeted by the sight of a laboratory for the production of sophisticated bombs. The real treasure was Ramzi Yusuf's laptop computer, which contained many details about several terror attacks that he had in the pipeline, particularly the air terror campaign, which was characteristically specific. This mission was to have been perpetrated by five members of Yusuf's terror cell, including himself, Murad, Shah, and two others whose identity is unknown; one of them was most probably Khaled Sheikh Muhammad, Yusuf's uncle.[75] All five were given code names on the computer and were supposed to plant bombs on eleven U.S. commercial airplanes, within a short period of time and simultaneously.

The cell's first member, under the code name Minkas, was to fly on a United Airlines flight on the Manila-Seoul-San Francisco route and to disembark in Seoul. The plane was to explode en route to San Francisco over the Pacific Ocean. Minkas was to continue on the Delta Airlines flight route via Seoul-Taipei-Bangkok and to disembark in Taipei. The aircraft was to explode in midair on the final leg to Bangkok. Minkas was to fly from Taipei to Singapore, and from there to a hideaway in Karachi.

The second member, Markoa, was to fly Northwest Airlines on the Manila-Tokyo-Chicago route, disembark in Tokyo after planting the bomb, and continue on the Northwest Airlines route via Tokyo-Hong Kong-New York, plant the bomb on the plane, disembark in Hong Kong, continue on to Singapore and from there flee to Karachi.

The third, "Obed" (the code name for Hakim Murad), was to fly on United Airlines via the Singapore-Hong Kong-Los Angeles route, plant the bomb on the aircraft, disembark in Hong Kong, and continue on the Hong Kong-Singapore-Hong Kong route, disembark in Singapore after planting a bomb on the plane, and continue on to Karachi.

The fourth, Majbos, was to fly the United Airlines route of Taipei-Tokyo-Los-Angeles, disembark in Tokyo after planting the bomb, continue on the United Airlines route of Tokyo-Hong Kong-New York, disembark in Hong Kong after planting another bomb and continue on to a hideaway in Karachi.[76]

The fifth, "Ziad" (apparently Ramzi Yusuf) had the most complex job. He was to fly Northwest Airlines on the Manila-Seoul-Los Angeles route, plant the bomb under his seat and disembark in Seoul. From there he was to take the United Airlines Seoul-Taipei-Honolulu route, disembark in Taipei after planting the bomb, and continue on to Bangkok on the United Airlines route of Taipei-Bangkok-San Francisco, disembark after planting another bomb and continue on from Bangkok to Karachi.[77]

The operation was almost in place and it appears that Murad ("Obeid") was supposed to launch the plan on January 21, about two weeks after the fire broke out in Yusuf's hideaway. Also found in the apartment were diagrams and manuals regarding the use of chemical and biological substances. In addition, the police discovered documents claiming credit for the attacks under the name of "The Fifth brigade of the Liberation Army." This is the name Yusuf used when he claimed responsibility for the Twin Towers attack. This name was also used when claiming responsibility for the attack on two U.S. citizens in Pakistan after Yusuf's extradition to the United States in February 1995. Osama Bin-Laden's name and phone number were found among Yusuf's belongings.

While Murad was caught a short time after the fire (January 11), Wali Khan succeeded in escaping from the detention facility where he was being held in Manila, flew to Malaysia where he was caught and extradited to the United States. Characteristically, Yusuf escaped and already on January 7 flew first class from Manila to Hong Kong, and from there to Karachi where he disappeared. The relentless Yusuf did not abandon his plans to carry out mega terror attacks, including those against aircraft. For this purpose he sent threatening letters to the Philippines government and demanded the release of Murad, whom he wanted to activate in continuation of a suicide assault against American targets. Yusuf linked up with several other collaborators in Pakistan, including Ishtihaqe Parker, whom he attempted to activate in the detonation of American commercial aircraft en route from Bangkok to the United States. He also considered attacking an Air France plane as an alternative. As his scheme did not succeed he returned to Pakistan to prepare for the renewal of his terror campaign.

Unfortunately for Yusuf, Parker eventually decided that Yusuf's plans for mass homicide were incompatible with Islam's values, and believed that his life was in danger. Parker, who was also aware of the high price of $2 million placed on Yusuf's head, called the American Embassy in Islamabad and reported Yusuf's whereabouts to the Embassy staff.[78] A special group of law enforcement staff arrived in Islamabad and in cooperation with Pakistani law enforcement agencies nabbed Yusuf at a guesthouse in Islamabad. Thus, the career of an international terrorist (as Yusuf proudly called himself) came to an end. He is undoubtedly one of the most cold-blooded and murderous individuals in the annals of modern international terror.

Yusuf's determination to perpetrate mass killings and his creativity in developing special methods of operation and means to facilitate the murderous vision of Fundamentalist Islamic zealots turned him into a role model for his followers, who were guided by the same principles, that is, that mass injury to non-Muslims is a good deed, regardless of sex, race or age.

Yusuf's sentence (240 years of imprisonment) was calculated according to the life expectancy of his dead victims at the Twin Towers. If he had been sentenced according to the number of lives he had planned to extinguish, his sentence would have reached tens of thousands of years.

The Millenium Attacks

Ahmed Rasem's terror cell exposed at the Canadian-U.S. border. On December 14, 1999, during a routine check by customs agents at the Canadian-U.S. border, Ahmed Rasem, a Canadian citizen of Algerian roots, was arrested while trying to pass the border between Vancouver, British Colombia, and Seattle. He had aroused the suspicion of the agents and a search of his car revealed some 50 kg of explosives and improvised detonators. Rasem tried to escape, but was apprehended. Investigations carried out after his arrest revealed that he was a member of an Algerian terror network that was active in several countries including Canada, the United States, Britain and France. Rasem was wanted for questioning in France due to suspicion that he had collaborated with the Algerian GIA organization, which perpetrated terror attacks in France during the years 1995-96. The initial suspicion was that he had planned to perpetrate a mega attack at the Space Needle in Seattle, which was to host the millennium celebrations that December 1999, but he subsequently confessed that his main target was to blow up the LAX airport in Los Angeles. In July 2001 two other Algerians, Hawari and Maskini, were tried for collaborating with Rasem. On April 6, 2002, Rasem was sentenced to 140 years of imprisonment and a large fine.

Due to his stiff sentence, Rasem decided to cooperate with his interrogators and divulged many details about his life after emigrating from Algeria to the West in 1992. He described his recruitment

Figure 3.6
Twin Tower Assaults from 1993 to 2001

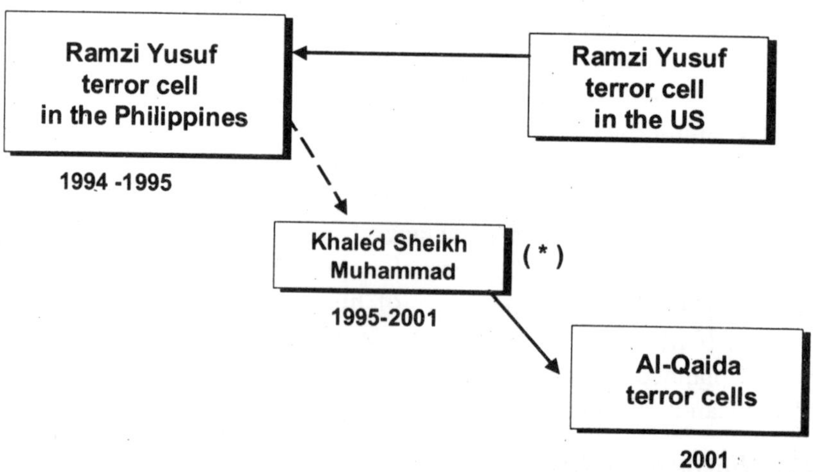

* Khaled Sheikh Muhammad belonged to Ramzi Yusuf's cell that planned the explosion of 12 U.S. airplanes and supervised the September 11 terror assault in 2001.

and training route in Afghanistan as well his plans to carry out terror attacks in the United States. Rasem also specified his links with activists in other Islamic terror networks in Europe. This testimony joined a long line of others describing the operation methods of the Islamic World Front functioning in Afghanistan under Bin-Laden's sponsorship.

Rasem's recruitment and training route according to his testimony at his trial in New York (July 2001). Ahmed Rasem, who arrived in Canada in 1994, was identified by Hanoushi, Imam of the mosque in Montreal, as a potential candidate for recruitment into the Global Jihad Movement.[79] Hanoushi encouraged Rasem to go to Afghanistan and provided him with a letter of recommendation which he handed over to Abu-Zubeida, Bin-Laden's deputy who was in charge of receiving young Muslim men joining the Global Jihad and sending them off for training in Bin-Laden's camps. In the beginning of 1998, Rasem traveled to Afghanistan and met with Abu-Zubeida who gave him a pass to join the Khaldun camp for training.[80] Rasem stayed in Afghanistan for six months, during which time he underwent training in terror and guerrilla warfare. He learned how to shoot, prepare explosive charges, act covertly, professionally gather intelligence and perpetrate attacks. He even underwent advanced training in sabotage at the Darunte camp and, according to his testimony, at its end was given $12,000 to prepare an infrastructure for terror attacks.[81]

At the Khaldun camp, about 100 young Muslims of different nationalities participated in the training; Jordanians, Egyptians, Algerians, Yemenites Saudi Arabians, and Muslims from European countries like Germany, France and Sweden. Rasem was instructed to organize a terror cell in Canada with other Algerians who had been trained with him at the camp and to prepare an infrastructure for perpetrating terror attacks in the United States.[82] The arrival of his peers was deferred due to the delay of some of the members in London, and others were afraid to travel to Canada. When Rasem realized that they would not be arriving to help him with preparations for the attack, he began to organize alternative local aid. He appealed to Hawari, an acquaintance of Algerian origins who was involved in criminal activity, to help him obtain forged documentation. Hawari introduced Rasem to another collaborator named Maskini, who mainly helped to procure forged documents.

Rasem gathered intelligence information about three airports. On one of his journeys from the Los Angeles Airport he left a suitcase unsupervised in a trolley in order to test the alertness of the security staff. His choice of this airport as a central target came from his understanding of its importance as a strategic, economic target and of the political repercussions if it were to be hit.[83]

Among his partners in the planning already in Afghanistan were Dr. Haider-Abu-Doha-and his deputy Mustafa Labasi. The two were at the camps in Afghanistan during his time there. Labasi actually lived with him for a time in Canada before moving to London, while Abu-Doha served as a trainer at the Afghanistan camps before moving to London. The two were senior members of the terror network subsequently busted in Britain at the beginning of 2001. An extradition order to the United States was issued against Abu-Doha, who was involved in Rasem's plans to attack the Los Angeles Airport, for his part in planning the attack.[84]

In his testimony, Rasem also exposed his link with Abu-Doha in Britain,[85] against whom charges were brought on August 28 for joining a conspiracy to bomb the airport in Los Angeles. Abu-Doha served as a liaison between Al-Qaida and the Algerian terror cell, which was supposed to act in the United States. Rasem described Abu-Doha as one of the key figures in the planning of the LA attack and noted that he had received his instructions from the latter. It is noteworthy that at the time of his arrest Rasem was carrying Abu-Doha's telephone number; he was in contact with a senior assistant at Bin-Laden's headquarters named Abu-Ja'afer, who lived in Peshawar and transferred instructions to whomever was conceived as a senior entity in the European network that coordinated its activities with the Al-Qaida command.[86]

Abu-Doha, suspected of being the mastermind behind the planned attack in LA, was held at the March prison in Britain prior to his extradition to the United States.[87]

The terror network arrested in Jordan on the eve of the millennium. From December 13, 1999, a thirteen-member terror network, mostly made up of Jordanians, Algerians and Iraqis, was arrested in Jordan. According to the charges, this network had twenty-eight members, some of whom still remain on the wanted list. The network planned to perpetrate a series of attacks in Jordan during the millennium celebrations as part of a combined assault staged by the Al-Qaida headquarters in Afghanistan. The attack targets were:

1. The Radisson Moriah Hotel in Amman.

2. The pilgrimage location in Martas that, according to Christian tradition, is the baptism site of Jesus in the Jordan River.

3. Tourists visiting Mount Nevo, which, according to Jewish tradition, is the burial site of Moses.

4. Israeli tourists at the Jordanian-Israeli border.[88]

Some members of the terror network underwent indoctrination and training at Bin-Laden's camps in Afghanistan, at the end of which they made their loyalty oath to Bin-Laden and to the ideal of the Global Jihad and returned to Jordan. Others trained at camps in Lebanon with the help of Hizballah people and Iranian elements.

The cell was financed by Abu-Katada the Palestinian (Omar Ben Omar), a Muslim cleric who was considered one of the most prominent radical indoctrinators in Europe.[89] The cell was also instructed to finance its activities through criminal activity, for example robberies.

The terror network in Jordan was headed by Abu-Hushar, who had been arrested in the past in Jordan (1993) and charged with perpetrating attacks against the throne, but the king mitigated his sentence and he was released. Abu-Hushar underwent training in Afghanistan and subsequently returned to Jordan, where he established the "The Army of Muhammad" organization, which was also made up of Afghan alumni.[90]

Another central activist alongside Abu-Hushar was Raed Hijazi, an American citizen of Palestini-origins, who was subsequently arrested in Syria and extradited to Jordan, where he was given the death sentence for his role in the operation.

The leaders of the Jordanian terror network were guided by Abu-Zubeida (Zeine Al Abadin, a thirty-one-year-old Saudi of Palestinian origin who was a senior activist in Al-Qaida; he was responsible for the activation of the two millennium cells in Jordan and in the United States). Abu-Zubeida was arrested more than two years later in Pakistan on March 28, 2002, and he remains one of the most senior terrorist activists in American hands.

The Palestini, Afghan, and Jordanian planners of the terror operation thwarted in Jordan had intended to cause multiple Israeli and American casualties. Only thanks to the Jordanian security forces was this conspiracy nipped in the bud, before it could cause casualties and leave any impression on public opinion in Israel and throughout the world.

Modus Operandi of the "Islamic Front"

- Detonating car bombs
- Suicide attacks in the air, on land and on the sea
- Assassinations
- Hijacking of airplanes
- Abductions
- Holding hostages for various purposes
- Poisonings and non-conventional attacks

Terror Cells Affiliated with Al-Qaida in Europe

Introduction

The Al-Qaida command considers Europe an important central arena to promote the concepts of the Global Jihad and realize the vision of the Islamic Caliphate throughout the world. Europe also constitutes a "Dar al-Harb" which, according to this prophecy, will become a "Dar al-Islam" as part of the world Islamic Caliphate. As a result of several conditions, there are some advantages for Europe to serve as the arena for the struggle of the International Islamic Front against the Western infidels. Among those conditions are:

1. The existence of large groups of Muslim minorities in several countries.

2. The leading of a traditional Muslim lifestyle anchored by mosques, cultural centers and voluntary, non-governmental (NGO) charities which provides optimal conditions for the operation of an identification system to recruit potential volunteers into the ranks of the Islamic revolution. Islamic Front "agents" are active through these institutions to recruit new "cadres" and convince them to explore the route of the "Islamic Jihad" as an ideological alternative to Western secular culture and as a solution to life's hardships. The Islamic insti-

tutions also constitute an important source of fund raising and the channeling of these funds to terror networks active throughout the continent.

3. The open democratic-liberal lifestyle in Europe that enables freedom of movement and easy transfer of activists, equipment and means between various countries and even outside of the continent.

4. A target audience for recruiting candidates into the ranks of the Global Jihad, which mainly includes first and second generation offspring of veteran emigrants. Most of them were born in Europe and grew up as local citizens, but many suffer from emigrant children's syndrome and harbor a grudge because of the difficulties their parents had in blending in or carry the stigma of "foreigners, the sons of foreigners." The sensations of insult and discrimination turn them into easy prey for tempting concepts like returning to one's roots, which is presented as an impetus to resolve their difficulties. Sometimes this is accompanied by a proposal to avenge themselves against the offenders, their families and traditions, as well as an indication of the Western lifestyle as a central cause of their tribulations.

5. The enlisting of young men who have deteriorated to the margins of society and crime as volunteers into the ranks of the Global Jihad. In European prisons tremendous effort is being made to recruit "born again" believers and even converts. Islam, with its militant, radical interpretation, offers a sense of new direction and meaning, content and a fresh and more promising order for them.

Bin-Laden and his associates regard these cadres as the avant-garde that will ignite the spark of revolutionary fervor and incorporate itself in the Global Jihad process, and in other ways including terror. An expression of this approach can be found in an intercepted conversation between two members of a terror cell in Italy, which went as follows: "God loves us because Europe is in our hands. Now we are the emigrants who are fighting the jihad. This is our role, our destiny, and we must accomplish it with honor. We must be like snakes, strike out at them and hide."[91]

Europe also serves as a central logistic rear guard for the Afghan alumni. The terror networks, mainly in North Africa and the Magreb, regard Europe as an arena for purchasing weapons for the struggles that their associates are conducting to achieve the collapse of "heretic" regimes in their own lands. The purchase of weapons and auxiliary fighting equipment and fundraising have become a routine part of their activities. This activity was combined with extensive criminal activity on the part of the network's members, who dealt in the theft of credit cards, the sale of forged documentation and drugs. Some of the income was sent to their countries of origin in order to finance the military struggle.

The composition of the terror cells of the Afghan alumni in various European countries was based on the country of origin. However, the joint experience of living together and in some cases even fighting together in Afghanistan has expanded the circle of participants to activists from other countries of origin, the adhesive substance being the concept of Global Jihad.

The alignment of terror networks in various European countries is extensive and is based on prior acquaintance, sometimes due to living for a prolonged period in a certain country or due to a concentration of emigrants in the same country. It is difficult to define "work distribution" between the various countries, because similar characteristics were identified in all of the countries where terror cells of this kind were apprehended, such as the purchasing of weapons, explosive substances or their components, the recruitment of new cadres, collecting funds in the form of contributions, distortion or the theft of credit cards, purchasing forged documentation or stealing authentic documentation, disseminating propaganda material and more. Nevertheless, it is possible to identify a "function" that the terror infrastructures played in several countries on the continent.

Characteristics of Terror Cells in Europe as a Model for Islamic Terror Cells

- Age group—early twenties to mid-thirties.
- Educated individuals, students, and sometimes academics in the areas of chemistry, engineering, computers.
- Successful, middle-class professionals, businessmen.
- Emigrants, sons of emigrants.
- Sometimes individuals with criminal records.
- Converts to Islam.
- Familiarity with the Western lifestyle.
- Awareness of their legal rights during interrogation.
- Alumni of training camps in Afghanistan, Bosnia and Chechnya.

- Active in recruiting candidates in mosques, Islamic centers, cultural centers and universities.

- Based on nostalgic feelings for their lands of origin and Islam, exploiting feelings of discrimination and alienation of emigrant children.

- Maintenance of strict compartmentalization.

- They tend to act in frameworks with a majority made up of a defined ethnic origin, but also include various nationalities.

Britain. Britain has played a special and central role as a basis for an ideological infrastructure and a site for activity in the area of propaganda. Britain, which has a large community of approximately 2 million Muslims, has become a focus of Islamic radicalism in Europe, due chiefly to lenient emigration laws combined with a willingness to offer political asylum to entities claiming to be politically persecuted by the regimes in their countries of origin, a strict adherence to individual rights, free speech and propaganda.

British liberalism ("Hyde Parkism") triggered a flourish of Islamic propaganda activity to terminate adversaries on the basis of race, religion and politics, hovering at the brink of incitement and even crossing the line from time to time. Britain has served as a central site for those requesting political asylum from among the Afghan alumni, war veterans and many emigrants from North Africa and the Magreb, who at some point were attracted to the concepts of the Global Jihad. The activities of central mosques in British cities, headed by fanatic spiritual mentors, have turned them into an attractive focus for young people who have undergone "ideological indoctrination" and semi-military training, which ultimately led them to Bin-Laden's training camps in Afghanistan.

For years radical Islamic clerics have been active in Britain, openly and rabidly inciting their audiences against the West, and some of them are even suspected of being involved in terror attacks of Afghan alumni. The most prominent is Omar Abu Omar ("Abu-Katada"), a forty-two-year-old Jordanian of Palestinian origin who is considered a central figure among Muslim leaders in Europe. Abu-Katada is an Afghan alumnus who fought alongside the local mujahidin during the eighties. He was granted political asylum because he claimed that he was being politically persecuted. For several years he was the editor of the Algerian GIA's *Al-Antsar* newspaper. He serves as the Imam of the Finsbury mosque and is considered the chief protagonist and instigator of the Global Jihad in Britain. He expresses open support for all Islamic organizations that back the war against the United States and calls for a jihad against Israel and Jordan. In an interview that he granted to the "Confrontation" program on Al-Jazeera television on March 9, 2000, Abu-Katada condemned the Arab states that prevent Muslims from fighting Israel. His ties with terror activists are extensive, and there is a death sentence pending against him for his part in aiding the millennium terror attacks in Jordan (at the end of 1999), because of his fatwa permitting the attacks planned there and his instructions to provide financial aid to this terror network. Incitement tapes and large amounts of money, which he claimed were designated for charity, were found at his home. Abu-Katada was arrested several times by the British, but was conditionally released until he finally "disappeared" at the end of 2002; apparently, he is under the supervision of the British authorities.

Another senior cleric is Mustafa Kamal Mustafa, "Abu-Hamza," the Egyptian leader of the Antsar A-Sharia (Supporters of the Sharia) organization founded in 1997. Abu-Hamza is an Afghan alumnus who lost one eye and a hand in the explosion of a letter bomb. He also served as the Imam at the mosque in Finsbury Park, north London. After his retirement from the Algerian GIA, he founded the *Antsar A-Sharia* bulletin, which was designated to protect Muslim rights in Britain. The aggressive stand taken by the paper called for a jihad against the United States and Israel and to kill Western tourists in Islamic states. Abu-Hamza justified the massacre carried out by the Jama'a al Islamiya terrorists in Luxor in November 1997 because the tourists were contaminating the Muslim society in Egypt. He is also suspected of involvement in the murder of Western tourists in Yemen in 1998. In the framework of his activities in Britain, he encouraged the enlistment of young Muslim men for training in Britain prior to their transfer to Bin-Laden's training camps in Afghanistan.

The Syrian Sheikh Omar Bakri, who emigrated to Britain after his deportation from Saudi Arabia, heads the mujahidin movement founded in 1996, and he also agitates for Global Jihad against the enemies of Islam, headed by the United States, Israel and all of their supporters.

Against the background of the vitriolic Islamic incitement in Britain, it is not surprising that the latter has become a hothouse for the cultivation of activists who are directly involved in the perpetration of terror or in the planning of terror attacks. Among these is Zakaria Musawi, who was arrested in the United States in August 2001 and was thus prevented from participating as the twentieth hijacker in the death flights of September 11. Even if it turns out that the suspicion in this matter is refuted, it is clear that he was an inseparable part of the terror network active in Britain. Musawi's friend Richard Colvin Reed, who aspired to blow up an American Airlines flight on December 22, 2001, by igniting shoes full of explosives, was also a member of one of the terror cells in the country. Jamal Begal, who was apprehended in Doha in July 2001 before he had a chance to realize the goals of the terror network he headed and carry out attacks in France, was also a member of the radical Islamic circles in Britain.

The principal role of Abu-Doha, who was one of the senior activists of the European terror network that functioned in Britain and was described in detail earlier, also testifies to the centrality of Britain in the deployment of the Afghan alumni in Europe. The transfer of some of the U.S. suicide team members through Britain and their stay in that country for short periods also corroborate the assessment that radical Muslims feel secure when active in this country.

Germany. Germany also constitutes a convenient base for the activity of radical Islamic entities in Europe. In certain cities mainly in the periphery, such as Hamburg and Frankfurt, the members of the Islamic Front acted out of a sense of security and made their preparations for a terror act to be enacted outside of the borders of that country.

The freedom of movement inside the country, the lack of close police/intelligence supervision over foreigners, especially if they had the status of students, and their proximity to target countries on the continent, mainly France and Italy, made Germany an attractive base.

The presence of a large Muslim community and of mosques, Muslim cultural organizations and charities, enabled them to assemble at these places, recruit new members, and mainly to operate their subversive activities under the cover of religious activity and free ritual customary in this country. The presence in Germany of Muslim businessmen from all over the world helped them to obtain donations without the supervision of the authorities. To date, Germany has not served as the site for a terror attack out of the fear that this kind of activity might impair the comfortable conditions that Germany has granted to the terror cells.

France. France, which houses a large community of Muslims including many from the North African countries, was a central focus for terror cells composed of Afghan and Bosnian alumni. France was undoubtedly a country of destination for them, mainly for the Algerian terror cells. During 1995 and 1996, terror attacks were perpetrated in France by the GIA, which were meant to express their protest against French support of the Algerian regime and "settle historical accounts" with the French occupation of Algeria until the sixties of the twentieth century.

The activity of terror cells that originated in the Magreb continued through the end of the nineties. A splinter group from the GIA called the GSPC had intended to perpetrate attacks in France during the World Cup soccer games in the summer of 1998, but they were thwarted, as well as subsequent attacks aimed at hitting Christian targets, in addition to American targets, in France. Al-Qaida-supported terror networks undoubtedly perceived France as a central target country for terror activities. The terror activities of these Al-Qaida-affiliated networks in Europe continued throughout the nineties, but gained considerable momentum in the second half of that decade due to Bin-Laden's firm standing in Afghanistan under Taliban sponsorship.

Europe experienced waves of terror and thwarted terror attacks throughout the nineties: for example, the wave of attacks perpetrated by the Algerian terror networks in France during 1995-1996, the intended terror attacks in France during the World Cup games in 1998, and the arrest of terror cells in Italy, Belgium and Germany which exposed the tip of the iceberg vis-à-vis the activities of Afghan alumni in Europe.

Aware that the time for direct confrontation with the United States was drawing near, the leaders of Al-Qaida in Afghanistan, directed by Bin-Laden and his associates, intensified the transfer of Afghan alumni to Europe in the form of organized Al-Qaida-supported terror cells in order to launch a terror campaign in Europe, mainly against American targets, but also against others. The operation methods that they planned to use indicated mass and indiscriminate terror, meant to kill many innocent citizens of various nationalities.

Relatively fewer attacks than planned were carried out in Europe by terror cells and groups affiliated with the Global Jihad. This achievement must be credited to the enforcement and thwarting activities of European security forces that acted both independently and via international cooperation. Their success saved many lives and, simultaneously, helped to curb the scope of malicious intent and murder looming over European heads due to expert terrorists from among the Afghan alumni, armed with a radical ideology and an apocalyptical vision. This danger, however, did not pass even after the end of the first round of fighting in Afghanistan, which brought about the banishment of the Taliban and severely impaired the infrastructure of Al-Qaida in Afghanistan. The chief remaining danger is the Al-Qaida-affiliated terror cells still located in Europe and in the rest of the world.

The exposure of these remaining terror cells in Europe, which began at the end of 2000 and continues to date, may reflect the scope of the threat. During this period a series of arrests of Global Jihad activists was conducted in Germany, Britain, Italy, Spain, France, Belgium and Holland. Their intention was to realize the terror policy conceived by Bin-Laden in order to cause political instability and an atmosphere of fear on the Continent. This activity was to be part of a process, which was intended to ignite the spark of Islamic revolution in Europe and be incorporated into a terror campaign planned for North America, Asia and the Middle East, alongside the September 11 attacks. It was meant also to trigger a religious war, which according to Bin-Laden's vision would ultimately lead to the reinstatement of the Islamic Caliphate in the world.

Central Al-Qaida-Affiliated Terror Cells Exposed in Europe since the Year 2000[92]

Germany. On December 24, 2001, Frankfurt police raided two safe houses in the city and arrested four individuals: two Iraqis, an Algerian and a Frenchman, who had in their possession weapons, forged documentation, and stolen credit cards. The weapons included rifles, grenades, 20 kgs of improvised explosives and homemade detonators. All four carried false papers under assumed names.[93] Their safe houses also revealed videotapes inciting for jihad and a tape containing preparatory material prior to perpetrating attacks. The tape presented targets, which included a cathedral and a Christmas market in Strasbourg.

Muhammad Ben Zakaria, dubbed "Milliani," was able to get away but was apprehended later in June 2001 in the Spanish city of Alhanta.

In the trial of the defendants held in Germany in April 2002, one claimed that a synagogue in Strasbourg was also among the targets. According to the charges brought against them, the terror cell operated was from Britain, from which they received instructions and funding.[94]

Britain. As a result of the investigation and the findings confiscated upon apprehension of the German cell in December 2000, London police carried out a series of arrests in February 2001 of terror cell members in England, which played a central role in activating terror networks in various European cities. This cell was led by Dr. Haider, also called Abu-Doha, and his deputy Mustafa Labasi. The thirty-six-year-old Abu-Doha of Algerian descent turned out to be high up in the terror networks active in Europe, and he was linked to several of them. He served as a trainer at the Khaldun camp in Afghanistan until 1999 when he moved to Britain and settled in London, apparently after coordinating the move with Al-Qaida headquarters. Labasi, his deputy, shared an apartment with Ahmad Rasem during his stay in Canada. Labasi is suspected of hosting some of the hijackers of the U.S. commercial airplanes in his home in London when they were en route to their suicide mission in the United States.

Italy. In April 2001, members of the The Salafi Group for Propaganda and Combat (GSPC) were arrested in Italy. A thirty-three-year-old citizen of Tunisian descent named Sa'id Sami Ben Khamis headed the cell. Together with his accomplices, he planned a suicide attack at the U.S. Embassy in Rome. Simultaneously, Italian security taped a telephone conversation between Khamis and his thirty-one-year-old Libyan partner Lased Ben Hanni, in which they discussed a plan to introduce cyanide into the air-conditioning system of some target, thus causing immediate death from asphyxiation of thousands of people, all in the name of the Islamic revolution in Europe.[95]

Spain. Several arrests of terror cells and activists connected to Al-Qaida were carried out in Spain. In June 2001, the head of the terror cell in Frankfurt, called "Milliani," was arrested, but he succeeded in breaking out of detention in December 2000. In July, six members of an Algerian cell were arrested. They dealt mainly with logistic and criminal activity in aid of the The Salafi Group for Propaganda and Combat. The group's members were experts in forging documents and carrying out credit card fraud.[96]

On November 13, 2001, an additional cell with eight members was discovered in Spain. A Spanish resident of Syrian origin named Amad A-Din Birkat Yirkam, also known as "Abu-Dahdah," led this cell. Some members had undergone training in Afghanistan, where they learned terror and guerrilla warfare and pledged their loyalty to the jihad. According to the charge sheet filed against all of the eight by the investigative Judge Garcon, they were suspected of having links with additional members of terror cells in Germany and France. The cell members worshipped at the central mosque in Madrid, where they were involved in their secret activities. They were careful to maintain a routine middle-class lifestyle, but at the same time dealt in subversive activity, which included recruiting young men for the Global Jihad network, raising funds for the purchase of weapons and explosives, and the use of fake credit cards to finance their activities. In 1997, Abu-Dahdah's telephone line was tapped. At this point it is not clear if any of the cell members had contact with Muhammad Atta during his two visits to Spain in 2000 and 2001. The charge sheet mentions a coded telephone conversation between Abu-Dahdah and an activist named "Shoukour," in which they discussed activity that is suspected of being connected to aviation targets.[97]

In April 2002, three businessmen were arrested in Spain, headed by Muhammad Ralev A-Zweidi (Abu-Talha), who, according to the charge sheet, led the financing network of Al-Qaida in Spain, which operated under the cover of a construction company. Zweidi, a Spanish citizen of Syrian descent, gave a large sum of money to Abu-Dahdah and his group in Spain and also transferred money to Al-Qaida people in various countries all over the world, including the United States, Belgium, Turkey, Jordan, Syria, Saudi Arabia and China.[98]

The Terror Network of Jamal Begal in France, Holland, and Belgium

On July 28, 2001, Jamal Begal, a thirty-six-year-old French citizen of Algerian descent, was arrested in Doha while en route from Afghanistan to Europe. In his interrogation he revealed the process of his recruitment into the ranks of the Global Jihad and his participation in the weekly sermons of Abu-Katada. After a preliminary "brainwashing" process in Britain, Begal traveled to Bin-Laden's training camps in Afghanistan in November 2000, where he underwent basic training in combat and sabotage, combined with indoctrination lessons, and then pledged his loyalty oath to Bin-Laden. At the end of his training, he was instructed by Abu-Zweida, Bin-Laden's senior deputy, to establish a terror network in Europe, whose mission was to perpetrate terror attacks at the U.S. Embassy and Cultural Center in Paris at the end of 2000 and the beginning of 2001.[99]

As a cover for his activities, Begal was instructed to open a business and Internet café, which would help him maintain e-mail contact with his operators in Afghanistan. Begal was arrested on the possession of false documents on his way from Pakistan to France, and was extradited to France in October 2001 to stand trial.

Begal's network had about twenty members and collaborators spread out in France, Holland and Belgium. Begal's arrest was kept under wraps, which enabled security forces in these countries, which were cooperating with each other, to place the cell members under surveillance and closely monitor their activities in an effort to thwart the attacks planned for Belgium and France. On September 13, about ten members were arrested in Belgium and Holland; some had in their possession weapons, forged documentation and Islamic incitement material.

The exposure of the arrests in the *La Mode* newspaper and on French television forced French security forces to bring the arrests of the remaining local cell members forward to prevent the destruction of incriminating evidence and their escape.

Prominent members of Begal's cell included: Nizar Terabelsi, a thirty-three-year-old former professional soccer player who had converted to Islam and volunteered to drive a car bomb in a suicide mission at the U.S. Embassy in Paris; Kamal Daoudi, a twenty-seven-year-old French student of Algerian descent, who was a computer expert. He underwent training in Afghanistan and lived in Begal's apartment in Paris. When the authorities came to arrest him, he eluded them and fled to Leicestershire, England, where he was arrested on October 25, 2001, and was extradited to France.[100]

The Incident of Richard Colvin Reed (The Man with the Explosive Shoes—The "Shoe Bomber")

On December 22, 2001, a suicide bomber named Richard Colvin Reed attempted to detonate American Airlines passenger flight 63 while en route from Paris to Miami. His shoes were loaded with one hundred to two hundred grams of explosives, which he intended to ignite in order to blow up the aircraft along with its 196 passengers and crewmembers about two hours before the scheduled landing in Miami. The alertness of a flight attendant, who was summoned to Reed's seat by a suspicious passenger, and the neutralization of the terrorist with the help of other passengers, prevented a grave disaster.

In his interrogation, Reed claimed that he was acting alone, but it is evident that he was a member of a terror cell affiliated with Al-Qaida, which sent him on the mission. Human hair belonging to someone other than Reed was detected on the explosive charge. Also, Reed was in constant contact with Pakistan via the Internet and apparently received instructions from his operators in this way. His personal background indicates a familiar pattern of activity of recruiting British citizens who had converted to Islam into the ranks of Al-Qaida and terror cells supported by the latter.

Reed was born in Britain. His father was of Jamaican roots and his mother was middle-class British. The father, a vagabond type who had also got entangled in crime, deserted his home and his pregnant wife. Reed was aware of the existence of his biological father, but he did not meet him until he was twelve. Reed grew up in England as a child of a mixed marriage. According to his father and other family members who were interviewed after his terror attempt, Reed was "a confused, lost, restrained, and angry young man."[101] At the age of 15, Reed was sent to a juvenile detention center. While there he was persuaded to convert to Islam and upon his release was attracted to radical religious Muslim circles in Britain and spent much of his time in mosques in the Brixton area.

The mosques served as centers for ideological indoctrination meetings, which were targeted at persuading young Muslims throughout Europe to join the Global Jihad. After undergoing the indoctrination process in London, Reed traveled to Pakistan and from there to Bin-Laden's camps in Afghanistan, where he passed through the "melting pot" of the Afghan alumni. In Britain he spent his time among the same radical circles that had produced notorious terrorists such as Zakaria Musawi, Jamal Begal and Nizar Terabelsi.

The attempted attack by Reed serves as indisputable evidence that Al-Qaida and its affiliated terror cells have not abandoned their intention to perpetrate additional deadly mega attacks. It testifies to the fact that despite the heavy blow sustained in the onslaught of the international allied forces led by the United States Al-Qaida's ability to persevere in the perpetration of terror attacks (particularly against transportation targets) has not been impaired. This also bears witness to the working pattern of Al-Qaida-affiliated terror cells, which is based on the activity of small terror cells with three to five members, having the capability to cause very heavy damage.

The alertness of the crewmembers and passengers, which helped to thwart the attempted American Airlines attack, provides additional evidence that public cognizance and decisive action have been a critical contribution and must continue in the war against terror.

Terror Cells Affiliated with Al-Qaida in Southeast Asia—Arrests

Arrests in Malaysia [103]

Starting from August 2001, Malaysian security forces carried out the arrests of radical Islamic activists, most of whom were members of the Kompulan Mujahidin Malaysia (KMM). This was accomplished in two waves: the first, between August and December 2001, was the arrest of KMM activists suspected of assassinating a Malaysian politician in Penang as well as being involved in an explosion in Jakarta, Indonesia; the second, between December 2001 and January 2002, was the arrest of members of an Islamic terror cell, some of which were affiliated with the Jama'a Islamiya and the KMM, and were also linked to Al-Qaida. To date, about sixty-eight suspects have been arrested in Malaysia, forty-five of whom were trained and fought alongside the mujahidin in Afghanistan during the eighties.

The Arrest of KMM Members

In August 2001, twenty-four individuals were arrested in Malaysia and accused of membership in the KMM. They were charged with involvement in a terror attack in Jakarta, a political assassination in Penang, Malaysia, and in maintaining contact with Islamic isolationists from the Abu-Sayyaf organization in the southern Philippines. The interrogation of the detainees indicated that most of them had trained and fought in Afghanistan and had links with Al-Qaida.

One of the detainees was Nick Adli Aziz, an organization leader and son of the spiritual mentor of the Pan Malaysian Islamic Party.

From Adli Aziz's arrest warrant interesting details can be gleaned about the KMM terror network in Malaysia.

According to this document, sixty-eight of the organization's members were arrested, forty-five of which had undergone training in Afghanistan during the eighties and nineties (This number also includes later arrests.) Nick Adli himself is accused of undergoing military training in Afghanistan during the years 1990-1996. In 1999, he visited southern Thailand, where he purchased weapons and explosives, and smuggled them into Malaysia. That same year he also visited the headquarters of the MILF in the Philippines and underwent training in the preparation of explosive charges. At the end of 1999 and early in 2000, Nick Adli Aziz sent sixteen KMM members to join members of the organization in Indonesia, in order to fight Christians in the Indonesian island of Ambons.

The Arrest of the Malaysian Terror Network (Singapore-Indonesian)

The spiritual and military mentor behind the organization is Abu-Bakhir Bashir, leader of the Jama'a al Islamiya, who lived in Malyasia for fifteen years and enlisted many followers for his radical views of Islam. Bashir is currently located in Indonesia. His deputy in terror activities is Hambali Norjaman Riduan, who presently leads the wanted list in Malaysia. Another key figure in the terror network is Yazid Sufat, a businessman and one of the senior leaders of the Jama'a al Islamiya, who is also wanted by the Malaysian authorities.

Malaysian Deputy Prime Minister Abdullah Ahmad Badawi revealed in an interview that since December 9, 2001, fifteen individuals had been arrested who were connected to Islamic terror organizations. Some were affiliated with the Jama'a al Islamiya network uncovered in Singapore. Members of the Malaysian network had purchased four tons of chemical substances of the ammonium nitrate type for the production of improvised explosives to be used in car bombs for attacks in Singapore.

The Malaysian authorities are also looking into the ties of some members with Al-Qaida members who participated in the suicide attacks on September 11. According to information in the possession of the authorities, during the summer of 2000 two of those involved in the September 11 attacks visited Malaysia. One of the detainees met with Khaled Al-Midhar and Nawaf Al-Hamzi, two of the hijackers of flight 77 that crashed into the Pentagon. The meeting was held in Kuala Lumpur and was filmed on video by Malaysian intelligence. The investigation indicates that it is possible that Ambali also met with the two in the apartment of Yazid Sufat in the suburbs of Kuala Lumpur. The purpose of their visit to Malaysia is not clear.

The Arrest of the Network in Singapore[104]

During December 2001, fifteen members of the Singapore Jamaa al Islamiya were arrested. They were busy with preparations to perpetrate attacks against U.S., British, Israeli and Australian targets in Singapore.

The Jama'a al Islamiya organization had a hierarchical structure led by a spiritual mentor. Beneath him was a "row," made up of an advisory council (based in Malaysia), which activated and coordinated the activities of the organization's representatives in Indonesia, Singapore and Malaysia (see figure 3.7).

The leader of the organization in Singapore was Haj Ibrahim Haj Maidin, (aged 51), who trained in Afghanistan in 1993. Under his leadership, there was a row, a local advisory council that activated different committees/units who dealt with communications, finances, security, operations and religion.

Under the sponsorship of the Jama'a al Islamiya at least three terror cells were active in Singapore, and were uncovered by the Singapore authorities. At the head of one of the Singapore terror cells were two foreigners, who were later apprehended: "Sami," (whose real name was Muhammad Mansur Jabara), an Al-Qaida member of Arab descent who used Canadian documentation; and "Mike" (Fathur Al Rozi), of Indonesian descent. The exposure of the network was initiated as the result of information transferred by the United States to the Singapore authorities about a videotape found in the rubble of the home of one of Bin-Laden's deputies in Afghanistan, Muhammad Atta, who was killed in the bombing.

The interrogation of the detainees in Singapore indicated that the terror cell members were busy preparing for attacks, and in this framework were gathering information about attack targets, preparing hideaways, and purchasing chemical substances for the preparation of improvised explosive charges to be planted as car bombs.

The Singapore network prepared several attack plans:

- An attack against a bus transporting American soldiers on furlough from the navy base to the subway in Yishun. This attack was to be perpetrated apparently through the use of a booby-trapped bicycle. A tape dealing with the preparation of the booby-trapped bicycle and another tape documenting the surroundings of the subway and parking sites for bicycles corroborate the assumptions regarding the characteristics of the attack.

- An attack on an American boat. A map was found in the possession of one of the detainees containing observation points of the "kill zone" along the navigation route of American vessels near the Singapore shore.

- An attack at the U.S. Embassy in Singapore using a truck bomb. Videotapes documenting the embassy compound were found. Cell members were asked to find hideaways to conceal the truck bomb and to purchase chemical substances to prepare explosive charges.

- Attacks at the Israeli embassy, British and Australian High Commissions buildings in Singapore, here, too, were to be through the use of a truck bombs.

- Intelligence was gathered about American businesses and apartment buildings where American citizens resided in Singapore.

The arrests of the network members apparently prevented a series of terror attacks whose preparations were in high gear.

The existence of identical videotapes in the possession of one of the detainees and in the rubble of Muhammad Atef's home in Afghanistan proves the link between the cell and its operators at Al-Qaida.

The Terror Infrastructure on the Island of Bali[105]

During the night of October 12, 2002, a series of mega terror attacks took place on the Island of Bali; two car bombs were detonated simultaneously and an explosion occurred at the American Consulate on the island. Earlier that evening, a bomb had exploded near the Philippine Embassy in Jakarta. In these deadly attacks some two hundred people were killed and another three hundred were injured. Most of the victims were Westerners who had come to spend their vacations on Bali. The attacks were focused on two popular nightclubs on the Kota Coast, which is considered a central tourist attraction. The attacks were perpetrated through the use of a suicide-bomber and a car bomb loaded with TNT, both detonated within seconds of each other. The explosions devastated the discotheques, causing the ceilings to collapse and a huge fire to break out. The results were multiple deaths and widespread destruction. About half of the victims were Australian citizens, who generally visited the island in droves, as well as tourists from the United States, Germany, New Zealand and Britain.

Although the organization refrained from claiming responsibility immediately after the attack, the Jama'a al Islamiya Organization, headed by Bashir, was suspected of orchestrating the attack. Omar al-Farouq, an Indonesian citizen who was one of the leaders of the Southeast Asian terror network and who was arrested in June 2002 in Indonesia, gave incriminating testimony regarding the involvement of Bashir in the Asian terror system. Bashir was subsequently interrogated. In November 2002, a suspect named Amrozi was arrested in Indonesia. He confessed to involvement in terror attacks in Bali and admitted that the goal of his six- to ten-member terror cell was to kill Americans.

From the analysis of the characteristics of the attacks in Bali, we can note the following facts: The complexity of the terror attacks, as well as their planning and execution, all indicate considerable professional, operative and logistic capabilities. It appears that this level of performance would require greater knowledge than that possessed by the Jama'a al Islamiya or any other local Indonesian group, so it is safe to assume that Al-Qaida was involved in the preparations.

From the modus operandi of Al-Qaida and its affiliates in the past, such as the attempted attack in Singapore which was thwarted in December 2001, it is probable that the attacks in Indonesia were supervised by foreign activists, command and demolition experts, as was the case in Singapore. It is believed that the mastermind behind the terror attack thwarted in Singapore was Khaled Sheikh Muhammad, who served as the overall supervisor and commander of the foreign experts. The "experts" were Fathur Al Rozi, dubbed "Mike"—an Indonesian citizen who served as the network's demolition expert and who was arrested in the Philippines in December 2001—and Muhammad Jabara, dubbed "Sami," a Canadian citizen of Kuwaiti descent, who served as a key figure in supervising the attack in the field. Jabara fled and was subsequently arrested in Oman.

The goals of the attack went beyond the drive to kill Westerners according to the Global Jihad doctrine: The attack, which was carried out in an Islamic country, was meant to challenge the legitimacy of the "heretic" Islamic regime in Indonesia, to shake the country's political and economical stability, and create an atmosphere of insecurity, while striking at the regime's susceptible underbelly via terrorism against tourists at a tranquil and unprotected site, which was relatively easy to penetrate. Another aim was to continue to generate friction and foster controversy between the Western and modern Islamic world, which does not share the radical orientation preached by the afghan alumni.

The murderous attack in Bali clearly proved that the assertion among leaders and the general public in countries in the area, according to which it was believed that the threat posed by the Al-Qaida terror network and its affiliates had been dealt with effectively, together with the claim that the Islamic terror network had been severely crippled, making it incapable of carrying out mega attacks, proved to be no more than a wishful pipedream. The terror

Figure 3.7
The Jama'a al Islamiya Network in Southeast Asia

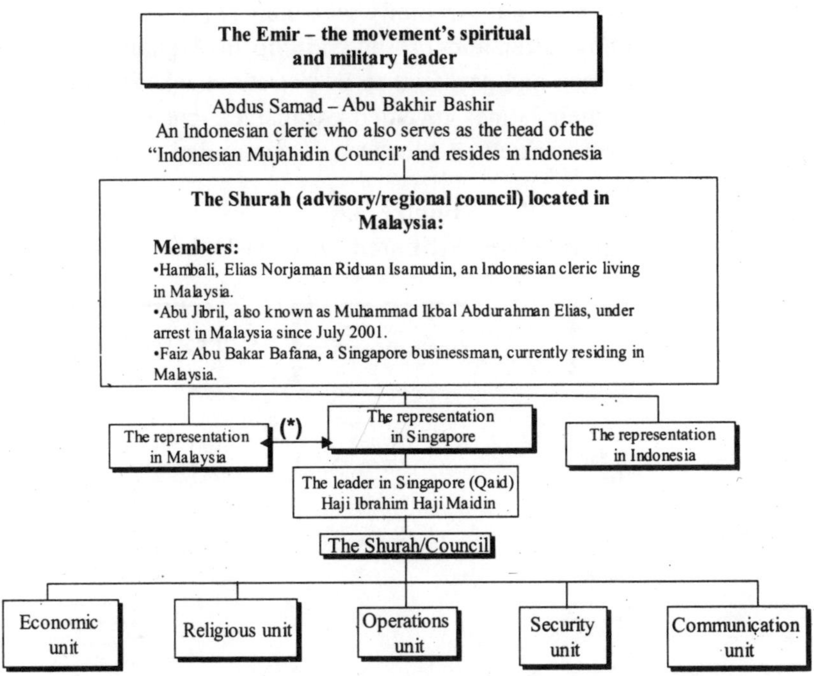

(*) It is possible that there is a joint representation for Malaysia and Singapore

attack on Bali triggered serious economic damage whose repercussions will undoubtedly be felt in the future as well, mainly in the area of tourism. It also represented a threat against the regime of President Magowuati, leader of one of the largest Muslim countries in the world. This constituted a blow to the Indonesian government, but also to Australia, whose citizens constituted the vast majority of the casualties. Australia, and even more so Indonesia, did not make a timely or concerted effort to join the world battle against terror, mainly because they did not suffer from any prior attacks initiated by the Afghan alumni. Nevertheless, the main lesson, which has proven itself again and again, is that no country or citizen in the world is immune to the long arm of terror, which has raised its ugly head repeatedly, each time in different countries and accentuates the need for worldwide cooperation to neutralize the venom of this diseased evil.

The Terror Cell Affiliated with Al-Qaida in Morocco

On May 12, 2002, a terror cell linked to Al-Qaida was arrested in Morocco. The cell members included three men and their wives. The members were Saudi Arabians who had come to Morocco at Al-Qaida's bidding, after undergoing training in Afghanistan. They married local women and prepared to perpetrate attacks in this country. A search of their homes revealed explosives, but it is not clear whether they were created in Morocco or smuggled into the coun-

Figure 3.8
Terror Cells Affiliated with Al-Qaida

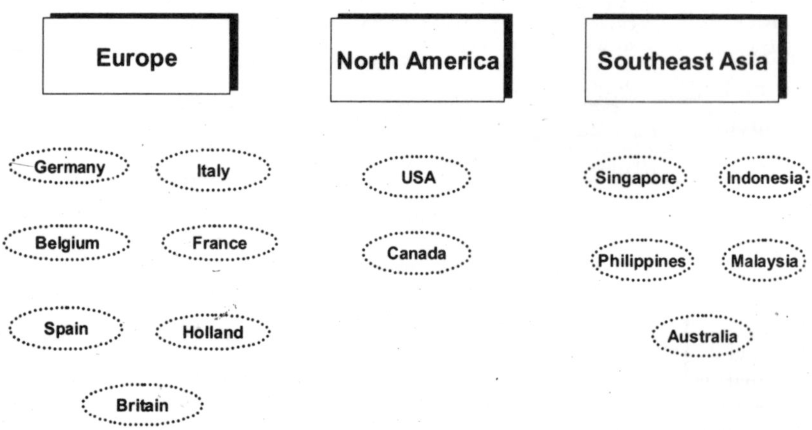

try. The cell's targets included churches, synagogues and tourist sites in Morocco. The "crowning glory" of the terror campaign was to have been suicide attacks against American and British warships that navigate the Straits of Gibraltar. These attacks were planned along the same lines as the attack on the *USS Cole* two years earlier. It appears that the planning of the attacks in Gibraltar involved the same commander[106]—Abdahlah Nashiri who had supervised the attack on the *USS Cole*.

After the discovery of the cell, the Moroccan police arrested additional suspects affiliated with the radical Islamic stream, including Afghan alumni of Moroccan descent. The arrests were conducted due to information received as the result of the interrogation of Moroccan detainees who had fought in the ranks of Al-Qaida in Afghanistan and were currently located at Guantnamu.[107]

The thwarted terror attack in Morocco and the suicide attack in Tunisia in April 2002 may indicate a trend on the part of Al-Qaida and its supporters to initiate activities in the Mediterranean basin as part of an overall attack against the NATO states. These attacks were meant to show that despite the blows sustained by the organization, it was still capable of carrying out mega terror attacks, including suicide attacks against members of the counter-terror coalition and their supporters among the Arab states.

Morocco, one of whose citizens (Sa'id Bahaji) collaborated with the Hamburg Group involved in the terror attack on the United States, is one of the Arab states that agreed to support the struggle against Islamic Fundamentalism. In this framework, and apparently in cooperation with the United States, Morocco extradited Muhammad Haider Zamar to Syria in December 2001. Zamar, a German citizen of Syrian descent, is the man who recruited Muhammad Atta into the ranks of Al-Qaida. This coordination with the United States, and apparently with Saudi Arabia as well, helped Morocco to thwart the terror campaign brewing on its home front.[108]

Notes

1. Yoram Schweitzer, The Bin-Laden Principle, www.ict.org.il. August 4, 2001.
2. Ibid.
3. Yossef Bodanski, *Bin-Laden, The Man Who Declared War on America*, Forum, Roseville, CA, 1999, p. 263.
4. Ibid.
5. Ibid., p. 233.
6. Peter L. Bergen, *Holy War—Inside the Secret World of Osama Bin-Laden Inc.*, Weidenfield & Nicolson, London, 2001, p. 118.

7. Ibid., p. 119.
8. *Al Halij*, United Arab Emirates, April 2, 2001.
9. *Newsweek*, March 19, 2001.
10. AFP, Paris, October 17, 2000.
11. *A-Zman*, London, November 5, 2000.
12. *A-Shark Al-Awsat*, London, November 13, 2000.
13. *A-Shark Al-Awsat*, London, November 12, 2000.
14. *Al-Haiat*, London May 4, 2002.
15. CNN, March 8, 2002.
16. *Washington Post* Internet, February 6, 2002.
17. *Yediot Aharonot*, Tel Aviv, December 14, 2001.
18. Ibid.
19. Al-Jazeera, October 7, 2001.
20. Abiensky Ze'ev, *Personal Terror, the Idea and Practice*, Hakibbutz Hameuhad Publishing, Tel Aviv, 1997, p.30.
21. Al-Jazeera, December 27, 2001.
22. *New York Times*, Internet, April 2, 2002.
23. *Yediot Aharonot*, Tel Aviv, December 14, 2001.
24. The data regarding the flights and suicide attackers are based on articles from *Time*, dated September 11, 2001, and from *Newsweek*, September 24, 2001, pp.32-33, 52-53.
25. CNN, March 8, 2002.
26. *Time*, November 2000, p. 23.
27. *Yediot Aharonot*, Tel Aviv, December 14, 2001.
28. *New York Times* Internet, April 16, 2002.
29. *New York Times* Internet, September 15, 2002, and *Time,* October 8, 2001, pp. 52-55.
30. The TV broadcast, "The Death Pilots," edited by Forrest Sawyer for CNN, the Geographical Society, and aired in the U.S. on March 10, 2002, and Lecture of Nancy Hartevelt Kobrin, Ph.D., Some Motivations and Personalities of the 9-11 Death Pilots: The Annihilation of Maternal Cameo as Resolution of Schizoid Dilemma, pp. 5-6.
31. *Time*, November 5, 2001, pp. 36-37.
32. The TV program "Death Pilots."
33. *New York Times* Internet, November 18, 2001.
34. The TV program "Death Pilots."
35. The weekly *Der Spiegel*, November 5, 2001.
36. *New York Times*, October 24, 2001.
37. *Time*, January 28, 2002, p. 26; *Ha'aretz*, January 17, 2002.
38. *New York Times*, October 24, 2001.
39. *Washington Post* Internet, June 19, 2002.
40. *Washington Post* Internet, June 12, 2002.
41. Profile report for CNN by the station reporter in Berlin, November 29, 2001.
42. Profile report for CNN by Dianna Muriel, December 11, 2001.
43. The German daily, *Build*, September 25, 2001.
44. The TV program "Death Pilots."
45. CNN, October 1, 2001.
46. *New York Post* Internet October 2, 2001.
47. *New York Times* Internet, October 8, 2001.
48. *Washington Post* Internet, September 27, 2001.
49. Yoram Schweitzer, Denying Responsibility and Liability, www.ixt.org.il, October 4, 2001.

50. The interview was aired on NBC television on April 17, 2002.
51. CNN, December 13, 2001.
52. CNN, December 13, 2001.
53. Al-Jazeera TV, "Under the Microscope" program, April 18, 2002.
54. Yoram Schweitzer, "Suicide Terrorism: Development and Characteristics," *Countering Suicide Terrorism*, ICT, The International Policy Institute for Counter-Terror, The Interdisciplinary Center, Herzliya, in cooperation with the A.D.L., 2001, 77.
55. Ibid., p. 78.
56. Eitan Azani, Suicide Attacks—The Phenomenon, Its Roots, Characteristics, and the Iranian-Lebanese Connection, MA thesis, Tel Aviv University, October 1997.
57. The data are taken from a database based on the Israeli press owned by Yoram Schweitzer.
58. Professor Dogul Ergil's lecture at the ICT Conference on Countering Suicide Terrorism, February 2000, in Schweitzer's article, pp. 83-84.
59. Walter Picuz, Mueller Outline Origin, Funding of September 11 Plot, *Washington Post* Internet, June 6, 2002.
60. Natan Guttman, *Ha'aretz*, Tel Aviv, September 30, 2001, A6; Natan Guttman, The Connection between the Airplane Hijackers Has Been Found: Letters of Guidance and Support in Arabic.
61. Ibid.
62. Al-Jazeera TV, April 17, 2002.
63. Ibid.
64. Laurie Mylroie, *The War Against America—Sadam Hussein and the World Trade Center Attacks—A Study of Revenge*, AEI Press, 2001.
65. Reeve, Simon, *The New Jackals, Ramzi Yusuf, Osama Bin-Laden and the Future of Terrorism,* Northeastern University Press, Boston, 1999, p. 125.
66. Ibid., p. 132.
67. Peter L. Bergen, *Holy War—Inside the Secret World of Osama Bin-Laden Inc.*, pp. 237-38.
68. Laurie Mylroie, The War Against America, p. 18.
69. Ibid., p 27.
70. Ibid., pp. 82-83.
71. Ibid., p. 78.
72. Reeve Simon, *The New Jackals, Ramzi Yusuf, Osama Bin-Laden and the Future of Terrorism*, p. 72.
73. Ibid., p. 76.
74. Ibid., pp. 79-80.
75. Ibid., pp. 85-86.
76. Ibid., p. 91.
77. Ibid.
78. Ibid., p. 101.
79. Josh Meyer, Terrorist Says Plans Didn't End with LAX, *Los Angeles Times*, July 4, 2001, p. 3. Hyperlink http://www.latimes.com.cgi-bin/print.cgi, www.latimes.com.cgi-bin/print.cgi.
80. Ibid., p.1.
81. Ibid., p. 2.
82. Ibid., p. 4.
83. Josh Meyer, Man Charged as Bomb Plot Mastermind, *Los Angeles Times*, July 16, 2001, p. 1.
84. *New York Times* Internet, July 4, 2001.
85. *Los Angeles Times* Internet, July 8, 2001.
86. *Washington Times* Internet, August 29, 2001.

87. *A Shark Al-Awsat*, September 1, 2000.
88. ABC network, January 25, 2000.
89. *Al-Hayat*, London, December 17, 1999.
90. The French News Agency, December 18, 1999.
91. *Washington Post* Internet, October 22, 2001.
92. Reuters, December 28, 2000.
93. *Ha'aretz*, Tel Aviv, April 16, 2002.
94. *Washington Post* Internet, October 22, 2001.
95. *Time*, November 5, 2001.
96. *Ha'aretz*, Tel Aviv, September 27, 2001.
97. *Ha'aretz*, November 21, 2001.
98. *Al-Hayat* Internet, April 28, 2002.
99. *Daily Telegraph* Internet, September 23, 2001.
100. *Time*, October 12, 2001.
101. *Maariv*, February 8, 2002, pp. 28-29.
102. Reuters, Malaysia, January 1, 2002; *The Straits Times* (Singapore), January 26, 2002; AP, December 6, 2001; *The Straits Times*, February 25, 2002; *The Sunday Times*, January 6, 2002.
103. *Washington Post*, February 25, 2002; *The Straits Times*, January 4, 2002; *The Straits Times*, January 5, 2002; *The Straits Times*, January 12, 2002; *The Straits Times*, January 26, 2002; Reuters, Malaysia, January 1, 2002; Singapore, Ministry of Information, Communications and Arts, Singapore Finds New Evidence of Clear Link between Detainees to Al-Qaida, January 24, 2002; *The Sunday Times*, January 13, 2002.
104. This section is based on *Yedioth Aharonot*, Tel Aviv, October 13-14, 2002; *Maariv*, Tel Aviv, October 13-14, 2002; *Sydney Morning Herald*, Australia, October 13, 2002.
105. AP, Morocco, June 11, 2002.
106. *Al Hayat*, London, June 14, 2002.
107. *Al Hayat*, London, June 13, 2002.

4

The Campaign against Terror and Its Threats

The Stages of the Campaign against Global Islamic Terror

The attacks of Al-Qaida in the United States constituted a sharp slap to world consciousness and intensified the real danger posed by the Afghanistan alumni to all lovers of liberty throughout the world, regardless of their religion. During the past decade, almost without interruption, the Afghan alumni in various locations all over the globe (and with even greater intensity since 1996 in Afghanistan) have concentrated on preparation of their terror infrastructure in Afghanistan. The inherent danger of the terror organizations founded by these Afghan alumni has been made amply apparent by the attacks perpetrated by terror cells acting in the name of the Global Jihad dogma. Nevertheless, the true dimensions of the danger posed by the radical ideology of the Afghan alumni, and mainly their clear intention to realize it, have not fully penetrated the consciousness of all of the decision makers in the West. Much of what has been said and written in the world media about Osama Bin-Laden, chiefly after the attacks in Kenya and Tanzania (August 1998), mainly addressed the mythical aspect of the phenomenon rather than the nature of the risks. Bin-Laden's declared intentions to incite an overall war between the Muslim world and the West and the extent of destruction that he planned to inflict on his enemies were perceived as exaggerated and unrealistic. Thus, it happened that the writing that had been on the wall for a long time turned to boiling lava in September 2001, necessitating immediate and drastic measures, which were extremely late in coming. It is possible to draw a comparison between contending with the phenomenon of the Afghan alumni and dealing with a malignant illness whose treatment has been neglected, and delayed discovery of acute symptoms necessitates drastic and unusual treatment.

It is possible to note three main stages in the world campaign against terror:

1. Destruction of the Al-Qaida infrastructure in Afghanistan and removal of the Taliban regime that offered the organization patronage.

2. A campaign against the Al-Qaida-affiliated terror cells.

3. A campaign against the countries that support terror.

The campaign against world terror is currently at the end of the first stage, while simultaneous steps that will serve the coming stages are being implemented: contending with Al-Qaida-affiliated Islamic terror all over the world, and making preparations in anticipation of the third stage of the campaign against countries that support terror, starting with Iraq under the leadership of Sadam Hussein. This campaign is global in nature and is being enacted on several levels simultaneously, including continued action against Al-Qaida remnants in Afghanistan, assisting the Philippine government in its battle against the Abu-Sayyaf organization, and worldwide intelligence and police activity to arrest members of terror networks (in Europe, the United States, Southeast Asia, and elsewhere), while forming a coalition and action patterns against countries that support terror.

A specification of the three stages involved in the campaign against terror follows.

Stage One

The first stage of the campaign against global terror necessitated aggressive military handling of the Taliban regime, which was under the leadership of Mullah Omar and which enabled Bin-Laden's terror industry to develop in the country without disruption. This intent was clear and vital from the very beginning of the campaign, despite various critics and protesters who claimed that the war's aims were undefined and it was not clear who the enemy was.

Implementation of this stage began with the launching of a military campaign in Afghanistan by the international coalition headed by the United States and its allies. The declared goal of the coalition against terror was to topple the regime of the Taliban under Mullah Omar's leadership because of his unrestrained policy vis-à-vis terror. The conversion of Afghanistan into an unrestricted living space for terrorists from all over the world who had undergone prolonged and professional training to carry out political assassinations was not to be endured. Afghanistan's support of terror differed from that of other countries that, in recent years, have been careful to avoid open identification with terror although behind the scenes they continue to support terror organizations. The Taliban, on the other hand, flaunted their support.

The campaign's objective was fully achieved with relative speed. It took about a month and a half to totally collapse the Taliban's military opposition and that of several thousand supporters from nearby Pakistan. This was followed by the introduction of a new temporary government composed of a coalition of local power brokers in Afghanistan.

The military campaign directed against Al-Qaida in Afghanistan took on a different character, as well as different standards to define victory. Al-Qaida is a decentralized body fighting guerrilla warfare and terror. The guerrilla concept adopted by the organization as its combat method enabled it to deploy its forces over an extensive geographic area and to hide in a twisted labyrinth of caves located in Afghanistan's mountainous region. The organization was able to pull back its splintered forces in order to avoid conquest by a stronger attacking adversary, and to smuggle its people into neighboring countries without having this appear as defeat, but rather as a desirable tactical withdrawal, even portraying it as a victory.

When attempting to calculate the account of Al-Qaida's profit and loss as a result of its terror campaign in the United States one year after its occurrence, it can be viewed as a tactical triumph but a strategic loss. The tactical victory is the result of Al-Qaida's success in surprising the United States, murdering thousands of its citizens in government and commercial centers, and causing its economy huge damage. It provided Al-Qaida with unprecedented media coverage which helped cultivate the powerful image of the Islamic Front headed by Bin-Laden, and granted them an important achievement from the standpoint of morale. On the other hand, Bin-Laden failed to achieve his main goal-that of prompting the United States to initiate a wide range of aggressive, unrestrained and indiscriminate actions against Muslims, in the hope of instigating a frontal collision between Islam and the other countries of the world. This confrontation, so desired by Bin-Laden, failed to materialize. In contrast, a wide international coalition came into existence that received the backing of Muslim countries and gave the United States and the coalition support in an overall military campaign against the Taliban regime. This campaign enabled the removal of the Taliban regime from Afghanistan and dealt a heavy blow to Al-Qaida's infrastructure in Afghanistan. Its bases and training camps were destroyed, and thousands of its documents were confiscated, thus revealing its plans and modus operandi. The organization suffered heavy losses among its leadership; several of its leaders were either killed or apprehended, and hundreds of its fighters were killed or taken prisoner. Thus, at least temporarily, Al-Qaida lost the activity base that constituted a vital component enabling it to build up its terror industry and spread it throughout the world without disruption. In addition, Al-Qaida sustained a blow to its prestige as a result of the successful military campaign waged against it by the United States in Afghanistan, which chipped away at the "invincible" image that the Afghan mujahidin and their leader Bin-Laden had carefully fostered since their triumph over the forces of the former Soviet Union.

It is important to emphasize clearly that the future of the overall campaign against the Afghan alumni, and Bin-Laden at their head, and its definition as a strategic victory, will first and foremost depend on the ability of the West to identify accurately the essential risks inherent to the phenomenon of the Afghan alumni and to provide an adequate and effective response to the threat that they pose. Failure to do so may provide Bin-Laden and his associates with additional victories and enable them to recover and cause even greater damage than they have to date.

The West must clearly comprehend that the strong blow sustained by Al-Qaida did not completely demolish its strength, and certainly did not diminish the power of the terror cells that have its support and whose activities are linked to that organization. These cells are waiting in many countries all over the world to continue and promote the agenda of the Global Jihad. These cells are composed of trained and determined fighters who are above all thirsty for revenge. The "nomadic" character of Bin-Laden's terror network, including its many branches, enables it to sustain these blows while continuing to operate. The survival of the senior commanders, including Bin-Laden and his deputy, Dr. Aiman A-Zawahiri, as well as several other senior operational activists, and the escape of several hundred Al-Qaida members from Afghanistan via Iran and Pakistan to countries that knowingly or unknowingly allow them to operate within their boundaries, have helped the organization to reorganize itself for continued terror activity.

The aborted terror attempt of Richard Reed to explode the American Airlines flight in the air (December 2001), the suicide attack near the synagogue in Tunisia which caused the death of nineteen people (April 2002), and the latest attacks in Bali (October 2002) and Mombassa (November 2002) constitute tangible testimony to this fact.

A Balance Sheet–Bin-Laden's Gains and Losses

Gains:

- The infliction of a massive blow to American prestige and to its economy.
- The launching of successful "propaganda by the deed."
- Increased recruitment for the Global Jihad.
- The unveiling U.S. vulnerability and Al-Qaida's capabilities at the same time.
- Igniting the aspired frontal confrontation with the West.

Losses:

- Loss of his home ground and main base of operations.
- Suffered a severe blow to his
    - Infrastructure
    - Commanding echelon
    - Foot soldiers
    - Economic assets and cash flow
- Placed the Islamic NGO's that provided him with aid under international observation.
- Placed the development and procurement of W.M.D. materials under strict international inspection.

Stage Two

The second stage of the campaign is associated with Al-Qaida and is dedicated to uprooting the bitter fruit of Bin-Laden's terror industry in Afghanistan. At this stage, Al-Qaida-affiliated terror cells must be eradicated all over the world. For over a decade, and with increased intensity since 1996, thousands of young Muslim men from all over the Arab world and from many countries over the globe were trained in terror and guerrilla warfare in Afghanistan, after which they were sent back to their native countries. Thus, a reservoir of trained terrorists loyal to the Global Jihad ideology was created. Each of these cells is comprised of a handful of activists "programmed" to perpetrate terror against Islam's adversaries, according to their conception.

The exposure of terror cells in Europe (Britain, France, Belgium, Italy, Spain, Germany), in Asia (the Philippines, Malaysia, Indonesia, Singapore, India), in the Middle East, (Jordan, Egypt, Lebanon and Israel), and in North America (the United States, Canada)—before and after September 11—provides ample evidence of the modus operandi, their intentions, targets and their inherent danger. The terror activities of these cells are incorporated with criminal activity: forged documents, stolen credit cards, weapon sales, thefts and robberies, and sometimes drug dealing. The growing cooperation between terror elements and the criminal world requires special attention and integrated handling by police and intelligence agencies worldwide.

The handling of the terror cells and their accomplices must be conducted on the local level by each country within its own borders and, at the same time, through international cooperation, which is an essential element for contending with the terror cells that maintain interpersonal contact and organizational links that disregard state boundaries. This handling must be conducted primarily by intelligence and prevention elements in cooperation with local police forces and international agencies such as the Interpol, in order to locate the terrorists and arrest them. The judicial authority must become involved in order to bring them to trial according to the legal system in each of the countries. Sometimes there is a need to extradite terrorists from one state, where they were caught, to another country, where they are wanted. Also, adaptation is required in local laws and in extradition agreements between the countries afflicted with terror.

The second stage began at the same time that the military campaign was launched, but it is expected to continue for years so that all of these terror cells, composed of trained and very patient members, with clearly defined missions, will be unable to realize their plots to deal their death blow to the liberal and free lifestyle. Even when it appears that Al-Qaida has been completely vanquished, the component of revenge may constitute a central motive for individual terror cells to persevere with the Global Jihad agenda.

Stage Three

This third stage must focus on the states that support terror, which are the core of the problem posed by international terror. The support of these states is the factor that has granted terror its scope of activity and power and its status as a regular player in international relationships. Without this support, terror would exist but at a much lower level than we are experiencing today. Therefore, maximum resources must be invested to deal with this issue and confrontation must be handled with political wisdom and through international coordination against those states that use terror in order to promote their political interests.

Due to the fact that the use of terror as an instrument by countries that support terror is generally based on rational considerations related to cost/benefit, it is necessary to significantly raise the cost while seriously diminishing the benefits.

The importance of using force in international relations has been evident since the beginnings of history. The use of military force in Afghanistan in the war against terror was an expression of this necessity to apply force from time to time. But in the campaign against countries that support terror there is a greater advantage to applying a system of general international sanctions against them than the use of military force. Validation for this can be found, for example, in the set of international sanctions applied against Libya when its involvement in the explosion of the Pan-American aircraft over Lockerbie became evident at the end of 1988. Effective application of the series of international sanctions declared by the Security Council (resolution no. 748 in March 1992) on the part of many countries is what converted Libya from the most brutal and active terror supporter in the history of international terrorism to a country that only passively supports terror.

The powerful intensity of the terror attack in the United States and its mammoth damage constituted a direct blow to the consciousness of a wide audience all over the world and shocked world leaders. Aside from its contributing to the creation of an international military coalition with wide political support, the attack also caused changes in the structure of international relations both on the bilateral and multilateral levels.

Thus, for example, unprecedented cooperation formed between two former rivals, the United States and Russia, in the war in Afghanistan. And as a result, unprecedented military cooperation between the United States and countries in the former USSR, such as Uzbekistan and Georgia, has also been initiated, with Russia's blessing. These countries have allowed American military forces to make use of bases in their territories to attack targets in Afghanistan. In return, the United States granted economic aid to these countries. This cooperation between the United States and Russia ultimately brought about the historical signing of a counter-terror cooperation agreement between the countries of the NATO Alliance (which was originally founded to balance the power of the Communist Bloc of the USSR and her satellite countries in the Warsaw Pact) and Russia.[1]

The relationship between the United States and China has also undergone changes as a result of the September 11 attack. Their relationship, which has often been overshadowed by a competition between two superpowers with different and often contradictory interests, had been tense due to the incident of an American intelligence aircraft caught in China, which caused a diplomatic crisis between the two countries. Facing the common threat of Islamic terror, the two countries reached a cooperative agreement. China, which is facing the threat of Islamic terror in the Xinjiang region, also supported the international coalition's activity against Islamic terror.

The relationship in the triangle of the United States-India-Pakistan has also experienced changes. Until September 2001 there had been a rapprochement between the United States and India at the expense of Pakistan, which was perceived by the United States as a country with a problematic policy vis-à-vis terror because of its support of the Taliban regime and Al-Qaida, and as a country that refused international supervision of its nuclear policy. Subsequently, a rapprochement occurred between the United States and Pakistan, which under the leadership of President Musharaf changed its declared policy in the area of terror and even helped in the removal of the Taliban regime in Afghanistan, in cooperation with the coalition states. In return, in an effort to improve its relationship with Pakistan the United States agreed to abolish the sanctions imposed upon that country. It is important to note that Pakistan has not yet abandoned the use of terror as part of its foreign policy, particularly in the bilateral status vis-à-vis India. Moreover, in Pakistan there are still elements that assist the Taliban and Al-Qaida, and the border area between Pakistan and Afghanistan serves as a haven for Al-Qaida personnel and perhaps even Bin-Laden, his deputy and Mullah Omar.

As a result of the September incidents, the situation between the United States and Saudi Arabia, a U.S. partner and important aspect of its Middle East policy, has undergone changes. Saudi Arabia, which was always perceived as an important country in U.S. considerations in the Persian Gulf and was granted special status in the structure of American foreign relations turned out to be a problematic country in matters related to terror.

Clearly, Saudi Arabia is a Islamic state with aspirations to lead the Sunni Muslim world. As such, for many years it has maintained a policy of export and of nurturing Sunni-Wahabi Islam. The realization of this policy has expressed itself in tremendous financial investment in cultural institutions, mosques, and in Islamic charities throughout the world, which serve as channels for the transfer of funds from Saudi Arabia to the boundaries of the Muslim world. These funds come from the royal family, wealthy businessmen, and the "Zakat" money (charity—one of the five commandments requires that every Muslim donate alms to the poor). Saudi Arabia's aspiration to reinforce its status as a leading entity in the Arab world has come up against a similar aspiration on the part of Shiite Iran. Since the rise of Khomeini to power in Iran, that country has acted to disseminate Shiite Islam throughout the Muslim world via terror activity and political subversion alongside the fostering of cultural institutions and Shiite centers. This fact has triggered competition between the two countries regarding hegemony in the Muslim world and has affected their support patterns for radical Islamic entities.

For many years, Saudi Arabia assisted Muslim groups fighting in the name of Islam, mainly at conflict areas like Bosnia and Chechnya, and in the past actively supported the Afghan mujahidin against the Soviets. Saudi Arabia offers the Palestinians active support and its funds have often served entities involved in terror, including suicide terror in Israel. The funds for Palestinian terror organizations are often channeled through charities active in Saudi Arabia and in the Gulf states. Among other considerations, Saudi aid for the Palestinians is meant to preserve Saudi Arabia's special status vis-à-vis Jerusalem, because the Saudi regime regards itself as the guardian of Islam's holy sites, including Jerusalem.

Several prominent charities operate under Saudi sponsorship such as the World Muslim League, the World Islamic Welfare Association, the Islamic Development Organization, Al-Haramin, and Al-Wafa. Some of these organizations are suspected of involvement in financing terror activities of Afghan alumni.

As a result of the September terror attacks and due to Saudi Arabia's involvement in funding terror entities directly linked to Bin-Laden, in addition to the fact that fifteen of the suicide hijackers were Saudis, this association came under sharp criticism by administration officials and in the House of Representatives; it was also reflected in the U.S media and may well effect a change in the action patterns inherent to the bilateral relations between the two countries.

For many years, the relationship between the United States and Iran has been affected by tension due to Iran's policy in several areas, including human rights, nuclear policy, and particularly its terror policy. Iran is the leader among the countries that support terror and in the past two years has been sharply chastised in U.S. State Department reports submitted to the Congress on patterns of global terrorism, for its role in spreading world terrorism. Although Iran condemned the terror attack in the United States and took a neutral stand vis-à-vis the activity of the Coalition Forces in Afghanistan, according to U.S. reports many of the Al-Qaida fighters fled to Iran on their way to seeking refuge in other countries.

The United States, which views Iran as a country that consistently supports terror, has named it one of the members of the "evil axis," and it is evident that in the future Iran will constitute a central target for attention among the countries that support terror. Syria and Lebanon, which host terror organizations that are on the American list of terror organizations, are perceived as targets for attention in one of the coming stages of the global war against terror, despite the fact that the two expressed support for the United States after the terror assault and have even assisted in the handling of some Afghan alumni located within their boundaries (State Department report, 2002).

Sudan and Yemen both rushed to offer practical and focused co-operation when the United States demanded assistance in contending with Al-Qaida within their boundaries. The depth and continuity of these efforts must be examined over time. However, the gesture clearly expresses a change in the policies of these countries, which formerly served as hothouses for Afghan alumni groups Even Libya under Qadaffi's leadership (after the verdict in the Lockerbie trial) is searching for ways to join the counter-terror coalition.

In the war against world terror, President Bush announced the necessity to fight the "axis of evil." He mentioned the names of three countries that constitute this axis: Iraq, Iran, and North Korea. With this declaration, President Bush expanded the definition of the targets of the counter-terror war and included the component of combating the spreading of non-conventional weapons to these countries, due to the fear that leaders may make direct or indirect use of this weaponry through terror organizations. Countries such as Iraq and Iran aspire to obtain non-conventional weapons and fight against international supervision of their activities, resisting any agreements to restrict distribution. Admittedly, these three countries have radical dictatorial regimes, and all three have been on the U.S. list of countries that support terror for many years, but their role in spreading terror at the current time is different and it dictates a different type of handling of each of these countries within the context of terror.

Iraq, or with greater accuracy the regime of Sadam Hussein, has been a U.S. target since the Gulf War. Despite the military defeat sustained by Sadam Hussein's army in the Gulf War of 1991, his regime remained standing, and Sadam Hussein still serves as the unshaken leader of this country. Iraq provides a haven for wanted terrorists and assists Palestinian terror organizations with funds and significant support for suicide attacks in Israel. Its efforts to develop nuclear power and its ties with terror organizations turn it into a prime target, alongside Iran, in what President Bush called "the evil axis." According to Sadam Hussein's action patterns in the political sphere to date, it will be vital to monitor closely the possibility that he might use terror organizations as his proxy in activities that include the activation of non-conventional weapons.

Future Terror Threats in the International Arena

The terror attack in the United States illustrated the destructive potential inherent to terror, which threatens the security, liberty, and economic welfare of citizens of all Western countries, and also most residents worldwide. Although it was the United States that endured the frontal attack dealt by terror, aspiring to undermine the Western secular and cultural lifestyle and to dictate its values through colossal violence, in actual fact this attack was directed at a much wider target audience than the citizens of the United States. This terror, which was meticulously planned through the use of relatively primitive means while exploiting American openness and, bluntly put, even U.S. naivety, must trigger a warning signal regarding the escalation potential of anticipated terror in the twenty-first century. Technological development both in the present and future may be maliciously exploited by the enemies of progress. The availability of combat means, industrial substances that can easily serve as the components of highly powerful explosives, and unconventional means in the hands of amoral countries, organizations and individuals could bring disaster upon all of humanity. Thus, the challenge posed by the events of September 11 surpasses the horrendous tragic dimension of the events themselves and obligates the free world to take a stand against terror, the sooner the better.

The understanding that there is a necessity to contend with the threat of world terror is the first essential step in order to take action to annihilate it or minimize it to as low a level of activity as possible. The main purpose today is to block its directions of development and its destructive activity trends, because the signs heralding enormous escalation are already evident. The looming concrete terror threats indicated on the basis of past and present experience are as follows.

Suicide Attacks

The suicide attacks of September 11, 2001, will serve as a source of inspiration for additional terror organizations in the future. This phenomenon is attracting new organizations and is spreading to new areas throughout the world due to the "invincible image" attributed to the suicide missions and because of the belief that this is a weapon that cannot be combated successfully. Thus, the tendency on the part of additional terror organizations, including secular ones, to make use of suicide attacks in order to instill fear in the adversary is increasing steadily. The success of countries suffering from suicide terror, such as Israel and Sri Lanka, in effectively contending with suicide attacks may serve as an important criterion to decrease the dimensions of this phenomenon.

It is important to understand that attacks by suicide terrorists are expected to continue being carried out, particularly by terror groups and cells from among the Afghan alumni, and also by other terror elements that will adopt this method of operation.

Mega Terror

The mega terror phenomenon appears to be the preferred pattern of activity of the "new terrorists," who are willing to carry out widespread massacres of unprecedented dimensions. Worthy of notice is the fact that in the past there have been quite a few terror attacks with multiple casualties, and some of those that were planned and failed also had the potential to cause many deaths, which would have won them the title of "mega terror." Among the terror attacks that caused hundreds of casualties were the detonation of the Air India flight by Sikh terrorists, in which 329 passengers and crewmembers perished (June 1985), the explosion of Pan-American flight 103 over Lockerbie, Scotland, in which 270 passengers, crewmembers and Lockerbie residents were killed, and the simultaneous suicide attacks in Beirut when 241 U.S. marines and fifty-eight French soldiers were killed. But even these horrendous incidents pale in comparison to the danger inherent to the use of non-conventional weapons.

Non-Conventional Terror

The threat related to the use of non-conventional weapons by a terror organization constitutes one of the gravest scenarios, which has caused responsible entities for security to lose more than a little sleep.

Despite the fact that the desire to obtain non-conventional weaponry is a recognized occurrence among various terror organizations, including Al-Qaida, it is possible to list only a very small number of incidents where terror organizations used non-conventional weapons to perpetrate attacks. A few examples in this category are:

- A group of fighters from the Tamil Tigers (LTTE), in June 1990, used chemical weapons in the form of chlorine gas in an attack on a military camp in Sri Lanka.

- The Japanese organization called Aum Shinrikyo perpetrated three of the most significant and prominent attacks using chemical weapons: (1) On June 27, 1994, the organization attempted to assassinate three judges through the use of sarin gas, which was cleverly introduced into a building in which the judges were present. Seven individuals were killed in this attack; (2) On March 15, 1995, the organization perpetrated an attack in the Tokyo subway, again using sarin gas. Twelve people were killed and about 5,000 were wounded. This non-conventional attack claimed the highest toll of victims to date; (3) On November 23, 1995, Chechen isolationists made an attack attempt in Moscow. The terrorists parked a van containing a barrel of radioactive substance at a park in Moscow. There were no known casualties.

- In the months of September-October 2001, envelopes containing anthrax were mailed within the United States. As a result of inhaling the anthrax five people died and twenty-five were wounded. To date, it is not clear who was behind this wave of attacks, although the main suspicion is that an American entity was responsible for them.

A review of non-conventional attacks that have taken place to date indicates attempts to use three areas of non-conventional weapons: chemical (chlorine and sarin gas), biological (anthrax), and radiological/nuclear. The range of terror organizations that have made use of these means (in Sri Lanka, Japan, Chechnya, and in the United States) indicates that the threat is universal. The organizations do not hesitate to use these weapons, each organization according to its technological and operational capabilities, and according to the adversary that it faces.

Despite the relative infrequency of non-conventional attacks in comparison to conventional attacks it is clear that the threat inherent to introducing non- conventional weapons into the repertoire of world terror is both strategic and real. Its significance clearly lies in the intensification of the dimensions of danger which terror poses against the stability of the world systems and the lives of large numbers of human beings. The attack on the subway in Japan clearly underscores the huge danger of mass attacks that can be perpetrated with chemical or biological weapons, as well as the tremendous difficulty in preventing or thwarting them. Despite the fact that the anthrax envelopes in the United States took a relatively low toll in human life, there was a significant psychological effect that necessitated protective preparations on the part of various U.S. authorities, which cost a small fortune.

The very precedent created by the use of non-conventional means in terror attacks and in the mass killings of September 11, has instigated a new reality, which may encourage terror organizations to perpetrate mega terror through non-conventional means as well.

The Non-Conventional Terror of Al-Qaida and Additional Islamic Terror Elements

The idea of using non-conventional combat substances was already examined by Ramzi Yusuf, pioneer of mega terror in the nineties. Yusuf explored the possibility of using a chemical weapon in order to assassinate President Clinton during his visit to the Philippines;[2] he also considered attacking the Twin Towers with toxic gas but dismissed the idea because it seemed too expensive, and he decided to perpetrate the attack with conventional explosives instead.[3]

Characteristically, Bin-Laden was the practical man who acted to obtain this type of weapon as a tool to promote his vision. During recent years indications have accumulated regarding Bin-Laden's efforts to obtain non-conventional combat substances. Thus, the Americans claimed that Bin-Laden funded the development of non-conventional combat substances in the "Shifa" pharmaceutical factory in Sudan, which served as a target for an American attack (August 20, 1998), in response to Al-Qaida's attacks at the American embassies in Kenya and Tanzania. The Americans claimed that traces of nerve gas VX were found at the attack site.[4] According to State Department publications, Mamdukh Salem, Bin-Laden's senior deputy who was arrested in Germany in October 1998 and extradited to the United States, was involved in the purchasing and logistics, including the procurement of non-conventional substances.

Additional indications of the efforts by Bin-Laden's men to obtain non-conventional weapons came to light in the trials of Al-Qaida members. In the trial of those charged with detonating the American embassies in Africa, the first witness, Jamal Ahmed Al-Fadel, who was a veteran member of Al-Qaida, revealed that Bin-Laden had tried to acquire uranium when he was living in Sudan in the early nineties.[5] The witness confirmed that he had served as a go-between in the initial attempts to purchase uranium, but he could not verify if the deals went through.

In the trial of Wadia Al-Haj, who had served as Bin-Laden's personal secretary, the charge sheet stated that Al-Haj had taken advantage of the fact that he carried an American passport for travels around Europe in order to purchase chemical weapons.[6]

A rare allusion to training in the use of explosives and non-conventional means at the Abu Habab camp, appeared in the charge sheet brought against Nabil Ukal, a Palestinian from the Gaza Strip, who was arrested in June 2000 by the Israeli security forces. The charge sheet stated that in March 1998, Ukal underwent advanced training in the use of chemical explosive charges at the Abu Habab camp. The charge sheet also stated that the camp commander warned Ukal "not to discuss the nature of the training with anyone."

The Algerian Ahmed Rasem, who stood trial in Los Angeles and was sentenced to 140 years in prison, stated that he had undergone advanced sabotage training at the Darunte training camp in Afghanistan. The training, which went on for six months, included light weapons and explosives, assassination training and intelligence gathering, and special instruction in the use of toxins while practicing cyanide poisoning on dogs.[7]

Rasem's testimony was borne out by the findings confiscated in some buildings in Kabul that served Al-Qaida. These findings included traces of chemical substances and documents, plus diagrams and explanations on how to assemble nuclear and chemical bombs. Two senior Pakistani nuclear scientists who were arrested in 2001 by their country's security services being suspected of leasing their services to Bin-Laden, confirmed Bin-Laden's efforts to obtain non-conventional weapons.[8]

Al-Qaida efforts to obtain non-conventional weaponry for practical use were also corroborated when Abdallah Al-Muhajir was arrested at Chicago's international airport on May 8, 2002. Muhajir is a thirty-two-year-old American citizen, born in New York as Jose Fediya, who converted to Islam in prison. Upon his release he found his way to Bin-Laden's training camps in Afghanistan and joined the ranks of Al-Qaida. He is an expert in chemistry and engineering, and in his role in the organization concentrated on the study and development of capabilities to construct a radiological bomb. According to U.S. Attorney General John Ashcroft, Muhajir's arrival in the United States was for the purpose of purchasing radiological substances in order to construct what is dubbed in journalistic terms as "a dirty bomb." Effective detonation of this bomb depends upon the quantity and quality of the radioactive material, but it can instantly cause massive deaths and trigger long-term genetic damage in those exposed to its radioactive fallout.[9] This type of attack can also contaminate a large area, which creates the necessity of sealing it off because of the difficulty in decontaminating it. No less devastating is the psychological damage to the stricken state as well as the effect of the event upon world population.[10]

Muhajir's arrest in Chicago joins a long line of indications testifying to Bin-Laden's practical intentions to obtain non-conventional weapons. Additional indications came in the form of the interrogation of Abu-Zubeida, one of the most senior Al-Qaida personnel under arrest in the United States, as well as in documents found in the organization's safe houses in Afghanistan. It is reasonable to assume that Al-Qaida and other terror organizations will act to obtain attack capabilities via non-conventional weapons, and this will undoubtedly constitute one of the central challenges with which mostly democratic countries will have to contend. Moreover, the very existence of these means in the possession of terror organizations and their threat to use them may constitute a means for extortion in order to achieve their goals or alternatively serve as a deterrent against countries taking steps to combat these terror organizations.

It is noteworthy that most of the concepts currently in use vis-à-vis non-conventional weapons are based on perceptions connected to the Cold War. The "balance of horror" that characterized this period was founded on a rational policy that was at the behavioral root of the involved countries, and which prevented the use of non-conventional weapons by the various sides. This assumption is not relevant to the behavioral patterns of a terror organization that gets its hands on non-conventional weapons, so concepts like "the balance of horror," "deterrent capabilities," the "first strike" and the "second strike" are incompatible with the new reality. The West must develop new concepts regarding methods to contend with the non-conventional challenge posed by terror organizations.

Cyber Terrorism

The Al-Qaida organization has already proved that despite its worldview, which regards Western culture as Islam's archenemy, it is well acquainted with the potential inherent in Western technology and has learned to exploit the latter for its own needs. Globalization and the communication era have opened action arenas for terror organizations like Al-Qaida, enabling them to exploit communication systems, information and funds, as well as supplier services to further their activities. The global communication system enables a subversive entity like a terror organization to exploit various functions that the system supplies to its users, to preserve a "low-profile signature" inside the system and turn the system itself including all its branches into an arena for activity and a target for attacks.

Cyberspace constitutes an optimal area for "nomadic entities," which can act from any location with no need for a territorial base or the development of a permanent and vulnerable infrastructure. Laptop computers, the satellite or cellular telephone and the Internet constitute the optimal action and combat arena for the "nomadic" entity. In this space, the state-oriented entity dependent upon technology becomes vulnerable and helpless vis-à-vis "nomadic" elements that thrive and act in space. This is true both of the lone hacker, who can challenge a national or global system, and of a terror cell manipulating the system for its own requirements, for malicious intent against that system or defined targets accessible through it.

The Information Age places new possibilities and action arenas at the disposal of terror organizations like Al-Qaida. The Internet, e-mail and the various communication networks will at times serve as an action arena and at other times constitute the target for the activities of these organizations.

John Arquilla and David Ronfeldt, researchers of the Rand Institute, point out two new concepts that describe the unique character of the war against modern Islamic terror. The first concept defines the battle as "netwars."[11] The researchers define the network wars as low-intensity social struggles conducted by networked organizations that act as small, decentralized units, and can be rapidly prepared for action at any location or time. The second concept is "networks," which characterizes the elements instigating the struggle in the networks.

In the broader connection, Arquilla and Ronfeldt describe the netwars as follows:[12]

> Netwar refers to an emerging mode of conflict and crime at societal levels, involving measures short of traditional war in which the protagonists are likely to consist of dispersed, small groups who communicate, coordinate and conduct their campaigns in an internetted manner, without a precise central command. Netwar differs from modes of conflict in which the actors prefer formal, standalone, hierarchical organizations, doctrines and strategies, as in past efforts, for example, to build centralized revolutionary movements along Marxist lines.

These organizations may act on behalf of negative goals, like the activity of Al-Qaida, or alternatively conduct a struggle for democracy and human rights, as is customary in various places in the world. The Information Age has opened up new arenas and unique "combat means" for terror elements that characterize this age.

The goal of the terror organizations is not to destroy the military capabilities of its adversaries but rather to influence their consciousness and impair their resolve from the point of view of determination and national strength. Thus, the terrorist aspires to impair and disrupt the lifestyle of the target countries, to spread fear and insecurity, and in this way to promote his interests. Therefore, the Information Age makes the society and economy of the modern Western state extremely vulnerable because of its great dependence on communication systems of all sorts for its daily survival.

There are several action patterns and central threats typical of the Information Age:

Information Combat. This concept contains many and varied components; one of the most central is combating an adversary's computer systems. In this modern era, most of a state's vital systems (infrastructure systems, economic systems, security systems, energy systems, transportation and more) are all based on computerized systems. Damage to these systems may paralyze them.

There are currently various methods to impair computerized systems, for example:[13]

- Spreading viruses to impair computerization systems by sending them from remote end points or by planting them in the system through an "agent."
- "Flooding" sites with electronic mail in order to cause their collapse.
- Planting worms in the computerizations systems. The worms reproduce infinitely and destroy the system (in 1994, the Internet system collapsed as a result of this phenomenon).

The ability to perpetrate terror attacks of this kind is currently in the hands of "hackers" and states, and can be adopted by terror organizations both via training the organization's computer experts and via the hiring of the services of external entities.[14]

Another component of informational combat is the area of psychological warfare. By its very essence, terror is meant to affect the adversary's consciousness, thus the Information Age provides terror organizations with the arena and optimal tools to realize their goals.

The Broadcast Media. Television and radio networks transmit messages and footage from the attack site to the entire world at real time, and provide terrorists with maximum media exposure. Broadcast and written media constitute an arena for terror organizations to transmit messages and wage psychological warfare. Osama Bin-Laden uses the media in this manner regularly. In recent years, the

Al-Jazeera network has become a major channel for this type of activity, and some Western networks also serve as important mouthpieces. Democracy and freedom of speech create an unrestricted communication arena that enables terrorists to exploit these values and use them for their own purposes.

Communication and information systems (based on the Internet) represent an important source for terror organizations to legally gather information prior to their attacks. Computerized financial systems enable the transfer of money, financing and logistical aid required for the support of terror activities. Modern communication systems allow terror organizations to communicate with their people all over the world in a rapid, efficient and safe way. For Al-Qaida use of the Internet for communication is essential; messages are encoded in a seemingly innocent way.

In summary, the Information Age and Cyber Space represent an ideal arena for terror organizations. The more developed a country becomes, the greater its vulnerability in the area of communication, and the more democratic it is in character and the more open its economy, so that the restrictions on accessibility and the use of these systems diminish. Terror attacks against communication systems are relatively easy to implement. The means required for these attacks are not particularly costly, and after the act the perpetrators are difficult to find. Today, existing solutions to protect systems provide only a partial response to a wide range of threats; the development of a defensive response is often infinitely more expensive than the development of the capability to cause the initial damage to the system.

Notes

1. Simon Reeve, The New Jackals, p. 76.
2. Ibid., p. 76.
3. Ibid., p. 108.
4. www.cnn.com, November 19, 1998.
5. Awad, Salah, *A-Sharq Al-Awsat* Internet, February 8, 2001.
6. Ibid.
7. Josh Meyer, Terrorist Says Plot Didn't End with Lax," *Los Angeles Times* Internet, July 4, 2001.
8. *Ha'aretz*, Tel Aviv, June 11, 2002.
9. Ibid.
10. Ibid.
11. John Arquilla and David Ronfeldt, Cyberwar is Coming!, article for Rand.
12. Ibid.
13. Yael Shahar, Information Warfare: The Perfect Terrorist Weapon, www.ict.org.il.
14. *Time*, Onward Cyber Soldiers, August 21, 1995, Vol. 146, No. 8.

Epilogue

The war against world terror is one that must be waged today by every human being on this globe who believes in human liberty and the individual's right to live his life according to his own beliefs without impairing his fellowman's right to live his life according to his own choice. The battle is over the right of residents of various countries in the world to personal security in their own lands, while traveling and when spending time abroad. In contrast, the goal of the terrorists is to impair personal security and force their worldview on their adversaries through the use of violence and coercion, without exception. In this struggle no one is immune, there is no distinguishing between enemy or ally, and anyone can be hurt by mass, indiscriminate terror, which seems to be the preferred action pattern of terrorists now and for the future as well. As terror is generally the weapon of the weak, the objective of the perpetrators is to diminish the inequality between them and their adversaries by spreading fear and horror in order to magnify their strength and create an image of power that far surpasses their actual force. For this purpose, they manipulate the media.

To a great extent, terror is psychological warfare. The terrorists' aim is for control over the mind and consciousness of the public observing the terror attack. The main message they seek to transmit is: "We have the power and ability to harm our adversaries whenever and wherever we choose, and no one is immune to us, not even the government that is supposedly protecting you." Thus, terror challenges the world's social order and the foundations of society and state, which is why the war against terror is not the sole legacy of the United States or any small number of countries. Countries all over the world may find themselves in a situation where they will have to become accustomed to armed guards and strict inspections at commercial centers, banks, malls, movie theaters and such, which have become prime targets for terror attacks due to the psychological effect that attacks at these locations can cause.

This struggle to influence public consciousness is being waged over television stations such as Al-Jazeera and via interviews in the Arab press, which serve as a platform for Al-Qaida spokesmen to spread their mega terror threats. Similar activities are conducted by other organizations such as the Lebanese Hizballah.

One of the objects of the battle for public consciousness is to arouse dissension between the United States and other countries or blocs of states while manipulating conflicting interests. For example, this is true of the ties between the United States and Europe, or the ties between the United States and Third World countries. There is also an attempt to exploit feelings of alienation and hostility that are harbored against the United States in Muslim communities and in many Third World countries that support the struggle led by Fundamentalist Islam.

Principles for the Handling of Terror from the Aspects of the Media and Morale

The Struggle over Consciousness

- Cooperating with the media rather than opposing or censoring it.
- The media are an important tool to convey contradictory messages.
- Exposure of the propaganda component in the adversary's activity (use of experts in the areas of communications, psychology, and counter-terror).
- Exposure of the adversary's actual size and power.
- Pointing out the components of the democratic dilemma and reinforcing the teaching of democracy in schools.
- Educating the public to be more vigilant and civically involved in counter-terror activity.

The attacks of September 11 have triggered a "revolution of consciousness," mainly among the terror organizations in regard to their ability to strike out at and contend with the most powerful of countries, let alone the weaker states. They have crossed out any moral or normative reservations vis-à-vis the "rules of the game" and the indiscriminate slaughter of innocent civil populations. The impact of the attacks affects not only the networks and Islamic terror organizations affiliated with the Afghan alumni, it may well radiate out towards established nationalist "secular" terror organizations and others such as the Spanish ETA, the Irish IRA and terror organizations in South America like the Colombian FARC and others. These organizations may decide to carry out terror attacks to inflict multiple casualties, because their outlook has been altered as a result of the fact that the "bar" applying to conventional attacks has been raised and is now higher than ever before. The model of the terror assault perpetrated in the United States is expected to trickle down to other arenas of the world including Europe, Africa, Latin America, and Asia, and its burgeoning has already been observed in the massive terror campaign that was planned for Singapore at the end of 2001.

The free world currently faces an unprecedented global threat, which imperils and undermines the very foundations of state and society. The war against terror currently being waged by the United States can be regarded as a kind of "Third World War," which in character may differ from past wars but in its achievements will affect the level of personal security and liberty of each and every citizen on the globe, and as such renders this campaign so vitally important.

Index